T0133954

EVOLUTIONARY COMPUTATION

The CRC Press
International Series on Computational Intelligence

Series Editor
L.C. Jain, Ph.D., M.E., B.E. (Hons), Fellow I.E. (Australia)

L.C. Jain, R.P. Johnson, Y. Takefuji, and L.A. Zadeh
Knowledge-Based Intelligent Techniques in Industry

L.C. Jain and C.W. de Silva
**Intelligent Adaptive Control: Industrial Applications in the
Applied Computational Intelligence Set**

L.C. Jain and N.M. Martin
**Fusion of Neural Networks, Fuzzy Systems, and Genetic Algorithms:
Industrial Applications**

H.-N. Teodorescu, A. Kandel, and L.C. Jain
Fuzzy and Neuro-Fuzzy Systems in Medicine

C.L. Karr and L.M. Freeman
Industrial Applications of Genetic Algorithms

L.C. Jain and B. Lazzerini
Knowledge-Based Intelligent Techniques in Character Recognition

L.C. Jain and V. Vemuri
Industrial Applications of Neural Networks

H.-N. Teodorescu, A. Kandel, and L.C. Jain
Soft Computing in Human-Related Sciences

D. Dumitrescu, B. Lazzerini, L.C. Jain, and A. Dumitrescu
Evolutionary Computation

B. Lazzerini, D. Dumitrescu, and L.C. Jain
Fuzzy Sets and Their Application to Clustering and Training

L.C. Jain, U. Halici, I. Hayashi, S.B. Lee, and S. Tsutsui
Intelligent Biometric Techniques in Fingerprint and Face Recognition

Z. Chen
Computational Intelligence for Decision Support

L.C. Jain
Evolution of Engineering and Information Systems and Their Applications

H.-N. Teodorescu and A. Kandel
Dynamic Fuzzy Systems and Chaos Applications

L. Medsker and L.C. Jain
Recurrent Neural Networks: Design and Applications

L.C. Jain and A.M. Fanelli
Recent Advances in Artifical Neural Networks: Design and Applications

M. Russo and L.C. Jain
Fuzzy Learning and Applications

J. Liu
Multiagent Robotic Systems

H.-N. Teodorescu and L.C. Jain
Intelligent Systems and Techniques in Rehabilitation Engineering

I. Baturone, A. Barriga, C. Jimenez-Fernandez, D. Lopez, and S. Sanchez-Solano
Microelectronics Design of Fuzzy Logic-Based Systems

T. Nishida
Dynamic Knowledge Interaction

C.L. Karr
Practical Applications of Computational Intelligence for Adaptive Control

EVOLUTIONARY COMPUTATION

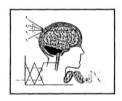

D. Dumitrescu
B. Lazzerini
L.C. Jain
A. Dumitrescu

CRC Press

Boca Raton   London   New York   Washington, D.C.

Library of Congress Cataloging-in-Publication Data

Evolutionary computation/D. Dumitrescu...[et al.].
      p. cm.—(CRC Press international series on computational intelligence)
      Includes bibliographical references and index.
      ISBN 0-8493-0588-8 (alk.)
      1. Evolutionary programming (Computer science) I. Dumitrescu, D. (Dumitru), 1949–
II. Series.
QA76.618. E882 2000
006.3—dc21   00-030348
                                                       CIP

Visit the CRC Press Web site at www.crcpress.com

© 2000 by CRC Press LLC

No claim to original U.S. Government works
International Standard Book Number 0-8493-0588-8
Library of Congress Card Number 00-030348
Printed in the United States of America   2 3 4 5 6 7 8 9 0
Printed on acid-free paper

To the new generation,

particularly to Irène, Andrei and Christian

Preface

Evolutionary computation is a relatively new, biologically motivated, optimization and search paradigm. It may also be considered as an optimization meta-heuristic.

Together with fuzzy systems and neural computation, evolutionary computation represents a new powerful, rapidly growing field of Artificial Intelligence, known as *intelligent computation*.

Evolutionary computation uses a biological metaphor to evolve a population of candidate (i.e., potential) solutions to a given problem. The underlying metaphor is that of biological reproduction, selection, and evolution.

The search process achieved by evolutionary algorithms may also be considered as the expression of a collective learning process in a solution population. This interpretation is consistent with some evolutionary models that emphasize the evolutionary role of learning processes in a population, as in the Baldwin evolutionary model and in new molecular theories of biological evolution.

The main classes of evolutionary algorithms are

- genetic algorithms,
- evolution strategies,

- evolutionary programming,

- genetic programming,

- learning classifier systems.

The roots of evolutionary algorithms are manifold. Examples are some numerical optimization procedures, early machine learning, automated programming research, and some (non-formal) models of biological evolution.

The aim of this book is to offer a presentation of the main ideas, models and algorithms of evolutionary computation.

To respect the historical perspective, we have kept the traditional classification of evolutionary algorithms. However, we tried to emphasize the unitary character of the field. Actually, the book is intended to offer a unitary treatment of evolutionary algorithms.

Evolutionary Computation contains an extensive treatment of the canonical (simple) genetic algorithm (using binary encoding) and of the corresponding selection and search operators.

Chapter 1 contains a review of evolutionary computation paradigms.

Chapter 2 is dedicated to genetic algorithms.

We devote Chapters 3, 4, and 5 to selection schemes. Selection mechanisms are coding-independent.

Recombination (crossover) and mutation operators are treated in Chapters 6 and 7, respectively.

The main theoretical result intended to explain how canonical genetic algorithms work is the *schema theorem*. Chapter 8 is dedicated to this theorem and its consequences.

Genetic algorithms using real-valued encoding are also considered in Chapter 9.

One important problem is the hybridization of an evolutionary algorithm with some powerful (general or problem-dependent) optimization heuristics.

Chapter 10 is dedicated to hybridization techniques, parameter setting, and (self-)adaptation.

Several approaches devoted to adaptive representation (messy genetic algorithms, delta coding, diploidy and dominance) are covered in Chapter 11.

Chapter 12 is dedicated to evolution strategies and evolutionary programming.

Some population models basically aimed at solving multi-modal optimization/search problems are presented in Chapter 13. Some parallel implementation models strongly related to these population models are also considered.

An evolutionary method for program discovery, namely, *genetic programming*, is described in Chapter 14.

Two classes of learning classifier systems, which evolve a population of rules intended to solve complex decision problems in a changing environment, are discussed in Chapter 15. These classes are the *Michigan* and the *Pittsburgh* (or *Pitt*) families of classifier systems.

A list of applications of evolutionary algorithms in several domains is provided in Chapter 16. Some applications, like pattern recognition and transition rule discovery in a cellular automaton, are treated in a more detailed manner.

******

Evolutionary Computation is intended for a large audience. Anyone interested in optimization/search problems can find useful ideas, methods, and algorithms.

The book will be of interest for scientists in any discipline. It could be used as a text for undergraduate or graduate courses in Evolutionary Computation or related topics. No particular prerequisites, except some basic concepts of mathematics (like linear algebra and probability theory) and computer programming elements are needed.

Contents

1   **Principles of evolutionary computation**..........1

   1.1   Introduction 1

   1.2   Genes and chromosomes....................................2

         1.2.1   Gene structure and DNA transcription.................2

         1.2.2   Gene expression as phenotypic traits 3

         1.2.3   Diploid and haploid genotypes............................5

   1.3   Early EC research...5

   1.4   Basic evolutionary computation models 7

         1.4.1   Genetic algorithms 7

         1.4.2   Evolutionary programming 7

         1.4.3   Evolution strategies 8

   1.5   Other EC approaches 9

         1.5.1   Genetic programming..9

         1.5.2   Learning classifier systems 10

1.5.2.1   Michigan approach 10

1.5.2.2   Pittsburgh approach 11

1.6   Structure of an evolutionary algorithm 11

1.6.1   Encoding solutions 11

1.6.2   Selection and search operators 13

1.6.2.1   Fitness function..................................13

1.6.2.2   Recombination operator....................13

1.6.2.3   Mutation operator 14

1.6.2.4   Selection..14

1.6.3   Innovative vs. conservative operators 15

1.6.4   Components of an EC algorithm........................15

1.7   Basic evolutionary algorithm...................................16

1.7.1.1   Termination condition.......................17

1.7.1.2   Result of an evolutionary algorithm ..17

References and bibliography...18

2   Genetic algorithms 21

2.1   Introduction...21

2.2   Problem representation and fitness function....................23

2.2.1   Representation...23

2.2.2   Fitness function 24

2.2.2.1   Chromosome evaluation 24

2.2.2.2   Implicit fitness and coevolution.........25

        2.2.2.3   Fitness landscape 25

2.3   Search progress 25

2.4   Basic elements of genetic algorithms......................26

2.5   Canonical genetic algorithm 28

      2.5.1   Representation 28

      2.5.2   Simple genetic algorithm....................28

      2.5.3   Replacement strategies 30

      2.5.4   Initial population 31

            2.5.4.1   Partially enumerative initialization....31

            2.5.4.2   Doping 32

2.6   Schemata and building blocks..............................32

      2.6.1   Notions concerning schemata...............33

      2.6.2   Building block hypothesis and schema theorem 36

      2.6.3   Implicit parallelism............................36

      2.6.4   Genetic drift....................................37

References and bibliography...37

3   Basic selection schemes in evolutionary algorithms................ 39

3.1   Introduction...39

3.2   Selection purposes..40

      3.2.1   Mating pool 40

3.2.2   Selection for recombination and
selection for replacement.................................41

3.3   Fitness function..42

   3.3.1   Fitness and scaling.................................42

   3.3.2   Implicit fitness cvaluation 43

   3.3.3   Coevolutionary fitness evaluation 44

3.4   Selection pressure and takeover time................................44

   3.4.1   Selection pressure.................................44

   3.4.2   Takeover time.................................45

   3.4.3   Selection pressure and search progress 46

3.5   Proportional selection 46

   3.5.1   Selection probability.................................46

       3.5.1.1   Basic definitions 46

       3.5.1.2   Average number of copies 47

   3.5.2   Proportional selection algorithm 48

   3.5.3   Premature and slow convergence......................50

       3.5.3.1   Premature convergence.....................50

       3.5.3.2   Slow convergence.................................51

       3.5.3.3   Takeover time for
proportional selection 51

   3.5.4   Variants of proportional selection......................52

       3.5.4.1   Stochastic sampling with
replacement.................................52

        3.5.4.2   Sampling rate assignment 53

        3.5.4.3   Stochastic universal sampling...........53

3.6   Truncation 54

References and bibliography..................................54

4 Selection based on scaling and ranking mechanisms 57

4.1   Introduction..57

4.2   Scale transformation 58

4.3   Static scaling mechanisms 59

      4.3.1   Linear scaling 59

      4.3.2   Power law scaling............................60

      4.3.3   Logarithmic scaling.........................60

4.4   Dynamic scaling...61

      4.4.1   Sigma truncation.............................61

      4.4.2   Window scaling...............................62

4.5   Noisy fitness functions................................63

4.6   Fitness remapping for minimization problems 64

4.7   Rank-based selection....................................65

      4.7.1   Linear ranking selection 66

        4.7.1.1   Selection probability for linear ranking 66

4.7.1.2   Range of parameter *Max*....................67

4.7.1.3   Another expression of selection
probability..69

4.7.1.4   Selection probabilities for the best
and worst individuals.........................69

4.7.1.5   Selection pressure and takeover time
for linear ranking 70

4.7.1.6   An example..71

4.7.1.7   Selection pressure and
population diversity 72

4.7.2   Nonlinear ranking..72

4.7.2.1   Exponential ranking..........................73

4.7.2.2   Geometric distribution ranking..........73

4.7.2.3   Biased exponential ranking...............74

4.7.2.4   General nonlinear ranking 74

4.8   Binary tournament...75

4.8.1   Deterministic tournament....................................75

4.8.2   Probabilistic tournament......................................76

4.8.3   Boltzmann tournament 77

4.9   *q*-tournament selection..78

4.9.1   Score-based tournament 78

4.9.2   Local tournament...79

4.9.3   Concluding remarks on tournament selection....80

References and bibliography...80

5 Further selection strategies 83

5.1 Introduction..83

5.2 Classification of selection strategies 84

5.3 Elitist strategies 86

5.4 Generation gap methods..87

    5.4.1 Overlapping and non-overlapping models 87

    5.4.2 Generation gap 88

5.5 Steady-state evolutionary algorithms...............................89

    5.5.1 Basic steady-state model 89

    5.5.2 Generalized steady-state algorithm 90

5.6 Generational elitist strategies in GAs...............................91

5.7 Michalewicz selection...92

5.8 Boltzmann selection..93

    5.8.1 Boltzmann selection by scaling.......................93

    5.8.2 Simulated annealing 95

    5.8.3 PRSA method..95

5.9 Other selection methods..96

    5.9.1 Greedy over-selection......................................96

    5.9.2 Coevolutionary selection models 97

5.10 Genetic drift 98

References and bibliography...99

6   Recombination operators within binary encoding 103

6.1   Introduction 103

6.2   One-point crossover 104

    6.2.1   Basic crossover operator 104

    6.2.2   Formal definition of crossover operator 106

6.3   Two-point crossover 107

6.4   *N*-point crossover 108

6.5   Punctuated crossover 110

6.6   Segmented crossover 112

6.7   Shuffle crossover 113

6.8   Uniform crossover 114

    6.8.1   Basic method 114

    6.8.2   Generalizations 115

6.9   Other crossover operators and some comparisons 115

    6.9.1   Multi-parent and one-descendent operators 116

    6.9.2   Reduced surrogate 116

        6.9.2.1   RRR operator 116

    6.9.3   Experimental and theoretical studies 117

        6.9.3.1   Comparative studies 117

        6.9.3.2   Positional bias and distributional bias 117

6.10 Crossover probability...118

     6.10.1 Setting crossover probability...................120

6.11 Mating...120

6.12 N-point crossover algorithm revisited............................121

6.13 Selection for survival or replacement 123

6.14 General remarks about crossover within the framework
of binary encoding 124

References and bibliography..125

7 Mutation operators and related topics 131

7.1 Introduction..131

7.2 Mutation with binary encoding......................................133

     7.2.1 Mutation rate 134

     7.2.2 Mutation rate values 134

7.3 Strong and weak mutation operators.............................135

     7.3.1 Selecting a position for mutation.....................136

     7.3.2 Strong mutation operator..................................136

     7.3.3 Weak mutation operator 138

     7.3.4 Mutation within a unique chromosome...........139

7.4 Non-uniform mutation 139

     7.4.1 Time-dependent mutation rate..........................139

          7.4.1.1 Fitness-dependent mutation rate 141

7.5 Adaptive non-uniform mutation.....................................142

7.6 Self-adaptation of mutation rate................................142

    7.6.1   Self-adaptation mechanism 143

        7.6.1.1   Mutation rate modification 143

        7.6.1.2   Transformed genotype 144

    7.6.2   Local mutation probabilities............................144

7.7 Crossover vs. mutation.......................................145

7.8 The inversion operator 146

7.9 Selection vs. variation operators 147

7.10 Simple genetic algorithm revisited 148

References and bibliography.....................................150

8 Schema theorem, building blocks, and related topics.. 153

8.1 Introduction..153

8.2 Elements characterizing schemata 155

8.3 Schema dynamics..157

8.4 Effect of selection on schema dynamics.......158

    8.4.1   Schema dynamics within selection..................158

    8.4.2   Dynamics of above/below-average schema 161

8.5 Effect of recombination on schema dynamics 163

    8.5.1   Schema disruption probability..........................163

    8.5.2   Actual disruption probability............................165

8.5.3   Survival probability 166

8.6 Combined effect of selection and recombination
on schema dynamics 166

8.6.1   Schema dynamics within selection
and crossover 167

8.6.2   Qualitative results concerning schema
dynamics 169

8.7 Effect of mutation on schema dynamics 170

8.8 Schema theorem 173

8.8.1   Schema dynamics within selection
and search operators 173

8.8.2   Approximating schema dynamics 174

8.8.3   Fundamental theorem 175

8.9 Building block 176

8.10 Building block hypothesis and linkage problem 177

8.10.1   Schema linkage 178

8.10.2   Concluding remarks 179

8.11 Generalizations of schema theorem 180

8.12 Deceptive functions 181

References and bibliography 184

9 Real-valued encoding 187

9.1 Introduction 187

9.2 Real-valued vectors 188

9.3 Recombination operators for real-valued encoding 189

    9.3.1 Discrete recombination 190

    9.3.2 Continuous recombination 191

    9.3.3 Complete continuous recombination 192

    9.3.4 Convex (intermediate) recombination 192

        9.3.4.1 One offspring 192

        9.3.4.2 Two offspring 193

        9.3.4.3 Random coefficient 193

        9.3.4.4 Local crossover 194

    9.3.5 SBX operator 195

    9.3.6 Multiple-parent recombination 196

    9.3.7 Fitness-based recombination 197

        9.3.7.1 Fitness-based scan 197

        9.3.7.2 Heuristic crossover 198

        9.3.7.3 Simplex crossover 198

        9.3.7.4 Random simplex crossover 199

9.4 Mutation operators for real-valued encoding 199

    9.4.1 Uniform mutation 199

        9.4.1.1 One-position mutation operator 200

        9.4.1.2 All-positions mutation operator 201

9.4.2   Non-uniform mutation 202

         9.4.2.1   A non-uniform mutation operator 202

         9.4.2.2   Generalized non-uniform mutation ..204

    9.4.3   Normal perturbation-induced mutation 206

         9.4.3.1   Multiplicative self-adaptation

                   procedure 207

         9.4.3.2   Additive self-adaptation procedure ..207

         9.4.3.3   Other self-adaptation procedures 208

    9.4.4   Cauchy perturbation 208

9.5   Concluding remarks 209

References and bibliography 211

10   Hybridization, parameter setting, and adaptation 213

10.1   Introduction 213

10.2   Specialized representation and hybridization

      within GAs 214

    10.2.1   Specific representation 214

    10.2.2   Hybridization 215

    10.2.3   Use of specific encoding and hybridization 216

10.3   Parameter setting and adaptive GAs 218

    10.3.1   Parameter setting in GAs 218

10.3.2   Parameter setting and

representation adaptation.................................219

10.3.3   Adaptive fitness of a search operator 221

10.4 Adaptive GAs...223

10.4.1   Adaptation problem...223

10.4.2   Adaptive techniques based on

fuzzy logic control...225

References and bibliography...225

11 Adaptive representations:

messy genetic algorithms, delta coding,

and diploidic representation 231

11.1 Introduction..231

11.2 Principles of messy genetic algorithms..........................233

11.2.1   Variable-length encoding 233

11.2.2   Linkage problem...234

11.2.2.1   Linkage within binary encoding 234

11.2.2.2   Solutions to the linkage problem 235

11.2.3   Messy encoding...236

11.2.4   Incompleteness and ambiguity 237

11.2.4.1   Dealing with over-specification.......238

11.2.4.2   Dealing with under-specification.....238

11.3   Recombination within messy genetic operators............239

    11.3.1   Recombination................................239

    11.3.2   Examples 240

11.4   Mutation...242

11.5   Computational models 243

11.6   Generalizations of messy GAs.........................244

11.7   Other adaptive representation approaches 245

    11.7.1   ARGOT system 246

    11.7.2   Dynamic parameter encoding..............246

11.8   Delta coding 247

    11.8.1   Real-valued delta coding 247

    11.8.2   Real-valued delta coding procedure................248

    11.8.3   The algorithm 250

11.9   Diploidy and dominance 252

    11.9.1   Haploid and diploid chromosome structures

             revisited 252

    11.9.2   Dominance.................................253

    11.9.3   Diploidic representation 254

    11.9.4   Triallelic representation................254

    11.9.5   Quadrallelic representation..............256

    11.9.6   Evolving dominance map 256

    11.9.7   Use of diploidy 257

References and bibliography................................257

12 Evolution strategies and evolutionary programming 261

12.1 Introduction 261

12.2 Evolution strategies 261

12.3 (1+1) strategy 263

    12.3.1   1/5 success rule 264

    12.3.2   Standard deviation adaptation 265

    12.3.3   Schwefel's version of the 1/5 success rule 266

12.4 Multimembered evolution strategies 268

    12.4.1   Representation of individuals 269

12.5 Standard mutation 270

    12.5.1   Standard mutation of the control parameters ...270

12.6 Genotypes including covariance matrix.
Correlated mutation 272

    12.6.1   Covariance matrix for mutation 272

    12.6.2   Correlated mutations 273

12.7 Cauchy perturbations 274

    12.7.1   Cauchy distribution 274

    12.7.2   Cauchy perturbation-induced mutation 274

12.8 Evolutionary programming 275

    12.8.1   Sequential machine model 276

12.8.2   Function optimization by evolutionary

          programming 278

12.9 Evolutionary programming using Cauchy perturbation..279

References and bibliography..279

13 Population models and

parallel implementations 283

13.1 Introduction..283

13.2 Niching methods 284

13.3 Fitness sharing..284

      13.3.1   Sharing function 286

      13.3.2   Niche count..286

      13.3.3   Shared fitness 286

13.4 Crowding..287

13.5 Island and stepping stone models................................287

13.6 Fine-grained and diffusion models 289

13.7 Coevolution..290

      13.7.1   Competitive models..290

      13.7.2   Cooperative models...290

13.8 Baldwin effect 291

13.9 Parallel implementation of evolutionary algorithms.......292

      13.9.1   Subpopulations with migration 292

13.9.1.1 Island model.................................293

13.9.1.2 Coarse-grained models 293

13.9.1.3 Fine-grained models 293

13.9.1.4 Diffusion model 294

13.9.1.5 Overlapping subpopulations

without migration...........................294

References and bibliography...................................294

14 Genetic programming.................................. **299**

14.1 Introduction...299

14.2 Early GP approaches.......................................300

14.3 Program-generating language 301

14.3.1 Terminal and function sets 301

14.3.2 Closure property...............................303

14.3.3 Problem language and

implementation language 303

14.4 GP program structures 303

14.4.1 Tree structures.................................304

14.4.2 Graph structures 304

14.4.3 Linear structures..............................305

14.5 Initialization of tree structures 305

14.5.1 Grow method...................................306

14.5.2 Full method.....................................306

14.5.3   Ramped half-and-half method.........................306

14.6 Fitness calculation...307

14.7 Recombination operators 309

14.7.1   Standard recombination operator 309

14.7.2   Brood recombination.....................................310

14.7.3   Selecting crossover points.............................311

14.7.4   Introns...312

14.8 Mutation...313

14.8.1   Mutation of tree-structured programs..............314

14.8.1.1   Macromutation..................................314

14.8.1.2   Micromutation 314

14.8.2   Mutation of linearly represented programs 315

14.8.3   Mutation strategies 315

14.9 Selection..315

14.9.1   Selection for recombination 316

14.9.2   Selection for replacement...............................316

14.10 Population models 316

14.11 Parallel implementation.....................................317

14.12 Basic GP algorithm...317

14.12.1 GP procedure setting 317

14.12.2 Generational algorithm...................................318

14.12.3 Steady-state GP algorithm..............................319

References and bibliography...320

15 Learning classifier systems 323

15.1 Introduction 323

15.2 Michigan and Pittsburgh families of

learning classifier systems 324

    15.2.1 Michigan approach 324

    15.2.2 Pittsburgh approach 325

15.3 Michigan classifier systems 326

    15.3.1 Structure of a Holland system 326

    15.3.2 Rules and messages 327

15.4 Bucket brigade algorithm 328

    15.4.1 Principle of the algorithm 328

          15.4.1.1 Bargaining procedure 329

          15.4.1.2 Bid and winning probability 330

    15.4.2 Updating strength of a winning classifier 332

    15.4.3 Updating strength of a producing classifier 333

          15.4.3.1 Income tax 334

          15.4.3.2 Property tax 334

    15.4.4 Updating strength for remaining situations 335

    15.4.5 Taxing the winners.

Updating strength revisited 336

          15.4.5.1 Remarks on bucket brigade

algorithm 336

15.5 Pittsburgh classifier systems 337

15.6 Fuzzy classifier systems...337

    15.6.1   Fuzzy Michigan classifier systems...................338

    15.6.2   Fuzzy Pittsburgh classifier systems.................338

          15.6.2.1   Learning fuzzy memberships...........339

          15.6.2.2   Learning fuzzy rules with fixed fuzzy membership functions......................339

          15.6.2.3   Learning fuzzy rules and membership functions separately 339

          15.6.2.4   Learning fuzzy rules and membership functions simultaneously 340

References and bibliography...340

16 Applications of evolutionary computation . 343

16.1 Introduction...343

16.2 General applications of evolutionary computation 344

16.3 Main application areas 346

16.4 Optimization and search applications 354

    16.4.1   Optimization..354

    16.4.2   Search 355

16.5 Choosing a decision strategy..355

16.6 Neural network training and design 357

    16.6.1   Neural network training using evolutionary computation................................357

16.6.1.1 General applications 358

16.6.1.2 Evolutionary algorithms as
training procedures 359

16.6.2 Establishing neural network architecture 359

16.7 Pattern recognition applications......................................360

16.7.1 A simple genetic algorithm for
fuzzy clustering 361

16.7.2 Other approaches..364

16.8 Cellular automata 365

16.8.1 Basic notions 365

16.8.2 Specification of a cellular automaton...............367

16.8.3 CA applications 369

16.8.4 Determining transition functions.....................370

16.8.4.1 CA rule detection 370

16.9 Evolutionary algorithms vs. other heuristics..................374

References and bibliography...374

Index 379

1

Principles of evolutionary computation

1.1 Introduction

Evolutionary computation (EC) represents a powerful search and optimization paradigm. The metaphor underlying EC is a biological one: that of natural selection and genetics.

There are a variety of classes of evolutionary computational models that have been proposed and studied. These models are usually referred to as *evolutionary algorithms*.

The main characteristic of evolutionary algorithms is the intensive use of randomness and genetics-inspired operations to evolve a set of candidate solutions.

Evolutionary algorithms involve selection, recombination, random variation, and competition of the individuals in a population of adequately represented potential solutions.

The candidate solutions to a certain problem are referred to as *chromosomes* or *individuals.*

Depending on the actual problem and the type of the adopted evolutionary algorithm, chromosomes are represented as bit strings, real-component vectors, pairs (triples, etc.) of real-component vectors, matrices, trees, tree-like hierarchies, parse trees, general graphs, and permutations.

Finite-state machine representations or sequences of symbols over finite alphabets may also be considered to encode solutions to specific problems.

1.2   Genes and chromosomes

Each cell of a biological organism contains a set of *chromosomes.* A chromosome is composed of *genes.* The genes are strings of DNA that encodes the synthesis of a specific protein. The DNA is the carrier of complete *genetic information.*

Each gene is located at a particular position, or *locus,* on the chromosome.

A gene may assume several values (or may have several forms). Each value of a gene is referred to as an *allele* of that gene.

1.2.1   Gene structure and DNA transcription

In the cellular *transcription* process a gene can be transcribed as RNA by the action of enzymes. The first transcription product is a polymer: *messenger* RNA (mRNA), which can be translated into protein via another form of RNA: *transfer* RNA (tRNA).

The genes are separated by sequences of DNA without transcriptional effect (*non-coding* DNA segments, or *junk* DNA). As junk DNA does not encode proteins and does not control the protein synthesis, its role is not very clear.

Each intragenic DNA sequence alternates sequences of *exons* and *introns*. Exons are expressed as the gene products (typically a protein molecule).

Introns are transcribed into mRNA but are removed from the transcript before translation to proteins. Therefore, introns may be considered as non-coding segments of genetic structure.

Introns probably have some effect in increasing the efficiency of protein synthesis. Also, introns may play a role in preventing damage to exons during recombination.

The role of non-translational segments of DNA (junk DNA, introns) is not completely elucidated and is still controversial.

1.2.2 Gene expression as phenotypic traits

The complete genetic information is called the *genome* of an organism. Many organisms have multiple chromosomes in each cell (*polyploidy* phenomenon).

The *genotype* represents the set of genes contained in a genome, i.e., the genetic program of an individual inherited from its parents as encoded in the DNA of that organism.

Mutation and recombination take place at the genome level. Therefore, the genome is the principal mechanism for inducing variability in a population.

A *phenotype* is the actualization of a genotype in a concrete individual, i.e., the set of all observable characteristics of an organism.

If the trait that a gene encodes (or co-encodes) actually appears (is manifested) in the phenotype, then that gene is said to be *expressed.* Usually many genes are *not* expressed.

Roughly speaking, a gene may be considered as encoding a single phenotypic trait. In fact, a gene can affect more than one phenotypic trait. Moreover, different genes can cooperate to produce one trait.

Therefore it is not generally possible to make one-to-one genotype-phenotype mappings because a gene can participate in the execution of multiple cellular or developmental programs.

When a single gene influences multiple phenotypic features of an organism we speak about *pleiotropy.* On the other hand, the term *polygeny* refers to the fact that a single phenotypical feature is the result of multiple gene interaction and cooperation.

Many significant novelties that appeared at different stages of the biological evolution (such as the eyes or the wings) involved the orchestrated expression of many different loci, a number of which act in the expression of multiple phenotypes.

The phenomenon dual to gene cooperation is *epistasis.* Epistasis designates the molecular mechanism that allows the expression of one gene to block the expression of other genes (i.e., one gene masks the phenotypic effects of other genes).

When there is no gene interaction the genes are called *orthogonal.* Orthogonality means that the semantics (or phenotypic effect) of one gene depend only on its value and is independent of the other genes.

1.2.3 Diploid and haploid genotypes

Doubling the number of chromosomes in somatic cells is called *diploidy*. In the case of diploidy, chromosomes are grouped in pairs. Most complex organisms have diploid or polyploid genotypes.

In *diploid* organisms, the cells contain two sets of chromosomes, i.e., the genotype of diploid organisms contains a pair of *homologous* chromosomes.

Haploid organisms carry only one set of genetic information, i.e., each cell contains a unique chromosome.

The chromosomes that make up a pair in a diploid genotype (the homologous chromosomes) bear similar or identical genes. Similar (homologous) genes have the same positions in the two chromosomes and carry information about the same function. However, their values (alleles) may be different. Only one of the two homologous genes is (phenotypically) expressed.

Homologous chromosomes encode the same set of individual features (traits), but the values of some characteristics may be different (the corresponding alleles are different). The question that arises is which of the contradictory features are transmitted to descendants (i.e., are actualized in the phenotype) or, stated otherwise, which genes are expressed.

The conflict resolution mechanism deciding which allele (gene value) is realized (expressed) in the phenotype is called *dominance*.

1.3 Early EC research

The mainstream instances of evolutionary computation models are traditionally considered to be

- *genetic algorithms,*

- *evolutionary programming*, and

- *evolution strategies.*

Other powerful, related evolutionary techniques are

- *genetic programming*, and

- *learning classifier systems.*

The common idea of all evolutionary algorithms is to evolve a population of candidate solutions to a given problem, by using search operations inspired by biology, like recombination, mutation, and selection.

The roots of evolutionary computation emerge from some evolution-inspired algorithms developed in the 1950s. The purposes of this research were *machine learning* and *numerical optimization.*

Let us recall some of the pioneering work in the field.

A.M. Turing (1950, 1992) considered the possibility of 'genetical or evolutionary search' for general machine intelligence purposes.

John von Neumann (1966) suggested the self-replicating automata as machine evolution implicit models.

Friedberg (1958) considered the use of the evolutionary process for machine-learning and problem-solving purposes. The aim was to teach a computer to generate programs for solving simple problems.

Box (1957) developed an evolutionary technique for the design and analysis of industrial experiments.

Bremermann (1962) developed an early evolutionary algorithm theory, and attempted to apply simulated evolution techniques to numerical optimization problems (convex optimization) and for solving nonlinear equations.

From the other founders of the field, let us mention Baricelli (1957) and Fraser (1957), who proposed to use simulated evolution for control purposes (controlled experiments).

1.4 Basic evolutionary computation models

In this section, the main streams of evolutionary computation models will be described briefly and their origins indicated.

1.4.1 Genetic algorithms

Genetic algorithms were developed by John Holland (University of Michigan in Ann Arbor) in the early 1960s (Holland, 1962). Holland's original intention was to understand the principles of adaptive systems.

Simple biological models based on the notion of survival of the best (the 'fittest') were considered to design robust adaptive systems.

Holland's method evolves a population of chromosomes (candidate solutions). The chromosomes are binary strings and the search operations are typically crossover, mutation, and (seldom) inversion. The chromosomes are evaluated by using a fitness function.

1.4.2 Evolutionary programming

Evolutionary programming was devised by L.J. Fogel (Fogel, 1962) as an attempt to simulate intelligent behavior by means of finite-state machines.

Intelligent behavior was viewed as the ability to predict the next state of the machine environment. When an input symbol is presented to the machine, the machine generates an output symbol, which is compared to the next input symbol.

The current output symbol represents a prediction of the next input symbol (describing the state of the environment). The quality of the prediction is measured by using a *payoff* function.

A population of machines is exposed to the environment (described by a list of input symbols). When all the symbols have been presented, the fitness of each machine is calculated by a function of the single prediction qualities. Offspring machines are generated through random mutation of parent machines.

The offspring machines are evaluated in the same way as their parents. The process is repeated until a new, not yet encountered symbol has to be predicted.

The best performing machine is selected to generate the new prediction.

The new predicted symbol is added to the already explored environment, and the process continues.

1.4.3 Evolution strategies

Evolution strategies (Rechenberg, 1965; Schwefel, 1975, 1977, 1981) originate in the work of Bienert, Rechenberg and Schwefel concerning a method to optimize parameters for aerotechnology devices.

The method focuses on building systems capable of solving difficult, real-valued parameter optimization problems. The natural representation is a vector of real-valued genes that are manipulated primarily by the mutation operator. Mutation perturbs the solution vector in various useful ways.

The main characteristic of evolution strategies is the self-adaptation of the strategy parameters, like the standard deviation of the mutation amplitude (the strategy step size).

1.5 Other EC approaches

In this section, two powerful EC paradigms, namely, genetic programming and learning classifier systems, are reviewed briefly.

1.5.1 Genetic programming

The aim of *genetic programming* (Koza, 1989, 1992) is to develop, in an automated way, computer programs for solving specific problems. Genetic programming is therefore a domain-independent approach to automatic programming.

Genetic programming is an evolutionary computation paradigm in which a population of computer programs are evolved to (approximately) solve problems.

In genetic programming, an individual is a computer program. The results produced by the execution of the program are evaluated. This evaluation represents the fitness value of the individual.

A tree-structured representation of the programs is generally used. Usually the representations are of variable size. Search operators for evolving programs are *recombination* and *mutation*.

Two-parent program trees may be used to create offspring by recombination. A subtree is chosen in each parent. The offspring are generated by substituting the chosen subtree from one parent into the other.

The mutation operator typically acts by selecting a node of the tree. The resulting subtree is replaced by a randomly generated subtree.

1.5.2 Learning classifier systems

Learning classifier systems (Holland, 1986) are dynamic, rule-based systems that learn by examples and induction.

Learning classifier systems use production rules of the form

$$if\ <condition>\ then\ <action>$$

A rule has the following meaning: The specified action is performed if the condition is true.

A production rule is called a *classifier*. The rules are adjusted by means of specific evolutionary procedures. Classifier systems may thus be considered as production systems using evolutionary algorithms for rule discovery.

In Holland's standard approach, the rules are encoded as binary strings. A performance (strength or fitness) measure is associated with each classifier.

There are two main techniques concerning learning classifier systems: the Michigan approach and the Pittsburgh (or Pitt) approach.

1.5.2.1 Michigan approach

In the *Michigan approach* (developed at the University of Michigan by Holland and Reitman, 1978), an individual of an evolutionary algorithm population encodes a single rule.

A *rule set* needed to solve a problem is represented by the *entire* population. The collection of rules is modified via interaction with the environment.

The problem is not to find the best rule but to obtain the best set of rules. Therefore, one must coevolve a set of cooperative rules that jointly are likely to solve the problem.

A usual evolutionary algorithm is not suitable because it converges toward a homogeneous population. A multi-modal evolutionary technique or another procedure preserving population diversity may be used. One method is to use a *credit assignment system* based on the reward the system obtains from the environment.

The *bucket brigade algorithm* is such a credit assignment procedure to update the rule strength (or fitness) at each generation.

The rule strengths are used to update the classifiers and to solve the conflict between contradictory rules.

1.5.2.2 Pittsburgh approach

The *Pittsburgh* (or *Pitt*) approach (developed at the University of Pittsburgh by Smith, 1980) considers that each individual represents an entire set of rules for the problem at hand.

As one individual represents a complete solution, the problem is to find the fittest individual. The Pittsburgh approach may include the use of a standard evolutionary algorithm.

The number of rules per chromosome is not necessarily constant. Search operators that change the number of rules in a given chromosome are often used.

1.6 Structure of an evolutionary algorithm

Evolutionary algorithms utilize the collective learning of a set of candidate solutions by imitating the process of natural evolution.

1.6.1 Encoding solutions

In many cases, the search is not performed directly in the (problem) solution space, but rather in the *representation* space.

Members of the population that encodes the solutions of an evolutionary algorithm are members of the representation space.

Each candidate solution is represented as an individual (or chromosome) of a population. Therefore, an individual encodes (or represents) a point in the search (or representation) space of a given problem.

New individuals are created in a given population by operators intended to model natural *crossover* (or *recombination*) and *mutation*. In this way, a new generation of solutions is obtained.

The individuals are compared by means of a *fitness* function. The recombination and survival are guided by the fitness value.

Let S denote the *solution space* of a given problem. The space of individuals will be denoted by X, and will be considered as representing the *search* (or *representation*) space of the system.

A problem solution s is encoded by an individual $C(s) \in X$, where C is the *encoding function*

$$C : S \to X.$$

Remarks

(i)   Sometimes the solution space S and the *representation space* X may coincide. This means that no supplementary solution encoding is needed.

(ii)   Members of the solution space S are sometimes referred to as *phenotypes*.

(iii)   Members of the representation space X are usually called *chromosomes, genotypes, genomes,* or *individuals*.

1.6.2 Selection and search operators

Let us denote by $P(t)$ the population of individuals at generation t, where $t = 0, 1, 2, \ldots$.

An offspring population is generated by means of *selection* and *search* (or *variation*) operators. The main search operators are *recombination* and *mutation*.

Other operators, like *inversion* or problem-specific operators, may also be useful.

1.6.2.1 Fitness function

The individuals of a population are evaluated by means of a real-valued *fitness function f*

$$f : X \rightarrow R.$$

A *survival* or *replacement* mechanism based on the fitness measure is applied to select the individuals of the new generation from offspring and parent populations.

The initial population $P(0)$ is usually generated at random. Sometimes specific knowledge about the problem domain may be used to start the search from an appropriate region in the search space.

Members of $P(0)$ are evaluated by using the fitness function.

1.6.2.2 Recombination operator

The *recombination* operator R is used to create new individuals by combining the genetic information of two or more parents.

We may define the recombination operator R as an application

$$R : X^p \rightarrow X^q.$$

In this case, the recombination operator realizes a (p,q) transformation where p parents are combined to obtain q offspring.

1.6.2.3 Mutation operator

The *mutation* operator M generates new individuals by (usually small) variations of a single individual.

Mutation aims to (re-)introduce variability in a solution population and to avoid search stagnation in a nonappropriate region of the search space.

This search stasis is known as the *premature convergence* of the search process.

The mutation operator may be represented as an application

$$M : X \rightarrow X.$$

1.6.2.4 Selection

We may consider two types of selection.

The *selection for recombination* operator is used to decide which members of the current population $P(t)$ will be used as parents of the new generation. Therefore, this operator selects the individuals entering the mating pool.

The *selection for replacement* operator is used to obtain which individuals from $P(t)$ and their offspring will effectively enter the new generation $P(t+1)$.

1.6.3 Innovative vs. conservative operators

Search operators may be classified as *innovative* operators and *conservative* operators.

Innovative operators ensure that the new aspects of the problem are taken into account.

A typical innovative operator is mutation. Several strong mutation operators may generate solutions completely uncorrelated with the original solution.

Conservative operators are used to exploit and consolidate what has already been obtained by the individuals in the population.

This aim is mainly achieved by the recombination of two or more solutions. Combining useful pieces of information from different individuals may result in better solutions.

1.6.4 Components of an EC algorithm

The main components of an evolutionary algorithm may be identified as follows:

* *representation scheme of potential solutions*;

* *population model*;

* *evaluation module*

    (realized by a fitness function or by other evaluation mechanisms);

* *search (variation) operators*;

* *parent selection strategy*

    (obtained by a selection for recombination operator);

- *survival strategy (environmental selection)*

  (obtained by a selection for replacement operator).

These components will be described in the various chapters of the book with reference to several evolutionary models.

1.7 Basic evolutionary algorithm

A general evolutionary algorithm using selection, recombination, and mutation may be outlined as below:

GENERAL EVOLUTIONARY ALGORITHM

begin

$t = 0$; $\{t$ is the generation index$\}$

initialise population $P(t)$;

evaluate $P(t)$; $\{$evaluate and select
individuals for
recombination
by using fitness$\}$

while (termination condition $\neq$ true) **do**

$P'(t) = $ recombine $P(t)$;

$P''(t) = $ mutate $P'(t)$;

evaluate $P''(t)$;

$P(t + 1) = $ select $(P''(t) \cup Q)$; $\{$select individuals for
replacement$\}$

$$t = t+1;$$

end while

end

Remarks

(i)   In the previous algorithm, Q is a set of individuals from $P(t)$ that are considered for replacement (survival).

(ii)   The extreme situations are

$$Q = \varnothing$$

and

$$Q = P(t).$$

1.7.1.1   Termination condition

The termination condition of evolutionary algorithms usually refers to a pre-specified number of generations.

According to the specific evolutionary algorithm, other stop conditions may be used, e.g., the number of successive generations for which no modification occurs in the population.

If we are able to formulate a criterion for optimal or acceptable solutions, it may be used to formulate a success predicate.

1.7.1.2   Result of an evolutionary algorithm

Basic methods to choose the result of an evolutionary algorithm are the following:

(i)   The solution is encoded by the best individual in the final population.

(ii)   The solution is given by the entire final population (e.g., classifier systems within the Michigan approach, or mixed strategies in game playing).

(iii)   The solution is given by a subset of the best individuals in the final population.

(iv)   The solution is given by the best individual found in the complete run of the evolutionary algorithm.

A *'caching the best'* mechanism, or an elitist selection strategy, is required in this case.

References and bibliography

Baricelli, N.A., (1957), Symbiogenetic evolution processes realized by artificial methods, *Methodos*, 9, 143-182.

Box, G.E.P., (1957), Evolutionary operation: A method of increasing industrial productivity, *Applied Statistics*, 6, 81-101.

Bremermann, H.J., (1962), Optimization through evolution and recombination, *Self-Organizing Systems*, M.C. Yovits, G.T. Jacobi, G.D. Goldstein (Eds.), Spartan Books, Washington DC.

Caporale, L.H., (Ed.), (1999), *Molecular Strategies in Biological Evolution*, The New York Academy of Sciences, New York.

Davis, L. (Ed.), (1991), *Handbook of Genetic Algorithms*, Van Nostrand Reinhold, New York.

Fogel, D.B., (1995), *Evolutionary Computation: Toward a New Philosophy of Machine Intelligence*, IEEE Press, Piscataway, NJ.

Fogel, L.J., (1962), Autonomous automata, *Industrial Research*, 4, 14-19.

Fogel, L.J., Owens, A.J., Walsh, M.J., (1966), *Artificial Intelligence through Simulated Evolution*, John Wiley, New York.

Fraser, A.S., (1957), Simulation of genetic systems by automatic digital computers, *Australian Journal of Biological Sciences*, 10, 484-491.

Friedberg, R.M., (1958), A learning machine, *IBM J. of Research and Development*, 2, 2-13.

Friedman, G.J., (1959), Digital simulation of an evolutionary process, *General Systems Yearbook*, 4, 171-184.

Glover, F., Laguna, M., (1997), *Tabu Search*, Kluwer Academic Publishers, Boston.

Holland, J.H., (1962), Outline for a logical theory of adaptive systems, *J. ACM*, 3, 297-314.

Holland, J.H., (1975), *Adaptation in Natural and Artificial Systems*, University of Michigan Press, Ann Arbor.

Holland, J.H., (1986), Escaping brittleness: The possibility of general-purpose learning algorithms applied to parallel rule-based systems, *Machine Learning*, 2, R.S. Michalski, J.G. Carbonell, T.M. Mitchell (Eds.), Morgan Kaufmann, Los Altos, CA, 593-624.

Holland, J.H., Reitman, J.S., (1978), Cognitive systems based on adaptive algorithms, *Pattern Directed Inference Systems*, D.A. Watermann, F. Hayes-Roth (Eds.), Academic Press, New York, 313-329.

Koza, J.R., (1989), Hierarchical genetic algorithms operating on populations of computer programs, *Proc. 11th Int. Joint Conf. on Artificial Intelligence*, N.S. Sridharan (Ed.), Morgan Kaufmann, San Mateo, CA, 768-774.

Koza, J.R., (1992), *Genetic Programming*, MIT Press, Cambridge, MA.

Rechenberg, I., (1965), Cybernetic Solution Path of an Experimental Problem, Royal Aircraft Establishment, Library Translation No. 1122, August.

Rechenberg, I., (1973), *Evolutionsstrategie: Optimierung Technischer Systeme nach Prinzipien der Biologischen Evolution*, Frommann-Holzboog Verlag, Stuttgart.

Schwefel, H.-P., (1975), Evolutionsstrategie und numerische Optimierung, Ph.D. Thesis, Technische Universität Berlin.

Schwefel, H.-P., (1977), *Numerische Optimierung von Computer-Modellen mittels der Evolutionsstrategie*, Birkhäuser, Basel.

Schwefel, H.-P. (1981), *Numerical Optimization of Computer Models*, John Wiley, Chichester.

Smith, S.F. (1980), A Learning System Based on Genetic Adaptive Algorithms, Ph.D. Thesis, University of Pittsburgh.

Turing, A.M., (1950), Computing machinery and intelligence, *Mind*, 59, 433-460.

Turing, A.M., (1992), Intelligent machines, *Mechanical Intelligence: Collected Works of A.M. Turing*, D.C. Ince (Ed.), North Holland, Amsterdam, 107-128.

van Laarhoven, P.J.M., Aarts, E.H.L., (1987), *Simulated Annealing: Theory and Applications*, D. Reidel Publishers, Dordrecht.

von Neumann, J., (1966), *Theory of Self-Reproducing Automata*, University of Illinois Press, Illinois.

2

Genetic algorithms

2.1 Introduction

Genetic algorithms (GAs) represent the main paradigm of evolutionary computation. Genetic algorithms consider a population of chromosomes (individuals) encoding potential solutions to a given problem.

Within the traditional GA model, the chromosomes are bit strings of a fixed length. Each chromosome represents a point in the search space.

The search progress is obtained by modification of the chromosome population. The most important search operator is traditionally considered to be *recombination* (*crossover*).

Random *mutation* of newly generated offspring induces variability in the population, preventing premature convergence. The *inversion* operator is rarely used and its role is not very well established.

A *fitness function* is used to measure the quality of each individual. The selection for crossover is based on the fitness value.

A probabilistic selection operator ensures the 'fittest' individuals the highest probability to produce offspring.

Iterative genetic search of a solution implies a compromise between two contradictory requirements: *exploitation* (or intensification) of the best available solution, and robust *exploration* of the search space.

Exploration may also be viewed as search *diversification*. The exploitation and exploration aspects of the search process correspond to the *local search* and the *global search*, respectively.

The search method has to achieve a balance between exploitation and exploration. If the obtained solutions are exploited too much, a *premature convergence* of the search process may occur. In this case, the search ceases to progress and the procedure eventually ends with an unacceptable solution.

On the other hand, if a special emphasis is placed on exploration, the information already available may be improperly used. In this case, the search process could become very slow.

Random search is a typical example of a search strategy that explores the search space by ignoring the exploitation of the promising regions of the space.

Genetic algorithms carry out a reasonable compromise between exploitation and exploration of the search space.

Holland (1975) pointed out that GAs achieve this compromise in a nearly optimal way.

2.2 Problem representation and fitness function

In this section, the encoding solution problem using binary chromosomes within standard genetic algorithms, and chromosome evaluation are considered.

2.2.1 Representation

To solve a particular problem it is necessary to give a suitable encoding (representation) of the problem, i.e., to specify the *encoding* function

$$C : S \rightarrow X,$$

where S is the solution space of the problem and X is the *chromosome* (or *search* or *representation*) space.

Remarks

(i)   As a chromosome encodes only one solution, in what follows the terms 'chromosome,' 'solution,' 'individual' will be considered as equivalent.

(ii)   Let us consider

$$c = C(S), \ s \in S.$$

The solution s may be interpreted as the *phenotype* associated with the *genotype* (or chromosome) c.

2.2.2 Fitness function

In order to compare chromosomes, they have to be evaluated somehow. Sometimes the problem allows defining of an evaluation function measuring the relevance of each chromosome.

2.2.2.1 Chromosome evaluation

To control the search progress, an evaluation of each chromosome appearing in the system is necessary. This evaluation is usually done by means of a quality (or *fitness*) function.

The fitness function depends on the user's ability to encode the problem adequately. For a numerical or combinatorial optimization problem, the fitness function usually coincides with the objective (criterion) function, or may be obtained from the objective function by some simple transformation.

For other problems the fitness function may be a cost function, a loss function, or may be obtained as a transformation of such a function.

Sometimes the quality of a solution may be evaluated by comparing it with a set of examples (test cases).

A genetic algorithm is an iterative, global search procedure whose goal is the optimization of the fitness function. The algorithm works in parallel on a population of candidate solutions (chromosomes) from the search space.

There must be enough fitness difference among individuals in the population to drive a real evolutionary search process. An algorithm where fitness is not sufficiently discriminatory may degenerate in a multi-member blind search.

2.2.2.2 Implicit fitness and coevolution

Normally the fitness measure of a chromosome is independent of the fitness of the other individuals in the population. However, it is possible to consider an *implicit fitness* function whose values depend on all the individuals in the population.

In this case, we have an *intrinsic adaptation* (Packard, 1988) that ensures the *coevolution* of the individuals (Kaufman and Johnsen, 1991).

2.2.2.3 Fitness landscape

The surface generated by the fitness function is sometimes referred to as the *fitness landscape*. When the objective function has the meaning of energy (or cost), the fitness landscape is interpreted as the *energy surface*.

A chromosome corresponds to a point of the fitness landscape. The fitness landscape structure may be relevant to the search progress.

The search may end prematurely by being trapped in a local optimum region of the fitness landscape.

2.3 Search progress

The dynamics of the search process of a genetic algorithm is obtained by chromosome recombination and modification.

At each iteration t, the algorithm creates a population that is interpreted as the *generation* at moment t. Mutation reintroduces lost genetic material into the population. Therefore, by mutation effect, no gene (allele) permanently disappears from the population.

Moreover, mutation may be responsible for exploring some promising regions of the search space.

Within the standard GA approach, all generations have the same size, i.e., the same number of individuals. Usually the new generation contains better individuals, i.e., individuals having a better adaptation (represented by the fitness function) to the environment.

With the increase of generations a tendency of evolution toward the global optimum of the fitness function may be observed.

2.4 Basic elements of genetic algorithms

Genetic algorithms involve a population of *independent* individuals representing problem solutions. The new generation $P(t+1)$ is obtained from the population $P(t)$ by means of the following steps.

1. **Evaluation**

   The genetic algorithm computes the quality (generally, the corresponding value of the fitness function) of each individual of the current population.

2. **Selection for recombination**

   The individuals of population $P(t)$ are selected for recombination according to their fitness.

   Selected individuals represent an intermediate population P^1.

   Individuals from P^1 will enter the mating pool with a given probability (crossover probability).

3. **Recombination and modification**

   The individuals from the mating pool are mated by using the recombination (or crossover) operator. A new intermediate population P^2 is obtained.

The resultant offspring (population P^2) are modified by means of the mutation and, possibly, inversion operators.

From an algorithmic point of view, the genetic operators are procedures that either modify locally the solutions (mutation and inversion operators) represented by chromosomes, or combine these solutions (crossover).

Recombination achieves gene transfer between two chromosomes.

Each genetic operator has a specific probability to be applied. These probabilities are parameters of the algorithm.

Let P^3 be the population obtained by applying mutation and, possibly, inversion to population P^2.

4. Selection for replacement and survival

The new generation $P(t+1)$ contains the individuals of the population P^3, and may include other selected individuals.

Several selection procedures are possible. For instance, (a subset of) the individuals from $P(t)$ that have not been selected for recombination might enter $P(t+1)$.

Some replacement methods are strictly *generational* procedures. Other methods allow generations to overlap. The *overlapping degree* between parent and offspring populations may be defined using the generation gap.

The *generation gap* is the percentage of the population to be replaced in each generation.

2.5 Canonical genetic algorithm

The canonical genetic algorithm is a simple instance of the general evolutionary procedure. Its replacement strategy is a generational one.

2.5.1 Representation

Within the canonical genetic algorithm, a fixed-size chromosome population is used (i.e., the number of chromosomes in each generation is constant).

The chromosomes are binary strings of constant length. The value of each gene is either 0 or 1.

It is sometimes useful to encode solutions in such a way that the genes are as orthogonal as possible (i.e., a gene's semantics depends only on its values, being independent of other genes).

2.5.2 Simple genetic algorithm

The search (variation) genetic operators are recombination (or crossover) and mutation.

There are different selection-for-replacement mechanisms.

The standard (canonical, simple) GA model starts with an arbitrary population of individuals.

A fitness-based selection of individuals is performed. The selected individuals are subject to crossover and mutation.

In the most usual case, generation $P(t+1)$ is composed of the offspring of generation $P(t)$.

The next generation completely replaces the parent generation. In this case, all parents are discarded.

The canonical genetic algorithm may be outlined as below.

CANONICAL (SIMPLE) GENETIC ALGORITHM

S1. Set $t = 0$.

S2. Initialize a chromosome population $P(t)$.

(Random initialization is the basic choice.)

S3. Evaluate $P(t)$ by using a fitness measure.

S4. **while** (termination condition not satisfied) **do**

   begin

   S4.1. Select for recombination chromosomes (individuals) from $P(t)$.

   Let P^1 be the set of the selected chromosomes.

   Choose individuals from P^1 to enter the mating pool (MP).

   S4.2. Recombine the chromosomes in MP forming population P^2.

   Mutate chromosomes in P^2 forming population P^3.

   S4.3. Select for replacement from P^3 and $P(t)$ forming $P(t+1)$.

S4.4.   Set $t = t + 1$.

end

Remark

The solution to the problem is usually considered to be the best individual of the last generation. But it is not guaranteed that a better individual has not been previously obtained. Therefore, it is useful to keep the best individual obtained up to each instant t (a supplementary 'caching the best' mechanism is thus needed).

2.5.3 Replacement strategies

The most common strategy to produce the new population is to use all the offspring generated (population P^3).

Let n be the population size. If the cardinality of P^3 is just n, then the old population is completely replaced by the new population.

In this case, step S4.3 may be written as

S4.3.   Set $P(t+1) = P^3$.

If the number of offspring is less than n, then the missing q individuals will be randomly selected from $P(t)$. One possibility is to select these individuals from non-mated members of P^1.

We may also assume that the best q individuals from $P(t)$ (or some randomly selected individuals) are unmodified when they enter the new generation. This may be the effect of a *reproduction* (or *clone*) operator. Note that, at the same time, these individuals may also be selected for recombination.

The considered strategies of selection for replacement are *generational*. Well-defined and distinct generations exist. An entire new generation is created from the old (parent) population. The offspring generation replaces the parent generation.

Remarks

(i)   Let us observe that a number of individuals can pass unmodified into the next generations via the reproduction operator.

(ii)   The main alternative to the generational replacement strategy (or to generational evolutionary algorithms) is the *steady-state* strategy.

In a *steady-state* selection, only one individual per generation is replaced. Usually the population's worst member is considered for replacement.

The parent selected for replacement is compared with the offspring obtained by recombination and mutation. If the offspring represents a fitness improvement, it will actually replace its parent.

2.5.4 Initial population

Most implementations of genetic algorithms use uniform random sampling to generate the first population. Several variants are possible.

2.5.4.1 Partially enumerative initialization

An alternative to random sampling is *partially enumerative initialization*. At least one instance of each possible schema (see next section) of a specified size is generated in the initial population.

In this way all good schemata needed to solve the problem can be represented in the initial population. So doing, the size of the initial population may be drastically reduced with respect to uniform random sampling.

2.5.4.2 Doping

The initial population may be occasionally *doped* with some very good solutions. These solutions may be generated by a different algorithm or may express the user's knowledge about the problem domain.

Of course, to avoid premature convergence, doping should be combined with an appropriate selection mechanism.

Ranking selection (see Chapter 4) may be such a mechanism. Tournament selection (see Chapter 4) is another useful and popular selection scheme.

2.6 Schemata and building blocks

Genetic algorithms work by using simple operations like chromosome copying, substring interchanging, and position modifying.

It is quite surprising how such elementary operations and the simple mechanisms considered above may achieve an efficient search.

A simple approach to explain how genetic algorithms work to achieve good and even excellent results has been considered by Holland (1975).

Holland proposed analyzing the complex behavior of genetic algorithms in terms of *schemata* and *building blocks*.

2.6.1 Notions concerning schemata

According to Holland's theory, genetic algorithms work by discovering, emphasizing, and recombining building blocks to obtain larger building blocks representing better solutions.

The idea is that acceptable solutions tend to combine to obtain good solutions.

Standard genetic algorithms use binary encoding. A chromosome is a string of fixed length. Each position of the string represents a gene. The value of a gene is either 0 or 1.

Let L be the chromosome length. In this case, the chromosome space X is the L-dimensional hypercube, i.e.,

$$X = \{0,1\}^L.$$

Each chromosome c is an element of X, i.e.,

$$c \in \{0,1\}^L.$$

A chromosome may be interpreted as a vector in the hypercube X representing the chromosome space.

Definition

A *schema* of the chromosome space X is a string of length L made up of the symbols 0, 1, $*$. The symbol asterisk represents a 'wildcard' (or 'do not care') matching both 1 and 0.

Remarks

(i)   A schema is an element of the set $\{0, 1, *\}^L$.

(ii)   A *schema* may be interpreted as a hyperplane of the search space.

Example

Let us consider the schema

$$S = 1 * * 0.$$

This schema represents four chromosomes that begin with 1 and terminate with 0. These chromosomes are

$$x_1 = 1000,$$

$$x_2 = 1010,$$

$$x_3 = 1100,$$

$$x_4 = 1110.$$

The chromosomes $x_1, \ldots, x_4$ are interpreted as the *instances* (or *representatives*) of the schema S.

Definition

The *well-defined symbols* (or specific positions) of a schema represent non-asterisk symbols in that schema.

Definition

A chromosome c is an *instance* of a schema S if the well-defined symbols of S coincide with the values in the corresponding positions of c.

We may also say that S *represents* the chromosome c.

Remark

A chromosome c with L genes is an instance of 2^L different schemata.

A schema is characterized by two elements: the *order* and the *defining length*.

Definition

The *order* of schema S is the number of well-defined symbols within S.

Definition

The *defining length* of a schema is the distance between the first and the last specific positions.

Example

For instance, the schema

$$S = * 0 * 1 0 1 * * 0 *$$

has order five.

The loci of the first well-defined symbol and the last well-defined symbol are 2 and 9, respectively. Therefore, the defining length of the schema S is seven.

Definition

The *fitness of a schema S* in a given population is defined as the average fitness of the instances of S in the population.

2.6.2 Building block hypothesis and schema theorem

The standard explanation of how genetic algorithms work is referred to as the *building block hypothesis.*

A *building block* is a short (small defining length), above-average, low-order schema.

According to the building block conjecture, genetic algorithms combine small building blocks into larger building blocks.

Informally stated, the *schema theorem* (Holland, 1975) asserts that short, above-average, low-order schemata acquire an exponentially increasing number of trials (instances) in the new generations.

On the contrary, below-average schemata tend to appear less frequently (have fewer instances) in the next generations.

2.6.3 Implicit parallelism

A genetic algorithm implicitly manipulates all schemata that are present in a given population. The schemata are only implicitly evaluated.

Let us consider a population of n individuals. The number of schemata processed at each generation is of the order n^3 (Goldberg, 1989).

The simultaneous implicit control and evaluation of a large number of schemata in a chromosome population are known as the *implicit parallelism* (Holland, 1975) of genetic algorithms.

The schema theorem ensures that the implicit parallelism is associated with fitness increasing in successive generations. The building blocks are combined into larger building blocks that converge toward the optimal solution.

Let us observe that no explicit operation is directly performed on building blocks or on other schemata by the genetic algorithm. No direct computation of the schemata fitness is made by the genetic algorithm.

2.6.4 Genetic drift

It is possible that some desirable properties of genetic algorithms are not observed experimentally. This deviation from the expected behavior of the genetic search may be generated by several factors. One of them is *genetic drift*.

Usually genetic drift is associated with a loss of diversity in a small population due to the random character of selection operators.

Genetic drift may cause an evolving population to cluster around a unique solution even if there are several solutions of interest in the search space.

Genetic drift and premature convergence of the search process are strongly correlated processes.

References and bibliography

Bäck, T., (1996), *Evolutionary Algorithms in Theory and Practice*, Oxford University Press, Oxford.

Bäck, T., Fogel, D.B., Michalewicz, Z. (Eds.), (1997), *Handbook of Evolutionary Computation*, Institute of Physics Publishing, Bristol, and Oxford University Press, New York.

Fogel, D.B., (1995), *Evolutionary Computation: Toward a New Philosophy of Machine Intelligence*, IEEE Press, Piscataway, NJ.

Goldberg, D.E., (1989), *Genetic Algorithms in Search, Optimization, and Machine Learning*, Addison-Wesley, Reading, MA.

Holland, J.H., (1975), *Adaptation in Natural and Artificial Systems*, University of Michigan Press, Ann Arbor (Second edition: MIT Press, 1992).

Kaufman, S.A., Johnsen, S., (1991), Co-evolution at the edge of chaos: coupled fitness landscapes, poised states and co-evolutionary avalanches, *Artificial Life*, 2, C.G. Langton, C. Taylor, J.D. Farmer, S. Rasmussen (Eds.), Addison Wesley, Redwood City, 325-369.

Michalewicz, Z., (1992), *Genetic Algorithms + Data Structures = Evolution Programs*, Springer-Verlag, Berlin.

Mitchell, M., (1996), *An Introduction to Genetic Algorithms*, MIT Press, Cambridge, MA.

Packard, N.H., (1988), Intrinsic Adaptation in a Simple Model for Evolution, *Artificial Life*, 1, C.G. Langton (Ed.), Addison Wesley, Redwood City, 141-155.

3

Basic selection schemes in evolutionary algorithms

3.1 Introduction

The aim of selection is to focus the search process on the most promising regions of the search space. Selection is based on the quality evaluation of the individuals expressed as their fitness or by a different means.

The selection task is to decide

(i)   whether an individual has to be modified by genetic variation operators, and

(ii)   whether it has to be kept in the population or replaced.

There are several selection operators but all of them are representation-independent. This characteristic gives selection a unique position among the EC operators.

As selection operators are general procedures, for each problem we have to make a decision about the most suitable selection operator. This decision is one of the most important because selection is highly responsible for the convergence of the search process.

This chapter is dedicated to a detailed presentation of some basic selection strategies. The chapter focuses on proportional selection and on several variants of this selection strategy.

Other topics of this chapter are

- fitness function,

- premature convergence,

- selection pressure, and

- truncation and scaling transforms.

3.2 Selection purposes

In this section, the basic aspects of the selection operation in an evolutionary algorithm are considered.

3.2.1 Mating pool

In order to ensure passage from the current population $P(t)$ to population $P(t + 1)$, it is necessary that a number of chromosomes be selected from the current population.

The selected individuals will act as the parents of the next generation. Operators of recombination, mutation, inversion, etc., may be applied to the selected individuals.

Let us suppose that the new population is obtained only as a result of recombination and mutation. Then, we will have two selections, a selection for recombination and another for mutation. Actually, the two selections do not apply strictly to the same population.

First, the selection operator is applied to population $P(t)$. The result is an intermediate population representing the *mating pool* of the system.

The recombination operator is applied on the mating pool. The population obtained by recombination is then subject to mutation.

3.2.2 Selection for recombination and selection for replacement

According to its goals, we have a *selection for recombination* (or *selection for mating*) and a selection from parent and offspring populations to produce the next generation (*selection for replacement*).

We will suppose that the purpose of using the evolutionary algorithm is the *maximization* of an objective function $J : U \to V$. This fact influences the way in which the selection is carried out.

Sometimes, however, we may want to apply the evolutionary algorithm to a minimization problem. In such a case, the problem needs to be reformulated as a maximization problem.

The aim of selection for recombination is twofold. On the one hand, selection has to provide high reproductive chances to the fittest individuals belonging to a given population.

On the other hand, selection must preserve population diversity in order to explore all the promising search space regions.

Due to the action of selection for replacement, the individuals that will contribute to the formation of the next generation are picked out of the current and offspring populations.

3.3 Fitness function

In this section, an axiomatic definition of the fitness function is given and some general methods to derive a fitness function are considered.

3.3.1 Fitness and scaling

In order to carry out selection, it is necessary to introduce a measure of the performance (quality or suitability) of the individuals. By selection we aim to maximize the performance of individuals.

The search concentrates, therefore, on those regions of the search space that correspond to maximum suitability. This concentration accomplishes the *exploitation* of the best solutions already found, which is exactly the purpose of selection.

In what follows, we will present different mechanisms of selection, stressing the advantages and limits of each of them.

For selection purposes, a performance value is associated with each individual in the current population $P(t)$. This performance value represents the *fitness* of the individual.

Usually a *fitness function* (or an *evaluation function*) is used to measure, in an explicit way, the chromosome performance. However, in some cases the fitness can be measured only in an implicit way using information about system performance.

Let X be the chromosome set and f the fitness function. Function f is a real-valued function on X. This function must reflect chromosome quality with respect to the current problem (for instance, the optimization of the objective function).

Further, if f is used to generate a selection probability, then f should have positive or zero values. Of course, this is not required in the opposite case (e.g., in rank-based selection schemes (see Chapter 4)).

For most applications, the fitness function is derived from the objective function. Usually the fitness function is defined as a composition of a transformation (scaling) function and the objective function.

The expression of the scaling function depends on the nature of the optimization (or search) problem.

For a maximization problem, the fitness function has to assume larger values for better individuals.

For minimization problems, smaller values have to be associated with better individuals. Actually, as evolutionary algorithms are maximization procedures, minimization problems are usually reformulated by remapping the fitness function (see Chapter 4). By remapping, the best individuals will assume the highest fitness values.

If the objective function has negative values, scaling also has the role of shifting the values of the fitness function to the positive domain.

3.3.2 Implicit fitness evaluation

For some problems the fitness of a chromosome is measured in an implicit way, by evaluating the quality (or the relevance) of the corresponding solution with respect to the current problem.

When a set of examples (*test cases*) is given, the fitness may be calculated using the solution error, i.e., the difference between the current solution and the correct (or desired) output. Another possibility is to simulate the system behavior generated by the current solution.

Implicit evaluation allows the use of evolutionary algorithms for solving problems for which an objective function is difficult or impossible to establish (designing very complex systems or playing games, for instance).

3.3.3 Coevolutionary fitness evaluation

Coevolutionary models may also represent a suitable tool for solution evaluation. In coevolutionary selection methods, individuals compete for selection without an explicit fitness value (Hillis, 1992, Angeline and Pollack, 1993).

According to the actual problem, two *cooperative* or *competitive* populations are considered. The fitness of one individual in the population is measured by the individual's relevance with respect to the other population.

3.4 Selection pressure and takeover time

Selection pressure and *takeover time* represent useful parameters characterizing the selection operators. They are directly correlated with the progress of the search process.

3.4.1 Selection pressure

The *selection pressure* of a selection operator may be defined as the degree to which highly fit individuals are allowed to produce offspring (copies) in the next generation.

Low values of selection pressure provide each individual in the population with a reasonable selection probability.

High values of selection pressure strongly favor the best individuals in the population. Therefore, selection becomes more and more elitist with an increase of the selection pressure.

3.4.2 Takeover time

Let us consider an evolutionary algorithm operating under selection alone (no variation operators, such as recombination or mutation, are allowed).

Consider an initial population that contains a single instance (or copy) of the optimal individual.

With the previous assumptions, the *takeover time* of a selection operator is defined as the number of generations required for the evolutionary algorithm to converge to a population consisting entirely of instances of the optimal individual.

Remarks

(i)   It is easy to see that selection pressure and takeover time are dual parameters. If the takeover time of a selection operator is small, then the selection pressure of the operator is large, and vice versa.

(ii)   Selection pressure gives an idea of how *greedy* the selection operator is in making the population uniform.

(iii)   Takeover time may be interpreted as a measure of how slow the algorithm convergence is.

3.4.3 Selection pressure and search progress

For a selection operator with high selection pressure the population diversity decreases quickly. Therefore, high selection pressure is generally associated with quick convergence of the search process.

In order to avoid the stagnation of the search process (stasis or premature convergence), highly disruptive search (recombination and mutation) operators are needed.

A selection scheme with high selection pressure has to be associated with high recombination and mutation probabilities.

If the number of allowed generations is small, a selection operator with high selection pressure is desirable to improve the search convergence.

3.5 Proportional selection

This section is dedicated to a particular selection scheme, namely, *proportional selection*. Implications of this scheme for search progress are investigated. Several variants of proportional selection are also considered.

3.5.1 Selection probability

Proportional selection is the most popular type of selection. Its basic probabilistic element, namely, selection probability, will be defined in what follows.

3.5.1.1 Basic definitions

Let us assume that the current population $P(t)$ has n chromosomes:

$$P(t) = \left\{ x^1, x^2, ..., x^n \right\}.$$

Definition

We define the *total fitness F* of the population as the sum of all individuals' fitness:

$$F = \sum_{i=1}^{n} f(x^i).$$

Definition

In the case of proportional selection, the *selection probability* of chromosome x^i is the number p_i defined as

$$p_i = \frac{f(x^i)}{F}, \quad i = 1, 2, ..., n.$$

3.5.1.2 Average number of copies

For a population of n chromosomes the selection operator is applied n times.

Each individual x^i will have an average number n_i of copies in the intermediate population given by

$$n_i = n p_i.$$

Using the expression of the selection probability we obtain:

$$n_i = \frac{n f(x^i)}{\sum_{i=1}^{n} f(x^i)}.$$

It follows that the proportional selection mechanism ensures an average number

$$n_i = \frac{f(x^i)}{\bar{f}}$$

of copies of chromosome x^i, where $\bar{f}$ is the average fitness value of the population.

3.5.2 Proportional selection algorithm

In order to ensure the selection of x^i with probability p_i (i.e., a uniform probability distribution), a *Monte Carlo* (or *roulette*) method can be used.

A spinning wheel is divided into n sectors. Each sector corresponds to a chromosome. The dimension of the ith sector is proportional to the selection probability p_i of chromosome x^i.

The wheel is turned n times. At each turn a chromosome is selected. The selected chromosome is copied into the intermediate population.

Selection based on the spinning roulette principle can be described by the following algorithm:

MONTE CARLO SELECTION ALGORITHM

(ROULETTE WHEEL SELECTION)

1.   For each chromosome x^i, $i = 1, 2, \ldots, n$, compute the number:

$$q_i = \sum_{k=1}^{i} p_k, \quad i = 1, 2, \ldots, n.$$

2.   **for** $i = 1, 2, \ldots, n$ **do:**

   2.1   Generate a random number g in the interval [0,1]. The random number g belongs to a uniform probability distribution.

   2.2   Selection rule:

   - if $0 \leq g \leq q_1$, then the first chromosome (x^1) is selected,

   - if $q_{i-1} < g \leq q_i$, $i = 1, 2, \ldots, n$, then chromosome x^i is selected.

Remarks

(i)   The previous selection rule represents a *stochastic sampling with replacement*. Although the method has zero bias, it allows a single chromosome to be selected more than once. This means that the best chromosomes may have more than one copy in the intermediate population, and therefore more descendents. Moreover, any individual with positive fitness could be selected to fill the entire population.

(ii)   There are several stable versions of the roulette mechanism (see Goldberg, 1989).

(iii)   Usually the standard variant given above is used.

In what follows, we will consider some drawbacks connected with proportional selection and various possibilities to ameliorate it.

3.5.3   Premature and slow convergence

The proportional selection mechanism is a natural one and has certain advantages that become apparent mainly in the schema theory.

This type of selection also has some disadvantages. It may induce both premature convergence as well as slow convergence.

3.5.3.1   Premature convergence

Let us consider a population having an individual whose fitness is much higher than the population's average fitness. According to proportional selection, this highly fit individual is likely to be selected several times. Its offspring will dominate the next generation and population diversity will decrease.

In this way one or a few comparatively highly fit (but not optimal) individuals may rapidly come to dominate the population. As a consequence, some regions of the search space are not explored any more during the optimization process, causing it to converge to a local optimum point.

To avoid local premature convergence of the search process we have to modify the way individuals are selected for mating. One basic idea is to adapt the fitness range by a *scale transform* and to prevent any individual from going over. By fitness scaling, the fitness values are adapted taking the population's average fitness into account.

A different idea is to use another stochastic selection mechanism instead of proportional selection, implemented by means of the roulette algorithm.

3.5.3.2 Slow convergence

Consider a homogeneous population where there are small fitness differences among individuals. Selection probabilities are approximately equal and there is no longer a real selection (selection becomes stagnant), but merely a random choice. Therefore, fitness uniformity implies vanishing selection.

After enough generations the average fitness could be high, and there might be little difference between the best and the average individuals. Selection is no longer able to drive the search process toward the global optimum point. The individuals will move very slowly in the search space. The search process has only a very slow convergence toward a global optimum point.

Slow convergence may be treated similarly to premature local convergence. The actual fitness range in the population is expanded. A mechanism to prevent very poor individuals from appearing should also be considered.

The problems generated by premature local convergence or by slow convergence can be treated by remapping the fitness function. *Scaling* is one of the most usual remapping techniques.

3.5.3.3 Takeover time for proportional selection

Goldberg and Deb (1991) have computed the takeover time for the proportional selection operator.

Consider a population of size n and the fitness function

$$f(x) = e^{cx}.$$

The takeover time τ for proportional selection (without fitness scaling) is

$$\tau = \frac{n \ln n}{c}.$$

If the fitness function

$$f(x) = x^c$$

is considered, then the takeover time is

$$\tau = \frac{n \ln n - 1}{c}.$$

3.5.4 Variants of proportional selection

To prevent an individual or a group of highly fit individuals from dominating the next generation, some modifications to the stochastic selection mechanism may be used.

3.5.4.1 Stochastic sampling with replacement

One possibility for avoiding the dominance of the fittest individuals is to diminish the selection probability of a given individual by a fixed positive constant each time the individual is selected.

This strategy may be considered a variant of the *stochastic sampling with partial replacement algorithm*.

3.5.4.2 Sampling rate assignment

Another possibility for ameliorating proportional selection is to assign a *target sampling rate* to each individual. The target sampling rate is a natural number indicating how many descendants (copies) of the individual are allowed.

The target sampling rate may be equal for all individuals in a population. In this way, the population diversity is preserved.

A dual solution is to rank individuals according to their fitness and to assign the sampling rate according to the rank. The best individual will have the greatest sampling rate.

The better an individual, the greater its sampling rate. This solution has an elitist flavor and ensures the exploitation of the promising solutions already found.

Selection is done using the spinning wheel procedure.

3.5.4.3 Stochastic universal sampling

A different strategy is to construct a spinning wheel with n sectors and n equally spaced pointers. The sector width is proportional to the selection probability of the corresponding individual.

A *single spin* of the wheel selects n individuals (not necessarily distinct). This single-phase selection algorithm has zero bias and may be considered as a version of the *stochastic universal sampling algorithm* (Baker, 1987).

Within universal sampling, each individual x^i is guaranteed to be selected at least k times, but not more than $(k + 1)$ times, where k is an integer proportional to the selection probability of x^i.

The method may be modified to allow the total number of selected individuals to be specified.

3.6 Truncation

Truncation selection (Mühlenbein and Schlierkamp-Voosen, 1994) is inspired by the breeding practice.

Truncation selection consists of selecting for recombination the best individuals and discarding the rest.

Selection quality is characterized by two parameters: response to selection and selection effectiveness.

The *response to selection* at generation $(t + 1)$ is the number $R(t)$ defined as the difference between the average fitnesses in the generations $(t + 1)$ and t, respectively.

We have

$$R(t) = m(t+1) - m(t),$$

where $m(t)$ is the average fitness of population $P(t)$.

The *selection effectiveness* is measured by using the *selection differential* $S(t)$, defined as

$$S(t) = M(t) - m(t),$$

where $M(t)$ is the average fitness of the selected individuals.

References and bibliography

Angeline, P.J., Pollack J.B., (1993), Competitive environments evolve better solutions for complex tasks, *Proc. 5th Int. Conf. on Genetic Algorithms*, S. Forrest (Ed.), Morgan Kaufmann, San Mateo, CA, 264-270.

Baker, J.E., (1985), Adaptive selection methods for genetic algorithms, *Proc. 1st Int. Conf. on Genetic Algorithms*, J.J. Grefenstette (Ed.), Lawrence Erlbaum Associates, Hillsdale, NJ, 101-111.

Baker, J.E., (1987), Reducing bias and inefficiency in the selection algorithm, *Proc. 2nd Int. Conf. on Genetic Algorithms*, J.J. Grefenstette (Ed.), Lawrence Erlbaum Associates, Hillsdale, NJ, 14-21.

Goldberg, D.E., (1989), *Genetic Algorithms in Search, Optimization, and Machine Learning*, Addison-Wesley, Reading, MA.

Goldberg, D.E., Deb, K., (1991), A comparative analysis of selection schemes used in genetic algorithms, *Foundations of Genetic Algorithms*, G.J.E. Rawlins (Ed.), Morgan Kaufmann, San Mateo, CA, 69-93.

Hillis, W.D., (1992), Co-evolving parasites improves simulated evolution as an optimization procedure, *Artificial Life*, 2, C.G. Langton, C. Taylor, J.D. Farmer, S. Rasmussen (Eds.), Addison Wesley, Reading, MA, 313-324.

Michalewicz, Z., (1992), *Genetic Algorithms + Data Structures = Evolution Programs*, Springer-Verlag, Berlin.

Mitchell, M., (1996), *An Introduction to Genetic Algorithms*, MIT Press, Cambridge, MA.

Mühlenbein, H., (1997), Genetic algorithms, *Local Search in Combinatorial Optimization*, E. Aarts, J.K. Lenstra (Eds.), John Wiley, New York, 137-171.

Mühlenbein, H., Schlierkamp-Voosen, D., (1994), The science of breeding and its applications to the breeder genetic algorithm (bga), *Evolutionary Computation*, 1, 335-360.

4

Selection based on scaling and ranking mechanisms

4.1 Introduction

Domination of a single, high-fit individual (as in proportional selection and in elitist selection schemes) and the quasi-random selection associated with the majority domination may sometimes mislead the search process. These extreme situations have to be equally avoided as potential sources of errors.

There are some methods for dealing with such problematic situations where individual effectiveness plays a very negligible role in selection.

Scaling transformation is one of these methods. Rank-based selection is another. In this chapter, both methods are considered.

Special attention is paid to selection methods based on the tournament concept.

The main topics of this chapter are

- static and dynamic scaling transforms;

- noisy fitness functions;

- linear and nonlinear ranking;

- biased selection;

- binary, deterministic, and probabilistic tournament;

- Boltzmann tournament;

- score-based and local tournament selection schemes.

4.2   Scale transformation

By scaling, we can modify the fitness function values as required to avoid the problems connected with proportional selection.

Scaling transformation may be *static* (generation- or time-independent) or *dynamic*. In a dynamic scaling transform, the scaling mechanism is reconsidered for each generation.

If a static scaling transform is used, the fitness values may rapidly converge to a restricted domain. As a consequence, selection pressure quickly decreases and some search space regions become inaccessible.

To prevent this behavior, a dynamic scaling transform (Baker, 1985) can be used. By scaling, differences between fitness function values can be modified in the desired manner.

Different, both static and dynamic, scaling transformations have been suggested. We will describe some of them in the following section.

4.3 Static scaling mechanisms

In this section, several static scaling procedures are considered. These procedures use some elementary real-valued functions (linear, power, or exponential).

4.3.1 Linear scaling

The linear scaling transformation is a one-variable real linear function S,

$$S(x) = ax + b,$$

where the coefficients a and b are real numbers.

The coefficients a and b do not depend on the problem in an explicit way.

The corresponding *transformed fitness* function *tf* is

$$tf(x) = S(f(x)).$$

Thus the evaluation (fitness) *eval(x)* of individual x becomes

$$eval(x) = tf(x)$$

$$= af(x) + b.$$

4.3.2 Power law scaling

The scaling transformation is the function

$$S(x) = x^u,$$

where u is a real number.

Usually, u is chosen close to 1.

4.3.3 Logarithmic scaling

Several logarithmic scaling transformations may be considered. An example is the *Boltzmann selection* (de la Maza and Tidor, 1993) that uses the transformation function

$$tf(x) = e^{\frac{f(x)}{T}},$$

where the parameter T, controlling the selective pressure, decreases during the search process.

We may use more sophisticated scaling transforms, but generally we do not have *a priori* arguments for choosing a particular type of function.

4.4 Dynamic scaling

In this section, several dynamic scaling mechanisms will be considered.

4.4.1 Sigma truncation

Sigma truncation (or *sigma scaling*) (Goldberg, 1989) incorporates some information about the current population $P(t)$. Within sigma scaling, a (reasonable) multiple of the standard deviation of the population fitness is subtracted from the fitness value.

Let T be the non-negative-valued function

$$T(x) = \begin{cases} x, & \text{if } x > 0, \\ 0, & \text{otherwise.} \end{cases}$$

The sigma truncation scaling function S is defined as

$$S(x) = T(x - (m_t - c\sigma_t)),$$

where

- m_t is the average fitness of the population $P(t)$,

- σ_t is the standard deviation of the population fitness at generation t, and

- c is a small integer representing a problem parameter (e.g., $c = 2$).

The transformed fitness function tf is

$$tf(x) = S(f(x)).$$

The evaluation *eval(x)* of individual x may be written as

$$eval(x) = tf(x)$$

$$= T(f(x) - (m_t - c\sigma_t)).$$

Let us observe that by this transform all negative fitness values are set to zero.

Sigma scaling keeps the selection pressure relatively constant rather than dependent on the fitness standard deviation in the population. Sigma transform restricts the effects that a single high-fit individual can have on the population.

Thus the evaluation of individual x after scaling will be

$$eval(x) = \begin{cases} f(x) - (m_t - c\sigma_t), & \text{if } f(x) > (m_t - c\sigma_t), \\ 0, & \text{if } f(x) \leq (m_t - c\sigma_t). \end{cases}$$

A different example of sigma scaling (Mitchell, 1996) is

$$eval(x) = \begin{cases} 1 + \dfrac{f(x) - m_t}{\sigma_t}, & \text{if } \sigma_t \neq 0, \\ 0, & \text{if } \sigma_t = 0. \end{cases}$$

4.4.2 Window scaling

Window scaling uses some information about the fitness in the last g generations, where $g \geq 1$.

If only the last generation $P(t)$ is taken into account, then the *dynamic window scaling* function is given by

$$eval(x) = f(x) - \min_{y \in P(t)} f(y).$$

Let us consider a more general (larger) *scaling window* W. The corresponding *dynamic window scaling* transform is

$$eval(x) = f(x) - \min_{y \in W} f(y),$$

where the scaling window W is the set of all individuals contained in the last g generations, $g \geq 1$.

4.5 Noisy fitness functions

Many real-world applications may be affected by noise, which can influence the fitness calculation.

The effects of noise in fitness calculation are considered in (Fitzpatrick and Grefenstette, 1988) and (Miller and Goldberg, 1996).

Noise can mislead the search process considerably. On the other hand, we sometimes try to detect robust solutions. Solutions that are very sensitive to small perturbations of their parameter values may not be useful in certain situations.

Noisy fitness functions may be interesting to cope with search/optimization problems where noise plays a significant role, or robustness is required.

Noisy fitness may be interpreted as a scale transformation

$$eval(x) = tf(x)$$
$$= f(x) + \delta,$$

where δ is a scalar noise.

When the aim is to detect robust solutions, noise is added to the phenotypic vector (solution) x (Tsutsui and Ghosh, 1997).

This may be obtained by considering an evaluation function of the form

$$eval(x) = f(x + a),$$

where a is a random vector having a specified distribution.

The obtained solutions are expected to be more robust against perturbations (noise) having the distribution of the vector a.

4.6 Fitness remapping for minimization problems

We have assumed that higher fitness values are assigned to better individuals. This assignment is suitable for maximization problems, which represent the situation implicitly considered in the book.

To solve minimization problems we have to transform the fitness function. One possibility is to consider the fitness transform

$$tf(x) = M - f(x),$$

where M is an upper bound of the objective function.

If the global maximum value of the objective function is unknown, we may use the fitness transform

$$eval\,(x(t)) = tf\,(x(t))$$

$$= M_t - f(x(t)),$$

where $x(t) \in P(t)$ and M_t is the maximum value of function f found so far (up to time t).

An alternative is to consider M_t as the maximum value of function f within generation $P(t)$.

Another plausible alternative is to consider the transformation

$$eval\,(x(t)) = \frac{1}{K + f(x(t)) - f_{\min}(t)},$$

where

- K is a positive constant, and

- $f_{min}(t)$ is the minimum observed value of function f up to time t, or the minimum value of function f within generation $P(t)$.

A further possibility is to consider a function of the form

$$eval\,(x) = \frac{1}{K + f(x)},$$

where K is a positive constant.

4.7 Rank-based selection

Rank-based selection mechanisms are focused on the rank ordering of the fitness of the individuals.

The individuals in a population of size n are ranked according to their suitability for the search purposes.

In what follows, the rank of the *least* fit is considered to be *one* and the rank of the *fittest* is considered to be n.

The selection probability is assigned to individuals as a function of their rank in the population.

Ranking selection is natural for those situations in which it is easier to assign subjective scores to the problem solutions rather than to specify an exact objective function.

Furthermore, while under proportional selection a small group of highly fit individuals might completely take over the population; ranking avoids premature convergence due to the domination of the best individuals.

Finally, we may note that ranking reduces the selection pressure when the fitness variance is high, and increases the selection pressure when the fitness variance is low.

4.7.1 Linear ranking selection

In linear ranking (Baker 1985), the selection probability of each individual is defined as a linear function of the individual's rank. Linear ranking may be implemented by specifying the expected number of offspring of the best individual of each generation.

4.7.1.1 Selection probability for linear ranking

Let us denote by *Max* the expected number of offspring of the best individual in the population.

The selection probability for individual x^i is defined as follows:

$$p_i = \frac{1}{n}\left[min + (Max - min)\frac{r_i - 1}{n-1}\right], \qquad (4.1)$$

where

- r_i is the rank of individual x^i, and

- *min* is the expected number of offspring of the individual with rank one (the worst individual in the population).

Remark

Max and *min* represent the *target sampling rates* of the best and the worst individual, respectively.

4.7.1.2 Range of parameter *Max*

The expected number of offspring of individual x^j is

$$n_j = np_j.$$

If the population size is constant, we have

$$\sum_{j=1}^{n} n_j = \sum_{j=1}^{n} np_j$$

$$= n.$$

From this equality and (4.1) we have

$$n\,min + \frac{1}{n-1}(Max - min)\sum_{j=1}^{n}(r_j - 1) = n. \qquad (4.2)$$

But

$$\sum_{j=1}^{n} (r_j - 1) = \sum_{i=0}^{n-1} i$$

$$= \frac{n(n-1)}{2}. \tag{4.3}$$

From (4.2) and (4.3), it follows that

$$min + \frac{1}{2}(Max - min) = 1.$$

Therefore, we have

$$min = 2 - Max. \tag{4.4}$$

From the condition

$$min \geq 0,$$

we obtain

$$Max \leq 2.$$

Since it is natural to suppose that

$$min \leq Max,$$

from (4.4) it follows that

$$Max \geq 1.$$

Thus we have established the inequality

$$1 \le Max \le 2.$$

4.7.1.3 Another expression of selection probability

Using (4.4), the selection probability may now be expressed as a function of parameter Max only. In this case, we may write

$$p_i = \frac{1}{n}\left[Max - 2(Max-1)\left(1 - \frac{r_i - 1}{n-1}\right)\right].$$

4.7.1.4 Selection probabilities for the best and worst individuals

The selection probability of the best individual obtained by setting

$$r_n = n$$

is

$$p_n = \frac{Max}{n}.$$

This expression is consistent with the meaning of Max.

For the worst individual we have

$$r_1 = 1,$$

and thus

$$p_1 = \frac{2 - Max}{n}.$$

Therefore, we have

$$p_1 = \frac{min}{n}.$$

The obtained condition

$$Max + min = 2$$

ensures that the population size is constant.

4.7.1.5 Selection pressure and takeover time for linear ranking

The parameter *Max* may be interpreted as expressing the selection pressure of the linear ranking selection.

Linear ranking increases population diversity by preventing the fittest individuals (or super individuals) from dominating the next generation. But by decreasing the selection pressure, linear ranking may have certain difficulties finding highly fit individuals. Therefore, the search process becomes slower.

Consider linear ranking selection with

$$Max = 2$$

in a population of size n.

The takeover time may be approximated (Goldberg and Deb, 1991) as

$$\tau \approx \frac{\ln n + \ln (\ln n)}{\ln 2}.$$

For linear ranking with

$$1 < Max < 2,$$

the takeover time is approximated as

$$\tau \approx \frac{2}{n-1} \ln (n-1).$$

4.7.1.6 An example

Let us consider a population having two individuals. Consider the case

$$Max = 2.$$

Let p_1 and p_2 be the selection probabilities of the worst and the best individual, respectively. Linear ranking gives

$$p_1 = 0$$

and

$$p_2 = 1.$$

Therefore, only the best individual will be selected in the mating pool (since its selection probability is 1).

If

$$Max = 1,$$

we obtain

$$p_1 = p_2$$

$$= \frac{1}{2},$$

i.e., both individuals will be selected.

4.7.1.7 Selection pressure and population diversity

The previous example enables us to view the relationship between selection pressure and population diversity within linear ranking. High selection-pressure values focus the search toward the best individuals. As a consequence, population diversity decreases.

Therefore, high selection pressure can be associated with local premature convergence of the search process. Conversely, low selection pressure can entail a uniform random selection. The search becomes inefficient.

We have to establish a balance between selection pressure and population diversity. We easily recognize here another aspect of the exploration–exploitation balance.

4.7.2 Nonlinear ranking

Nonlinear ranking assigns each individual a selection probability that is a nonlinear function of the individual's rank.

Let us consider a population of size n. The rank of the least fit individual is considered to be 1. The rank of the fittest individual is defined to be n.

4.7.2.1 Exponential ranking

An example of nonlinear ranking is

$$p_i = \frac{1}{c}\left(1 - e^{1 - r_i}\right),$$

where c is a normalization factor.

If we consider

$$r_i = 1,$$

we obtain

$$p_i = 0.$$

Therefore, within this selection scheme, the probability of selecting the worst individual (i.e., $r_i = 1$) is zero.

4.7.2.2 Geometric distribution ranking

Another selection scheme (Whitley and Kauth, 1988) uses the geometric distribution

$$p_i = a(1 - a)^{n - r_i},$$

where a is a parameter of the method, $a \in (0, 1)$.

Let us suppose that x^i is the best individual, i.e.,

$$r_i = n.$$

It follows that

$$p_i = a.$$

Therefore, a is the probability of selecting the best individual in the population.

4.7.2.3 Biased exponential ranking

Another exponential ranking scheme computes the selection probability using the selection bias constant a:

$$p_i = \frac{a-1}{a^n - 1} a^{n-r_i},$$

where $0 < a < 1$.

4.7.2.4 General nonlinear ranking

In principle, any increasing nonlinear function can be used for nonlinear ranking.

Let

$$g : \{1, ..., n\} \to [0,1]$$

be such an increasing function.

In this case, we may define the probability selection as

$$p_i = g(r_i), \quad i = 1, 2, ..., n.$$

4.8 Binary tournament

Tournament selection (Goldberg and Deb, 1991) is a very popular ranking method of performing selection.

Binary tournament implies that two individuals directly compete for selection. Tournament may be done with or without *reinsertion* of the competing individuals into the original population.

4.8.1 Deterministic tournament

Binary tournament selection is based on direct pairwise comparison of individuals and the selection of the most successful one. Such a competition may be referred to as a *trial*.

This type of selection implies the following operations:

(i)   Two chromosomes are chosen at random from the population.

(ii)   The fitness of the chosen chromosomes is calculated.

(iii)   The most successful chromosome (the winner) is selected. (The winner is copied into the intermediate population on which the recombination and modification operators will act.)

The two chromosomes are usually returned to the original population (tournament with reinsertion) and they may be selected again.

The described mechanism must be applied *n* times in order to generate an intermediate population made up of *n* chromosomes (not necessarily distinct copies of the chromosomes existing at the time *t*).

We may also consider that the winner is allowed to mutate. The result of mutation is returned to the population, replacing the loser of the tournament.

A slightly modified variant is to allow each chromosome to compete with a randomly selected chromosome.

Both variants allow a deterministic selection of the winner. Stochastic mechanisms for winner selection are sometimes useful. Such a tournament scheme will be described in Section 4.8.2.

4.8.2 Probabilistic tournament

We may consider a stochastic tournament selection, replacing step *(iii)* of the deterministic tournament by step *(III)*, as follows:

(III)   A random number $R \in [0, 1)$ is chosen at random. If $R < p$, where p is a parameter (for example, $p = 0.3$), the less fit individual is selected.

Otherwise, the fitter of the two individuals is selected.

This selection scheme may be generalized by admitting that the parameter p decreases with time.

We may also use a Boltzmann (or simulated annealing) tournament scheme (see Section 4.8.3).

The selection probability p may decrease with the generation index according to the law

$$p(t) = p_0\, e^{-ct},$$

where

• $p_0 \in (0, 1)$, and

- c is a positive constant.

This mechanism ensures the search progress, maintaining population diversity for the first stages of the search process. As the search advances, the probability of maintaining the best solutions increases.

A smoother selection probability decreasing scheme is

$$p(t) = p_0 \frac{c}{1 + \ln t},$$

where $c > 0$.

4.8.3 Boltzmann tournament

Goldberg (1990) and Mahfoud (1993) considered *Boltzmann tournament selection*. Suppose f is a function to be *minimized*. Depending on the problem, f may be interpreted as objective, energy, or cost function.

Let x be the current solution and y an alternative solution.

In a binary tournament with y, the individual x wins (is selected) with probability

$$p(x) = \frac{1}{1 + e^{\frac{f(x) - f(y)}{T}}},$$

where T is the temperature, which is reduced in a predefined manner in successive iterations.

Such competition is referred to as the *Boltzmann trial*.

The winner of the trial will be the current solution in the next trial.

4.9 *q*-tournament selection

Binary tournament may be generalized to an arbitrary tournament group size q, $0 \leq q \leq (n - 1)$.

In this section, several variants of many individual tournaments are presented.

4.9.1 Score-based tournament

For each individual x in a population, a group of q individuals is randomly chosen from the population. The number q is called *tournament size*. The chromosome x will compete with each individual in the tournament (or sample) group.

The problem is how to sample individuals for the tournament group from the population. Usually this sampling is uniformly random. However, better results are expected if the sample members are chosen so as to induce a great diversity within the tournament group (Rosin and Belew, 1995).

Within *disassortative* sample selection, the first member of the tournament group is randomly chosen. Each successive member of the sample is the most different (in terms of a suitable distance) from those already in the tournament group.

As a tournament result, a *score* is assigned to x. The score is a natural number between 0 and q representing the number of wins earned in the competition. Selection is made on the basis of these scores.

As all individuals in the population are involved in tournament, selection chooses the best subset of given size from the population.

We may consider tournament selection as a *score-based ranking selection*.

Tournament selection, like other ranking selection schemes, is less subject to rapid takeover by good individuals.

The tournament size q may be used to adjust the selection pressure. A small tournament size is associated with low selection pressure. In particular, the tournament size $q = 0$ corresponds to a random selection (no selection pressure). The selection pressure increases with the tournament size q.

Remark

For practical purposes, we may choose $q \in \{6, ..., 10\}$. A selection with $q \geq 11$ is usually considered relatively hard selection.

4.9.2 Local tournament

Different variants of q-tournament have been proposed. One of them is *local tournament selection* (Brindle, 1981).

Local tournament chooses q individuals from the population randomly. The individuals are selected with uniform probability but without reinsertion. The selected individuals play a tournament.

The winning individual is the best individual in the group, i.e., the individual having the highest fitness value. This is a *deterministic* tournament.

The tournament may be probabilistic as well. In a probabilistic tournament, the probability of an individual winning is generally proportional to its fitness.

4.9.3 Concluding remarks on tournament selection

Tournament selection tends to become the mainstream selection strategy. This happens because it does not require a global fitness comparison of all individuals in a population.

Tournament selection accelerates the evolution process. Parallel methods using tournament selection strategies are natural and simple to implement.

References and bibliography

Bäck, T., Hoffmeister, F., (1991), Extended selection mechanisms in genetic algorithms, *Proc. 4th Int. Conf. on Genetic Algorithms*, R.K. Belew, L.B. Booker (Eds.), Morgan Kaufmann, San Mateo, CA, 2-9.

Baker, J.E., (1985), Adaptive selection methods for genetic algorithm, *Proc. 1st Int. Conf. on Genetic Algorithms*, J.J. Grefenstette (Ed.), Lawrence Erlbaum Associates, Hillsdale, NJ, 101-111.

Baker, J.E., (1987), Reducing bias and inefficiency in the selection algorithm, *Proc. 2nd Int. Conf. on Genetic Algorithms*, J.J. Grefenstette (Ed.), Lawrence Erlbaum Associates, Hillsdale, NJ, 14-21.

Brindle, A., (1981), Genetic Algorithms for Function Optimization, Technique Report TR81-2, Department of Computer Science, University of Alberta, Edmonton.

de la Maza, M., Tidor, B., (1993), An analysis of selection procedures with particular attention paid to proportional and Boltzmann selection, *Proc. 5th Int. Conf. on Genetic Algorithms*, S. Forrest (Ed.), Morgan Kaufmann, San Mateo, CA, 124-131.

Fitzpatrick, J.M., Grefenstette, J.J., (1988), Genetic algorithms in noisy environments, *Machine Learning*, 3, 101-120.

Goldberg, D.E., (1989), *Genetic Algorithms in Search, Optimization, and Machine Learning*, Addison-Wesley, Reading, MA.

Goldberg, D.E., (1990), A note on Boltzmann tournament selection for genetic algorithms and population-oriented simulated annealing, *Complex Systems*, 4, 445-460.

Goldberg, D.E., Deb, K., (1991), A comparative analysis of selection schemes used in genetic algorithms, *Foundations of Genetic Algorithms*, G.J.E. Rawlins (Ed.), Morgan Kaufmann, San Mateo, CA, 69-93.

Hammel, U., Bäck, T., (1994), Evolution strategies on noisy functions: How to improve convergence properties, *Parallel Problem Solving from Nature*, 3, Y. Davidor, H.-P. Schwefel, R. Männer (Eds.), Springer, Berlin, 159-168.

Koza, J.R., (1992), *Genetic Programming*, MIT Press, Cambridge, MA.

Mahfoud, S.W., (1993), Finite Markov chain models of an alternative selection strategy for the genetic algorithm, *Complex Systems*, 7, 155-170.

Michalewicz, Z., (1992), *Genetic Algorithms + Data Structures = Evolution Programs*, Springer-Verlag, Berlin.

Miller, B.L., Goldberg, D.E., (1996), Genetic algorithms, selection scheme, and the varying effect of noise, *Evolutionary Computation*, 4, 113-131.

Mitchell, M., (1996), *An Introduction to Genetic Algorithms*, MIT Press, Cambridge, MA.

Mühlenbein, H., (1997), Genetic algorithms, *Local Search in Combinatorial Optimization*, E. Aarts, J.K. Lenstra (Eds.), John Wiley, New York, 137-171.

Rosin, C.D., Belew, R.K., (1995), Models for competitive co-evolution: Finding components worth feating, *Proc. 6th Int. Conf. on Genetic Algorithms*, L.J., Eshelman (Ed.), Morgan Kaufmann, San Mateo, CA.

Tsutsui, S., Ghosh, A., (1997), Genetic algorithms with a robust solution searching scheme, *IEEE Trans. on Evolutionary Computation*, 1, 201-208.

Whitley, D., (1989), The GENITOR algorithm and selective pressure: why rank-based allocation of reproductive trials is best, *Proc. 3rd Int. Conf. on Genetic Algorithms*, J.D. Schaffer (Ed.), Morgan Kaufmann, San Mateo, CA, 116-121.

Whitley, D., Kauth, J., (1988), GENITOR: A different genetic algorithm, *Proc. Rocky Mountain Conf. on Artificial Intelligence*, Denver, 118-130.

5

Further selection strategies

5.1 Introduction

This chapter explores the relationship existing among several selection schemes. To make this relationship clearer, various dichotomies of selection schemes are considered (elitist vs. pure, generational vs. nongenerational, conservative vs. extinctive, and dynamic vs. static).

Generation gap and overlapping degree of a selection scheme are defined.

Steady-state evolutionary algorithms are described.

Other selection schemes considered in this chapter are

- generational elitist strategies,

- Michalewicz selection,

- Boltzmann scaling,

- simulated annealing,

- PRSA selection,

- coevolutionary models,

- greedy over-selection.

The chapter concludes with some remarks on genetic drift due to the stochastic nature of the selection operator.

5.2 Classification of selection strategies

There are many different replacement and survival strategies. The simple genetic algorithm uses a complete generational replacement scheme. According to this scheme, distinct and well-separated generations exist.

Within the generational replacement scheme, a new population of offspring replaces the parent population. The basic alternative to the generational replacing rule is steady-state selection.

A possible taxonomy of selection schemes may be obtained according to the following independent classification axes (Bäck and Hoffmeister, 1991):

(i)   *Elitist* vs. *pure*

In a *pure* selection strategy, all members of a population are allowed to be selected according to a well-defined stochastic mechanism.

It would be interesting to keep the best individual of each generation. Such a strategy is called *elitist*. It seems natural that the best individual of a generation should survive unchanged into the next generation.

Another suggestion is that only a restricted part of the population be replaced within each generation.

Let r be a number defining the replacement rate. In this case, rn individuals are chosen from the population.

The rn descendants of the selected individuals will replace their parents in the new population.

Another possibility is that the offspring replace other members of the population, namely, those closest to the offspring themselves.

If the chromosomes are binary encoded, chromosome proximity can be calculated using the Hamming distance.

(ii)   *Generational* vs. *nongenerational*

Some selection strategies are *generational*, in the sense that the set of parents (mating pool) is determined once and remains fixed until a new population of offspring has been generated.

An entire new population is created from the old one and completely replaces it.

In *nongenerational* strategies, the parents are selected in different moments and the offspring are inserted into the population as they are generated.

(iii)   *Conservative* vs. *extinctive*

From another point of view, selection strategies may be classified as conservative and extinctive.

A *conservative* selection guarantees each individual a non-zero selection probability.

In certain *extinctive* strategies, the selection of the best individuals is given up in order to prevent premature convergence.

Proportional selection is conservative. Linear ranking selection is conservative for *Max* < 2 and extinctive for *Max* = 2. Deterministic binary tournament is extinctive, whereas probabilistic tournament is conservative.

(iv)   *Dynamic* vs. *static*

Depending on the selection probabilities, a selection method may be *dynamic* or *static*. *Dynamic* selection requires that the selection probabilities depend on the fitness values actually present in the population, varying across generations.

Tournament selection, sigma truncation, and window scaling selection are dynamic.

Remark

For all selection strategies, we may consider a supplementary '*caching the best*' mechanism. Within elitist strategies, such a mechanism is useless because the best individual in the population is automatically preserved.

5.3   Elitist strategies

Elitist strategies are methods of biased parent selection. Some of the best individuals in the population may be chosen to enter the new generation. Such individuals may be lost later, if they are not selected for mating or if they are disrupted by recombination or mutation.

In evolutionary algorithms, the *expected lifetime* of an individual is typically one generation. An elitist strategy links the lifetime of individuals to their fitness. Highly fit individuals can have a lifetime longer than one generation.

An elitist strategy allows copying the best member(s) of a generation into the next generation. Thus elitist strategies are techniques to preserve good solutions in a population for longer than one generation.

In elitist strategies, the search tends to be more exploitative than explorative. Although an elitist strategy may increase the premature convergence problem, elitism seems to improve the evolutionary algorithm performance in many cases.

Elitist strategies are suitable to find a global optimal solution but may fail for problems in which multiple optimal solutions are required.

5.4   Generation gap methods

In this section, the characterization of selection schemes that allow parent and offspring populations to compete for survival is considered. In such situations, the concept of generation is not sharp.

5.4.1   Overlapping and non-overlapping models

Within the canonical genetic algorithm, the offspring completely replace the parent population in the new generation. Such a model is also called non-overlapping.

In a *non-overlapping model*, parents and offspring never compete for survival. The entire parent population is replaced by the offspring population.

In an *overlapping model*, parents and offspring compete for survival. The selection pool for deletion (replacement) is comprised of both parents and offspring.

5.4.2 Generation gap

The *generation gap* (De Jong, 1975; De Jong and Sarma, 1993) is defined as the replacement rate, i.e., the percentage of the population selected from the current population to be replaced in each generation.

The remainder of the population is (randomly) chosen to survive intact in the next generation.

Let us denote by G the generation gap (replacement rate).

The case

$$G=1$$

corresponds to the canonical genetic algorithm (generational selection). All individuals in a population $P(t)$ compete for mating selection. The offspring produced by recombination and mutation will replace the entire population $P(t)$.

The *overlapping degree OV* between the parent and offspring populations may be defined as

$$OV=1-G.$$

For the canonical genetic algorithm we have

$$OV=0.$$

Therefore, the value $G = 1$ is associated with a non-overlapping system.

Non-overlapping models are similar to *generational* ones. Usually, as we have seen before, a generational model is considered to be a system where the parent population remains fixed until the new generation is complete.

If

$$G = \frac{1}{n},$$

a single individual is selected to produce a single offspring. The offspring will replace a member of the current population. This is the case of the *steady-state* evolutionary systems.

We may observe that the axes (dichotomies) generational/nongenerational and non-overlapping/overlapping are not completely independent. However, they are not identical. We can merely consider them as expressing facets of a more general dichotomy.

5.5   Steady-state evolutionary algorithms

The steady-state model is the main alternative to the generational replacement strategy.

5.5.1   Basic steady-state model

In *steady-state* evolutionary algorithms, only one individual is usually replaced in each generation. Typical examples of steady-state systems are *steady-state GA* (Syswerda, 1989) and the *GENITOR* system (Whitley, 1989).

One offspring resulting from recombination and mutation of the fittest individuals will generally replace the population's worst member, if the offspring represents a fitness improvement (compared to the worst member of the current population). This is also the selection mechanism of the $(\mu+1)$ evolution strategy (Schwefel, 1981) (see Chapter 12).

Within a steady-state algorithm, the genetic operators are applied asynchronously and there is no explicit mechanism for producing generations. This feature explains the name of the strategy.

In a more general case, the selected individual is not the best in the current population. One individual may be chosen by using an appropriate selection mechanism. The selection probability is proportional to the individual's fitness.

A further generalization is obtained if m individuals, where m is less than, or equal to, the population size n, are allowed to be replaced in the population.

5.5.2 Generalized steady-state algorithm

The generalized steady-state algorithm may be outlined as below.

GENERALIZED STEADY-STATE ALGORITHM

P1. m individuals are sampled from the current population with a probability proportional to their fitness.

P2. m offspring are generated by applying variation operators to the selected individuals.

P3. The offspring are inserted into the new population and other m members are discarded.

Remarks

(i) The deletion of the m individuals may be accomplished, for instance, by selecting them from the worst members following the inverse fitness ranking.

(ii) It is also possible to consider a tournament replacement scheme. In this case, the m offspring and the m poorest individuals compete to enter the new population.

Remark

In the steady-state algorithm without duplicates (Syswerda, 1989), the offspring that are duplicates of individuals in the population are immediately discarded. The method is not applicable when probabilistic or noisy evaluation functions are used.

Remark

The steady-state selection technique is useful for evolving *learning classifier systems*, where a problem solution is represented by the entire population (Michigan approach). Replacing a small number of rules is more beneficial than replacing the whole population.

5.6 Generational elitist strategies in GAs

Generational GAs consider only selection for mating (not for survival). There is no guarantee that the highly fit individuals will survive into the next generation. The use of an elitist strategy may overcome this drawback.

Let us note that steady-state evolutionary algorithms and, generally, overlapping systems, use an implicit elitist selection mechanism.

5.7 Michalewicz selection

Michalewicz (1992) proposed a mechanism of selection that independently chooses a number of r chromosomes (not necessarily distinct) for reproduction and r different chromosomes for removal.

These selections are carried out based on chromosome fitness. An individual whose fitness is above average has a higher probability of being selected for recombination. The chromosomes with below-average fitness have a higher probability of being selected for deletion.

The new population $P(t + 1)$ is made up of $(n - r)$ chromosomes of the old population (that is, all the members of $P(t)$, excepting those selected for deletion) and r descendants of the r selected parents.

Let us note that each individual selected for modification may be used for only one genetic operation (mutation, crossover, inversion, etc.). This strategy represents a method that is dynamic, generational, conservative, and elitist.

Three intermediate populations are a result of selection:

P_1: comprises the r parents,

P_2: includes the r chromosomes to be discarded,

P_3: is made up of the $(n - r)$ chromosomes that have to be copied into $P(t + 1)$.

Remarks

(i) The populations P_1 and P_2 are not necessarily disjoint.

(ii) It is possible that both a chromosome and its offspring enter population $P(t + 1)$. A chromosome whose fitness is above average may be selected both in P_1 and in P_3. In this way, one or more descendants of the chromosome will enter $P(t + 1)$.

A non-standard strategy concerning the search operators is considered. If three search operators (namely, mutation, crossover, and inversion) are used, then the crossover will be applied to one subset of P_1, mutation will be applied to another subset, and the inversion operator to the remaining individuals in P_1.

5.8 Boltzmann selection

There are several types of *Boltzmann selection*. The common idea is to find a method to control the selection pressure. It is generally convenient to have a low selection pressure in the early stage of the search process.

The selection pressure is controlled by varying the temperature parameter according to a given schedule.

The temperature is gradually lowered, which gradually increases the selection pressure. As selection pressure increases, the highly fit individuals will be favored, thus enhancing system stability.

5.8.1 Boltzmann selection by scaling

The *Boltzmann selection* method proposed by de la Maza and Tidor (1993) and Prügel-Bennett and Shapiro (1994) is a scaling method that assigns the individual $x \in P(t)$ the expected value

$$eval(x) = \frac{e^{\frac{f(x)}{T}}}{A},$$

where

- f is the fitness (to be *maximized*),

- T is a temperature-type parameter,

- *eval* is the transformed fitness function, and

- A is a normalization factor, which denotes the average over the population $P(t)$. We have

$$A = E\left(e^{\frac{f(x)}{T}}\right)_{x \in P(t)},$$

where E is the *mean value* operator.

Remark

The temperature parameter T is correlated with the selection pressure. High initial temperature corresponds to low selection pressure (each individual has a reasonable probability of being selected). As the temperature is lowered, the selection pressure increases and the search concentrates on the most promising regions of the search space.

5.8.2 Simulated annealing

Simulated annealing (Aarts and Korst, 1989; Ingber and Rosen, 1992) may supply an acceptance (winning) scheme in a binary tournament.

Let x denote the current solution.

According to the *Metropolis* acceptance scheme, the new candidate solution y wins the tournament (i.e., is accepted in the system as the current solution) with a probability given by

$$p(y) = \begin{cases} 1, & \text{if } f(y) < f(x), \\ e^{-\dfrac{f(y)-f(x)}{T}}, & \text{if } f(y) \geq f(x). \end{cases}$$

We recall that within this acceptance mechanism, function f has to be *minimized*.

5.8.3 PRSA method

Parallel recombinative simulated annealing (PRSA) (Mahfoud and Goldberg, 1995) processes the entire population $P(t)$ in parallel, using recombination and mutation.

The method pairs all individuals, at random, for recombination. After crossover and mutation, offspring compete against their parents in Boltzmann trials. Winners enter the new generation.

Several competition schemes are possible between two parents and two offspring.

In *double acceptance/rejection*, the parents compete as a team against the offspring. The fitness of a team is the sum of its members' fitness values.

In *single acceptance/rejection*, on the contrary, two separate competitions occur, in which each parent competes against one child.

5.9 Other selection methods

In this section, other selection methods will be considered. One is the rank-based greedy selection procedure. Another is a coevolutionary selection method.

5.9.1 Greedy over-selection

Complex problems usually entail large populations and exceedingly time-consuming fitness calculations. To enhance evolutionary algorithm performance, *greedy over-selection* (Koza, 1992) may be used. The method greedily over-selects the fittest individuals in the population.

To implement over-selection, the individuals in the population are sorted in descending order of their fitness. The best individuals are placed in the set $S1$, whereas the remaining individuals represent the set $S2$.

For a given percentage a of the time, an individual is selected from $S1$ according to its fitness, for $(100 - a)$ % of the time an individual is selected from $S2$.

Koza proposed the value

$$a = 80$$

for the parameter a.

It is also considered that $S1$ represents 32% from the individuals in the population, i.e.,

$$\frac{\operatorname{card} S1}{\operatorname{card} S1 + \operatorname{card} S2} = 0.32.$$

This heuristic may be called the *Koza 20-80 rule*.

The considered parameters have no particular justification. They represent a modality to realize greedy over-selection of the fittest individuals.

5.9.2 Coevolutionary selection models

Coevolutionary models may also represent a suitable tool for fitness evaluation and selection. Sometimes providing an adequate fitness function may be very difficult. This may happen, for example, in complex systems when the number of test cases is very large.

In coevolutionary methods for fitness computation, individuals compete for selection without an explicit fitness value (Hillis, 1992, Angeline and Pollack, 1993).

More precisely, two different populations are considered. These populations may be *cooperative* or *competitive*. One population may contain, for instance, solutions to an optimization problem and the second may represent constraints of the problem.

The fitness of an individual in a population is defined as its relevance with respect to a subpopulation of the other population.

The fitness of a game-playing strategy may be computed by playing the strategy against a (sub-)population of opposing strategies.

5.10 Genetic drift

Analysis of the selection schemes (Prügel-Bennett and Shapiro, 1994, 1997; Mühlenbein, 1997) emphasizes that the change of the population mean fitness depends on the population fitness variance. The fitness variance is reduced at each generation by the effect of two independent factors. One factor is the *selection pressure*, which favors better individuals in the population by producing multiple copies of them. The other factor is *genetic drift*, due to the stochastic nature of the selection operator.

The loss of population diversity due to genetic drift has a direct effect on the performance of the evolutionary algorithm. It is one of the factors responsible for the premature convergence of the search process.

A method for calculating genetic drift in terms of changing in the population fitness variance is proposed by Rogers and Prügel-Bennett (1999). Exact analytical expressions of genetic drift can be derived for any selection scheme.

Using these expressions the effect that genetic drift has on the convergence of an evolutionary algorithm may be quantified. Some comparisons under varying generation gaps can be made.

References and bibliography

Aarts, E.H.L., Korst, J., (1989), *Simulated Annealing and Boltzmann Machines: A Stochastic Approach to Combinatorial Optimization and Neural Computing*, John Wiley, Chichester.

Angeline, P.J., Pollack, J.B., (1993), Competitive environments evolve better solutions for complex tasks, *Proc. 5th Int. Conf. on Genetic Algorithms*, S. Forrest (Ed.), Morgan Kaufmann, San Mateo, CA, 264-270.

Bäck, T., Hoffmeister, F., (1991), Extended selection mechanisms in genetic algorithms, *Proc. 4th Int. Conf. on Genetic Algorithms*, R.K. Belew, L.B. Booker (Eds.), Morgan Kaufmann, San Mateo, CA, 2-9.

Baker, J.E., (1987), Reducing bias and inefficiency in the selection algorithm, *Proc. 2nd Int. Conf. on Genetic Algorithms*, J.J. Grefenstette (Ed.), Lawrence Erlbaum Associates, Hillsdale, NJ, 14-21.

de la Maza, M., Tidor, B., (1993), An analysis of selection procedures with particular attention paid to proportional and Boltzmann selection, *Proc. 5th Int. Conf. on Genetic Algorithms*, S. Forrest (Ed.), Morgan Kaufmann, San Mateo, CA, 124-131.

De Jong, K.A., (1975), An Analysis of the Behaviour of a Class of Genetic Adaptive Systems, Ph.D. Thesis, University of Michigan, Ann Arbor.

De Jong, K.A., Sarma, J., (1993), Genetic gaps revisited, *Foundations of Genetic Algorithms*, 2, L.D. Whitley (Ed.), Morgan Kaufmann, San Mateo, CA, 19-28.

Fitzpatrick, J.M., Grefenstette, J.J., (1988), Genetic algorithms in noisy environments, *Machine Learning*, 3, 101-120.

Goldberg, D.E., (1989), *Genetic Algorithms in Search, Optimization and Machine Learning*, Addison-Wesley, Reading, MA.

Goldberg, D.E., (1990), A note on Boltzmann tournament selection for genetic algorithms and population-oriented simulated annealing, *Complex Systems*, 4, 445-460.

Goldberg, D.E., Deb, K., (1991), A comparative analysis of selection schemes used in genetic algorithms, *Foundations of Genetic Algorithms*, G.J.E. Rawlins (Ed.), Morgan Kaufmann, San Mateo, CA, 69-93.

Hillis, W.D., (1992), Co-evolving parasites improve simulated evolution as an optimization procedure, *Artificial Life*, 2, C.G. Langton, C. Taylor, J.D. Farmer, S. Rasmussen (Eds.), Addison-Wesley, Reading, MA, 313-324.

Ingber, L., Rosen, B., (1992), Genetic algorithms and very fast simulated re-annealing: a comparison, *Math. Comput. Modelling*, 16, 87-100.

Koza, J.R., (1992), *Genetic Programming*, MIT Press, Cambridge, MA.

Mahfoud, S.W., (1993), Finite Markov chain models of an alternative selection strategy for the genetic algorithm, *Complex Systems*, 7, 155-170.

Mahfoud, S.W., Goldberg, D.E., (1995), Parallel recombinative simulated annealing: a genetic algorithm, *Parallel Comput.*, 21, 1-28.

Michalewicz, Z., (1992), *Genetic Algorithms + Data Structures = Evolution Programs*, Springer-Verlag, Berlin.

Miller, B.L., Goldberg, D.E., (1996), Genetic algorithms, selection scheme and the varying effect of noise, *Evolutionary Computation*, 4, 113-131.

Mitchell, M., (1996), *An Introduction to Genetic Algorithms*, MIT Press, Cambridge, MA.

Mühlenbein, H., (1997), Genetic algorithms, *Local Search in Combinatorial Optimization*, E. Aarts, J.K. Lenstra (Eds.), Wiley, New York, 137-171.

Prügel-Bennett, A., Shapiro, J.L., (1994), An analysis of genetic algorithms using statistical mechanics, *Physical Review Letters*, 72, 1305-1309.

Prügel-Bennett, A., Shapiro, J.L., (1997), The dynamics of a genetic algorithm for simple random Ising systems, *Physical Review*, D, 104, 75-114.

Rogers, A., Prügel-Bennett, A., (1999), Genetic drift in genetic algorithm selection schemes, *IEEE Trans. on Evolutionary Computation*, 3, 298-303.

Rosin, C.D., Belew, R.K., (1995), Models for competitive co-evolution: Finding components worth feating, *Proc. 6th Int. Conf. on Genetic Algorithms*, L.J., Eshelman (Ed.), Morgan Kaufmann, San Mateo, CA.

Schwefel, H.-P., (1981), *Numerical Optimization of Computer Models*, John Wiley, Chichester, UK.

Syswerda, G., (1989), Uniform crossover in genetic algorithms, *Proc. 3rd Int. Conf. on Genetic Algorithms*, J.D. Schaffer (Ed.), Morgan Kaufmann Publishers, San Mateo, CA, 2-9.

Tsutsui, S., Ghosh, A., (1997), Genetic algorithms with a robust solution searching scheme, *IEEE Trans. on Evolutionary Computation*, 1, 201-208.

Whitley, D., (1989), The GENITOR algorithm and selective pressure: Why rank-based allocation of reproductive trials is best, *Proc. 3rd Int. Conf. on Genetic Algorithms*, J.D. Schaffer (Ed.), Morgan Kaufmann, San Mateo, CA, 116-121.

Whitley, D., Kauth, J., (1988), GENITOR: A different genetic algorithm, *Proc. Rocky Mountain Conf. on Artificial Intelligence*, Denver, 118-130.

6

Recombination operators within binary encoding

6.1 Introduction

The selection operator is employed to focus the search upon the most promising regions of the search space. However, selection alone cannot introduce into a population individuals that do not appear in the intermediate population.

In order to increase population diversity, other operators are used. These are *search* (or *variation*) operators.

By perturbing and recombining the existent individuals, the search operators allow the search process to explore the neighboring regions or to reach further promising regions. The most frequently used search operators are *recombination, mutation,* and *inversion.* The typical recombination operator within binary encoding is also called the crossover operator.

The *crossover operator* achieves the recombination of the selected individuals. The operator combines segments (substrings) belonging to the chromosomes corresponding to parents.

The operator imitates the natural inter-chromosome crossover. Normally the (2,2) crossover type is used. This means that two offspring are obtained from two parents.

The crossover creates an information exchange between the parent chromosomes. The descendants obtained by crossover will possess features from both their parents.

The role of recombination is to act as an impetus to the search progress and to ensure the exploration of the search space.

Due to the great importance of recombination, various crossover operators have been proposed. In what follows, we will describe the most often employed variants of crossover within the binary encoding framework.

6.2   One-point crossover

There are several different ways in which the recombination of the genetic material of two chromosomes can be created. John Holland (1975) considered the *one-point crossover* operator. This operator is described below.

6.2.1   Basic crossover operator

Let L be the length of the chromosomes in a population.

A *crossover point* (or *breakpoint*) is an integer number $k \in \{1, 2, ..., L - 1\}$.

The number k indicates the position within the chromosome where the string is cut so that the resulting segments should recombine.

Let us consider two chromosomes:

$$x = x_1 x_2 \; ... \; x_k x_{k+1} \; ... \; x_L$$

and

$$y = y_1 y_2 \; ... \; y_k y_{k+1} \; ... \; y_L.$$

As a result of recombination, the two chromosomes exchange the substrings occurring after point k.

The offspring chromosomes will be

$$x' = x_1 x_2 \; ... \; x_k y_{k+1} \; ... \; y_L$$

and

$$y' = y_1 y_2 \; ... \; y_k x_{k+1} \; ... \; x_L.$$

Example

Let us consider the chromosomes:

$x:$ $x = 1\,1\,0\,0\,1$

$y:$ $y = 1\,0\,1\,1\,0$

As a result of the crossover with $k = 2$, the following descendants are created:

x': $x' = 1\ 1\ 1\ 1\ 0$

y': $y' = 1\ 0\ 0\ 0\ 1$

For a given pair of chromosomes, the crossover point is selected at random.

6.2.2 Formal definition of crossover operator

Let X be the set of chromosomes having fixed length L. By C we denote the (2,2) crossover operator

$$C : X \times X \to X \times X.$$

To describe the action of the operator C, we consider again two chromosomes:

$$x = x_1\, x_2\, \dots\, x_L$$

and

$$y = y_1\, y_2\, \dots\, y_L.$$

In this case, we have

$$C(x,y) = (x', y'),$$

where

$$x' = x_1 \ldots x_k\, y_{k+1} \ldots y_L,$$

$$y' = y_1 \ldots y_k\, x_{k+1} \ldots x_L,$$

and k is a random number from the set $\{1, 2, \ldots, L - 1\}$.

Remark

The number k is a realization of a random variable having uniform distribution on the set $\{1, 2, \ldots, L - 1\}$.

6.3 Two-point crossover

As in nature, recombination can take place by using one or two crossover points. When more crossover points are used, the resulting segments (substrings) recombine according to a given rule.

Let us consider the two-point crossover operator. This kind of crossover occurs by selecting two crossover points at random and exchanging the segments between such points.

Therefore, from the chromosomes

x :

y :

two descendants of the following type will result:

x':

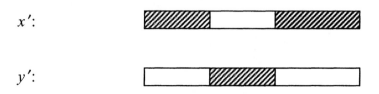

y':

According to Syswerda (1989), for some particular applications two-point crossover performs consistently better than one-point crossover.

6.4 *N*-point crossover

In the case of three crossover points, the offspring will have the form:

x':

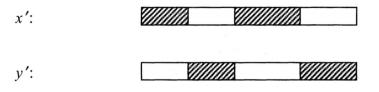

y':

Considering four crossover points, the descendants will have the form:

x':

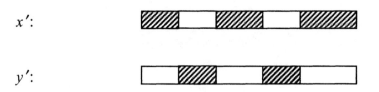

y':

The generalization to a number of N $(1 \leq N < L)$ crossover points is obvious.

As an effect of recombination, some schemata may be disrupted and others may be constructed. Analysis of disruptive aspects is useful to compare various crossover operators.

Multipoint crossover is justified by the fact that certain combinations of genes cannot occur if we use one-point crossover only.

In order to prove this, let us consider a population containing two successful schemata:

$$S_1 = (0\ 1\ *\ *\ *\ *\ *\ *\ *\ 1\ 1)$$

and

$$S_2 = (*\ *\ *\ 1\ 0\ 1\ *\ *\ *\ *\ *).$$

By mating two chromosomes that represent these schemata, we are not able to obtain a chromosome that would represent the following schema:

$$S_3 = (0\ 1\ *\ 1\ 0\ 1\ *\ *\ *\ 1\ 1).$$

This is because schema S_1 would be disrupted. On the other hand, schema S_3 can be obtained using two-point crossover. However, there are schemata that cannot be produced by using only two crossover points. It follows that multiple-point crossover is required.

The existence of a certain asymmetry between one-point crossover and mutation represents another argument in favor of the multiple point crossover.

Indeed, the expected number of chromosomes that will undergo mutation increases with the length of the chromosomes. On the other hand, one-point crossover is not sensitive in any way to the increase of the chromosome length, while the multiple-point crossover is.

Remarks

(i)   The value $N = 2$ (two-point crossover) is frequently used in applications because this choice minimizes the disruptive effects.

(ii)   There is no consensus about the advantages or disadvantages of using more than two crossover points.

6.5 Punctuated crossover

An *adaptive crossover*, called *punctuated crossover*, was proposed by Schaffer and Morishima (1987). This approach implies identifying a mechanism by which the fitness of the descendants obtained by using several crossover points is taken into account. The distribution of the crossover points self-adjusts in accordance with the results already obtained. This is achieved by recording the crossover points in the chromosome.

If a certain crossover point has generated a very poor offspring, this crossover point will not be considered further (the point dies). If the fitness of the descendant is good, the crossover point is maintained as active.

In this way, the crossover points will undergo an evolutionary process, meaning that they self-adjust according to the previous dynamics of the search process.

Punctuated crossover (Schaffer and Morishima, 1987) encodes the crossover points in each chromosome string.

More precisely, a binary substring, called *punctuation list*, is used to indicate the position of crossover points for a multipoint crossover operation. The punctuation list is incorporated in the genotype.

The resulting chromosome representation is a string c of length $2L$:

$$c = x_1 \ldots x_L\, k_1 \ldots k_L,$$

where k_i is a punctuation mark that indicates a crossover position.

If

$$k_i = 1,$$

then the position i is a crossover point.

If

$$k_i = 0,$$

the position i is not a breakpoint.

The bits of the *strategy parameter vector k* are interpreted as *crossover punctuation*.

Remarks

(i)   The genotype considered for punctuated crossover assumes the form:

$$c = (x, k).$$

(ii)   This representation allows the punctuation list to be modified (i.e., evolved) by the variation operators. Therefore, the number and location of crossover points can be manipulated during the search process.

The set of crossover points used in the recombination of two chromosomes is the union of the breakpoints on each chromosome.

During initialization the probability of generating a value

$$k_i = 1$$

is small (for instance, $p_i = 0.04$).

The usual mutation operator is also applied to the strategy parameter vector. In this way, self-adaptation of the number and location of crossover points is achieved.

6.6 Segmented crossover

Segmented crossover (Eshelman, Caruana, and Schaffer, 1989) is a variant of the N-point crossover. The number of crossover points is not constant.

A probability s that a substring has its right extremity in a certain position subsequent to its beginning is considered.

Starting from the first position

$$i = 1$$

of the chromosome, a real number $q \in [0,1]$ and a natural number

$$j, \ i < j \leq L,$$

are randomly generated.

The number q is considered as the probability of accepting j as a crossover point.

Depending on the relationship between s and q, the point j is accepted or not. In this way, the number of crossover points may vary.

Usually, j is accepted as a breakpoint if the condition

$$q \leq s$$

is fulfilled.

6.7 Shuffle crossover

Shuffle crossover (Eshelman, Caruana, and Schaffer, 1989) tries to eliminate the positional bias (mainly from one-point and N-point crossover operators) and to ensure a greater diversity of the offspring.

The shuffle crossover operator is applied together with any other crossover operator as a supplementary mechanism.

The process unfolds according to the following recipe:

(i)   The genes of the two parent chromosomes x and y are shuffled at random, using a permutation operator. The initial position of each gene is stored. As a result, the chromosomes x_1 and y_1 are created.

(ii)   The two chromosomes x_1, y_1 recombine using a crossover operator (two-point crossover, for instance). Let x_2 and y_2 be the two descendants thus obtained.

(iii)   The inverse permutation is applied to unshuffle the positions of the chromosomes x_2 and y_2. As the result of restoring the original symbol ordering, the offspring x_3 and y_3 are obtained.

Remarks

(i)   The shuffling operator is a variant of the N-point crossover operator.

(ii)   The shuffling operator is independent of the number of crossover points.

(iii)   Shuffle crossover may be useful to counteract the tendency in N-point crossover ($N \geq 1$) to disrupt high-defining length schemata more than it disrupts low-defining length schemata.

6.8 Uniform crossover

Uniform crossover (Ackley, 1987; Syswerda, 1989) does not use predefined crossover points.

For each gene of an offspring, a global parameter indicates the probability that this gene should come from either the first or the second parent.

Therefore, each position of a descendant is calculated separately.

6.8.1 Basic method

For each position of the first descendant, the parent that will contribute the value of that position is chosen (with a given probability p).

For the second offspring, we take the value of the corresponding position from the other parent.

We can also consider a mechanism in which the genes of each offspring are calculated independently. Thus, one parent can grant the value of a gene in both descendants.

The uniform crossover with probability p generates an average number pL of crossover points. Uniform crossover is a generalization of the multiple-point crossover.

The advantage of uniform crossover lies in the fact that it can combine features irrespective of their relative position. For certain problems, this ability compensates for the disadvantage of destroying building blocks. It was noticed, however, that, in certain cases, uniform crossover is less successful than two-point crossover.

6.8.2 Generalizations

A different variant of uniform crossover may be considered. According to this variant, a decision to insert a crossover point is made independently at each string position.

Spears (1995) investigated another simple generalization called *one-bit-self-adaptation*.

Within one-bit-self-adaptation, a one-bit strategy parameter is added to an individual. The strategy parameter indicates whether uniform crossover or two-point crossover has to be performed on the parents.

Ties are solved randomly.

6.9 Other crossover operators and some comparisons

Several uniform and non-uniform crossover operators are reviewed in this section. The positional and distributional bias of crossover operators are defined.

6.9.1 Multi-parent and one-descendent operators

Various aspects of crossover operators are often modified to enhance performance. One possibility is to use more than two parents.

Examples of crossover operators involving multiple parents are

- *multi-parent uniform crossover operator* (Furuya and Haftka, 1993);

- *diagonal crossover operator* (Eiben, van Kemenade, and Kok, 1995); and

- *scanning crossover operator* (Eiben, van Kemenade, and Kok, 1995).

A different possibility is to discard one of the offspring generated by crossover and retain only one. This technique can substantially reduce the population diversity.

6.9.2 Reduced surrogate

The *reduced surrogate* technique (Booker, 1987) restricts the crossover points to those positions where the parent chromosomes have different symbols.

This strategy increases the probability of generating offspring that are different from their parents. In this way, the population diversity increases.

6.9.2.1 RRR operator

The *random respectful recombination* (RRR) operator (Radcliffe, 1991) produces an offspring by copying the symbols at positions where the parents are identical. The remaining positions are filled with randomly generated values.

This operator allows the offspring to have genes that are not carried by either parent.

6.9.3 Experimental and theoretical studies

The problem of comparing various crossover operators is a very important one. The comparison can be done using experimental results. Crossover operators may also be characterized in terms of positional and distributional bias.

6.9.3.1 Comparative studies

Eshelman, Caruana, and Schaffer (1989) carried out a comparative experimental study of the various crossover operators. The results could not set a hierarchy of crossover operators.

It was remarked that each operator is suitable for certain classes of problems, while having poor results for other classes. The results showed that the weakest crossover operator seems to be the one-point crossover.

Theoretical studies done by Spears and De Jong (1991), Vose and Liepins (1991), and Booker (1993) supply a measure of potential schemata disruption due to recombination operators.

The disruption measure enables us to infer that two-point crossover is the best choice for minimizing disruptive effects.

6.9.3.2 Positional bias and distributional bias

The tendency of any search operator to produce a certain outcome more easily than others may be considered as an inductive *bias*. Random search, for instance, has no bias. Actually, an efficient search operator should have a bias.

A crossover operator may have a *positional bias* and a *distributional bias*.

Let us denote by $P(S)$ the probability that a set S of symbols is transmitted intact from a parent during recombination. The *positional bias* characterizes the dependence of $P(S)$ on the relative positions of the symbols in S on the string.

One-point crossover has a strong positional bias. This is also valid for N-point crossover. It may be noted that the positional bias depends on N. In contrast, uniform crossover has no positional bias.

The *distributional bias* refers to the probability distribution F for the number of the transmitted symbols. A crossover operator has distributional bias if the probability distribution F is not uniform.

One-point crossover and two-point crossover do not have a distributional bias.

For $N > 2$, the N-point crossover operator has a distributional bias.

The uniform crossover operator has a significant distributional bias.

6.10 Crossover probability

The crossover operator is applied to the individuals of the intermediate population established through the action of the selection operator. Let us denote by p_c the probability of applying crossover. The crossover probability p_c is one of the most important parameters of a genetic algorithm.

Let us consider a population $P(t)$ having n chromosomes. The selection operator will generate an intermediate population P^1 also containing n chromosomes.

We recall that selection does not generate new chromosomes (new potential solutions); it merely copies some chromosomes to the intermediate population.

Generally, not all the chromosomes of $P(t)$ will be copied into P^1. Further, more copies of some chromosomes from $P(t)$ may appear in P^1.

The probability that each individual of P^1 will be selected for mating is constant and equal to p_c.

Let V be an n-dimensional random variable that indicates for each individual the number of copies in the *mating pool*.

The expected value of the variable V is

$$m = \sum_{i=1}^{n} i^0 \, p_c$$

$$= n \, p_c.$$

The result is that np_c is the expected number of chromosomes selected for mating.

In order to accomplish a uniform selection with probability p_c for each chromosome in the intermediate population, a real number $q \in [0,1]$ is generated at random.

If

$$q < p_c,$$

then the corresponding chromosome will be considered for mating (will enter the mating pool).

6.10.1 Setting crossover probability

The crossover probability generally assumes values of the order of magnitude 10^{-1}. The actual value of the parameter p_c depends on the current problem.

It is reasonable to admit that the crossover probability belongs to the domain [0.2, 0.95].

If, for instance, we have $p_c = 0.3$, this means that 30% of the individuals of a population will undergo crossover.

6.11 Mating

A mating procedure determines which chromosomes are recombined to generate offspring.

The main mating strategies are (Goldberg, 1989)

- *Random mating*

  Mates are selected randomly with equal probability.

- *Inbreeding*

  Similar parents are intentionally mated.

- *Line breeding*

  A unique high-fit individual is bred with a base population and the offspring are selected as parents.

- *Outbreeding*

  Very different individuals are mated.

- *Self-fertilization*

  An individual is combined with itself.

- *Cloning*

  An individual is copied without modifications.

- *Positive assortive mating*

  Similar individuals are mated.

- *Negative assortive mating*

  Dissimilar individuals are mated.

Remarks

(i)   Random mating is used in most implementations of genetic algorithms.

(ii)   Mating very similar individuals may make the search process stick in a local optimum point (premature convergence).

6.12 *N*-point crossover algorithm revisited

By means of the crossover operator, new chromosomes are introduced within a population. The *N*-point crossover operation is done according to the following procedure.

N-POINT CROSSOVER ALGORITHM

P1.   For each chromosome from the intermediate population P', do P1.1. and P1.2.

     P1.1. A random number q is generated in the interval $[0,1]$.

     A uniform distribution in the given interval is considered for generating q.

     P1.2. If $q < p_c$, where p_c is the mating probability, the respective chromosome is considered for mating. Otherwise, this chromosome does not enter the mating pool.

P2.   Let m^* be the number of chromosomes selected at step P1.

If the number m^* is even, then the selected chromosomes are paired. The pairs are formed at random.

If m^* is odd, then either a selected chromosome is discarded, or a new chromosome from the intermediate population is added.

Addition or deletion of a new chromosome is decided at random (by generating a supplementary random number).

P3.   Crossover is applied on the pairs established at step P2.

In order to do this, the following steps are needed:

     P3.1. For each pair, an integer number k, $1 \le k < L$, is generated, where L is the chromosome length.

     The number k indicates the position of the crossover point.

     If crossover with $N \ge 2$ crossover points is required, then the numbers $k_1, k_2, \ldots, k_N$ are randomly generated.

These numbers indicate the positions of the crossover points.

The mating of the current pairs is carried out taking the identified crossover point(s) into account.

P3.2. The descendants obtained at step P3.1 become potential members of the population $P(t+1)$ (candidates for mutation).

P3.3. The parents of the newly generated chromosomes are discarded from P'.

P3.4. The chromosomes left in P' are added to the population $P(t+1)$ (as candidates for mutation).

6.13 Selection for survival or replacement

Any genetic algorithm has to specify to what extent the individuals of the generation $P(t)$ have to be found in the generation $P(t+1)$ (that is, how many chromosomes survive unmodified from one generation to another).

Within the canonical genetic algorithm, it is assumed that the generation $P(t+1)$ is made up of newly generated members plus those chromosomes of the intermediate population P' that have not undergone mating. Thus, the number of individuals belonging to each generation is constant.

Another possibility is to copy a fixed number of individuals from $P(t)$ into $P(t+1)$ without modifying them. These individuals are the best ones of the generation $P(t)$. They will be allowed to take part in the selection for recombination and mutation.

6.14 General remarks about crossover within the framework of binary encoding

There is no convincing theory or heuristics that would completely justify the use of a particular crossover operator. The choice of the crossover operator is done independently for each problem and it is based on the results obtained in relation to that particular problem.

Spears (1995) performed an experiment to determine the best crossover operator for solving multimodal optimization problems. The conclusion was that the key feature of the considered self-adaptation method is not to provide the possibility of adapting by choosing the best operator, but rather to let the algorithm access two different crossover operators. This enables the algorithm to achieve a better exploitation during the search. Thus it seems desirable to consider simultaneously various potentially useful recombination operators.

Independent of their form, crossover operators have several characteristics that make them extremely useful in the search process.

The following discussion points out the role traditionally associated with crossover in genetic search and optimization using binary encoding:

(i)   Offspring completely different from their parents can be obtained by means of crossover. It follows that the crossover operators are, to a high degree, responsible for increasing diversity of a given population.

(ii)   The crossover algorithm is an extremely important component of a genetic algorithm. If we eliminate the crossover operator from a genetic algorithm, then the resulting procedure loses, to a large extent, its genetic nature.

It is traditionally recognized that the use of a crossover operator distinguishes genetic algorithms from the other search and optimization algorithms.

(iii)   In a genetic algorithm, giving up crossover induces a performance decreasing.

(iv)   Crossover is regarded as an essential characteristic of genetic algorithms. It is responsible for a significant acceleration of the search process.

(v)   Mutation, the other important search operator, is traditionally considered a method of restoring diversity in a population in which, due to sheer chance, a position has the same value in all or many individuals.

(vi)   Crossover is considered to be the most successful search component. It acts by bringing about the rapid combination of what is best in an initial population and the proliferation of the most promising building blocks, in accordance with the schema theorem.

(vii)   Some experimental results point out the fact that the crossover probability is less important than we would expect.

References and bibliography

Ackley, D.H., (1987), *A Connectionist Machine for Genetic Hill-climbing*, Kluwer, Boston, MA.

Angeline, P., (1996), Two self-adaptive crossover operations for genetic programming, *Advances in Genetic Programming*, 2, P.J. Angeline, K.E. Kinnear, Jr. (Eds.), MIT Press, Cambridge, MA, 89-109.

Bäck, T., (1992), The interaction of mutation rate, selection and self-adaptation within a genetic algorithm, *Proc. 2nd Conf. on Parallel*

Problem Solving from Nature, R. Männer, B. Manderick (Eds.), North-Holland, Amsterdam, 85-94.

Bäck, T., (1996), *Evolutionary Algorithms in Theory and Practice*, Oxford University Press, New York.

Booker, L.B., (1987), Improving search in genetic algorithms, *Genetic Algorithms and Simulated Annealing*, L. Davis (Ed.), Morgan Kaufmann, San Mateo, CA, 61-73.

Booker, L.B., (1993), Recombination distributions for genetic algorithms, *Foundations of Genetic Algorithms*, 2, L.D. Whitley (Ed.), Morgan Kaufmann, San Mateo, CA.

Davis, L. (Ed.), (1991), *Handbook of Genetic Algorithms*, Van Nostrand Reinhold, New York.

Dumitrescu, D., (2000), *Genetic Algorithms and Evolution Strategies*, Blue Publishing House, Cluj-Napoca, 2000.

Eiben, A.E., Raué, P.-E., Ruttkay, Zs., (1994), Genetic algorithms with multi-parent recombination, *Parallel Problem Solving from Nature*, 3, Yu Davidor, H.-P. Schwefel, R. Männer (Eds.), Springer, Berlin, 77-87.

Eiben, A.E., van Kemenade, C.H.M., Kok, J.N., (1995), Orgy in the computer: multi-parent reproduction in genetic algorithms, *Proc. 3rd European Conf. on Artificial Life*, Springer, Berlin, 934-945.

Eshelman, L.J., Caruana, R.A., Schaffer, J.D., (1989), Biases in the crossover landscape, *Proc. 3rd International Conference on Genetic Algorithms*, J.D. Schaffer (Ed.), Morgan Kaufmann Publishers, Los Altos, CA, 10-19.

Furuya, H., Haftka, R.T., (1993), Genetic algorithms for placing actuators on space structures, *Proc. 5th Int. Conf. on Genetic Algorithms*, S. Forrest (Ed.), Morgan Kaufmann, San Mateo, CA, 536-542.

Goldberg, D.E., (1989), *Genetic Algorithms in Search, Optimization, and Machine Learning*, Addison-Wesley, New York.

Goldberg, D.E., Deb, K., Thierens, D., (1993), Toward a better understanding of mixing in genetic algorithms, *J. Soc. Instrum. Control Eng.*, 32 (1), 10-16.

Goldberg, D.E., Richardson, J., (1987), Genetic algorithms with sharing for multimodal function optimization, *Proc. 2nd Int. Conf. on Genetic Algorithms*, J.J. Grefenstette (Ed.), Lawrence Erlbaum Associates, Hillsdale, New York, 41-49.

Grefenstette, J., (1986), Optimization of control parameters for genetic algorithms, *IEEE Trans. on Systems, Man and Cybernetics*, 16, 122-128.

Grefenstette, J., (1995), Virtual Genetic Algorithms: First Results, Navy Center for Applied Research in AI, Report AIC-95-013.

Holland, J.H., (1975), *Adaptation in Natural and Artificial Systems*, University of Michigan Press, Ann Arbor (Second edition: MIT Press, 1992).

Hong, I., Kahng, A., Moon, B., (1995), Exploiting synergies of multiple crossover: initial studies, *Proc. IEEE Int. Conf. on Evolutionary Computation*.

Janikow, C.Z., Michalewicz, Z., (1991), An experimental comparison of binary and floating point representation in genetic algorithms, *Proc. 4th Int. Conf. on Genetic Algorithms*, B. Belew, L.B. Booker (Eds.), Morgan Kaufmann, San Mateo, CA, 31-36.

Manderick, B., Weger, M., Spienssens, P., (1991), The genetic algorithms and the structure of the fitness landscape, *Proc. 4th Int. Conf. on Genetic Algorithms*, R.K. Belew, L.B. Booker (Eds.), Morgan Kaufmann, CA, 143-150.

Mühlenbein, H., (1992), How genetic algorithms really work. Part I: Mutation and hillclimbing, *Parallel Problem Solving from Nature*, 2, R. Männer, B. Manderick (Eds.), Elsevier, Amsterdam, 15-25.

Radcliffe, N.J., (1991), Forma analysis and random respectful recombination, *Proc. 4th Int. Conf. on Genetic Algorithms*, R.K. Belew, L.B. Booker (Eds.), Morgan Kaufmann, San Mateo, CA, 222-229.

Schaffer, J.D., Caruana, R.A., Eshelman, L.J., Das, R., (1989), A study of control parameters affecting online performance of genetic algorithms for function optimization, *Proc. 3rd Int. Conf. on Genetic Algorithms*, J.D. Schaffer, (Ed.), Morgan Kaufmann Publishers, Los Altos, CA, 51-60.

Schaffer, J.D., Morishima, A., (1987), An adaptive crossover distribution mechanism for genetic algorithms, *Proc. 2nd Int. Conf. on Genetic Algorithms*, J.J. Grefenstette (Ed.), Lawrence Erlbaum Associates, Hillsdale, NJ, 36-40.

Schraudolph, N.N., Belew, R.K., (1990), Dynamic parameter encoding for genetic algorithms, CSE Technical Report, CS90-175, University of San Diego, La Jolla.

Schraudolph, N.N., Belew, R.K., (1992), Dynamic parameter encoding for genetic algorithms, *Machine Learning*, 9, 9-21.

Shaefer, C.G., (1987), The ARGOT strategy: adaptive representation genetic optimizer technique, *Proc. 2nd Int. Conf. on Genetic Algorithms*, J.J. Grefenstette (Ed.), Lawrence Erlbaum Associates, Hillsdale, NJ, 50-58.

Smith, J.E., Fogarty, T.C., (1997), Operator and parameter adaptation in genetic algorithms, *Soft Computing*, 1, 81-87.

Spears, W.M., (1992), Adapting crossover in a genetic algorithm, Report AIC-92-025, Navy Center for Applied Research in Artificial Intelligence, USA.

Spears, W.M., (1995), Adapting crossover in evolutionary algorithms, *Proc. 4th Ann. Conf. on Evolutionary Programming*, J.R. McDonnell, R.G. Reynolds, D.B. Fogel (Eds.), MIT Press, Cambridge, CA, 367-384.

Spears, W.M., De Jong, K.A., (1991), On the virtues of parameterized uniform crossover, *Proc. 4th Int. Conf. on Genetic Algorithms*, R.K. Belew, L.B. Booker (Eds.), Morgan Kaufmann Publishers, San Mateo, CA, 230-236.

Syswerda, G., (1989), Uniform crossover in genetic algorithms, *Proc. 3rd Int. Conf. on Genetic Algorithms*, J.D. Schaffer (Ed.), Morgan Kaufmann Publishers, San Mateo, CA, 2-9.

Thierens, D., Goldberg, D.E., (1993), Mixing in genetic algorithms, *Proc. 5th Int. Conf. on Genetic Algorithms*, S. Forrest (Ed.), Morgan Kaufmann, San Mateo, CA, 38-45.

Vose, M.D., Liepins, G.E., (1991), Schema disruption, *Proc. 4th Int. Conf. on Genetic Algorithms*, R.K. Belew, L.B. Booker (Eds.), Morgan Kaufmann Publishers, 237-242.

7

Mutation operators and related topics

7.1 Introduction

In classical genetics, a mutation is identified (at the level of its functional consequences) by an altered phenotype. In molecular genetics, mutation refers to any alteration of a segment of DNA, the carrier of genetic information.

It is currently accepted that spontaneous mutagenesis is normally not adaptive (i.e., does not pay attention to particular needs in order to cope with specific environmental requirements). Moreover, mutations providing a selective advantage are usually considered to be quite rare.

Some changes may destroy the genome structure. Other changes tend to create and integrate new functions. The equilibrium *fidelity-exploration* is governed by the selection pressure.

Changes representing a selective disadvantage occur considerably more often and can affect life processes at various degrees. The extreme situation, in which genetic alteration leads to lethality, is observed relatively frequently. It follows that tolerable overall mutation frequencies should normally be smaller than one mutation per genome and per generation.

This is a very restrictive condition that puts serious restrictions on the size of viable genomes. For higher organisms, the condition has been mitigated by the introduction of *diploidy* (see Chapter 11).

Diploidy represents a supplementary adaptation mechanism. A feature may disappear when the environmental conditions require that it does and may reappear when the changes in the environment make it useful again.

Genetic algorithms based on diploidy are suitable for dealing with difficult problems, such as non-stationary optimum problems.

Often, the alteration of the DNA sequence remains without immediate consequences on life processes. Mutations of this kind are called *neutral* or *silent*.

Neutral mutations may, at some later time, exert an evolutionary role in conjunction with some additional mutations. On the other hand, silent genome changes may not be silent in their effects on the local rate of DNA sequence change. Therefore, a selection process can exist to take both aspects of silent changes into account.

A new perspective (Caporale, 1999) emphasizes that some mutations are orders of magnitude more likely than other changes. Their probability may be so high that we can predict them.

The genomes for which probable mutations provide effective responses to environment challenges will be favored.

The genomes may also evolve mechanisms to overcome predictable challenges. As most challenges are not predictable, the genome may develop abilities to adapt and evolve.

This ability may be viewed as a *learning* mechanism. The Baldwin effect is such an example of a learning process (see Chapter 13).

In this chapter, several mutation operators are considered. The problem of adapting or self-adapting mutation operators is also addressed.

A simple (canonical) genetic algorithm with crossover and mutation is considered.

Other topics included in this chapter are

- self-adaptive and local mutation rates,

- inversion operator,

- crossover vs. mutation,

- selection vs. search operators.

7.2 Mutation with binary encoding

Within the framework of binary encoding, mutation is usually considered as the second genetic operator from the point of view of importance and usefulness. The effect of this operator is to change a single position (gene) within a chromosome.

By means of mutation, individuals that could not be generated through other mechanisms are introduced in the population. The mutation operator assures that the full range of allele values is available to the search.

7.2.1 Mutation rate

We consider a binary representation of chromosomes. In this case, as a result of applying the mutation operator to a chromosome, a single position (bit) of the chromosome is complemented.

Mutation is a probabilistic-type operator.

The probability of applying the operator is called *mutation probability* or *mutation rate* and is denoted by p_m.

The mutation operator acts on individual bits, irrespective of their position in the chromosome. Each bit of a population may undergo mutation. So, within a chromosome, more positions that undergo a mutation may exist.

We consider a population of n individuals, each individual having fixed length L. For each position (bit), there is the same probability p_m to undergo mutation.

As nL is the total number of bits in the population, it follows that the average number of positions that will undergo a mutation is

$$B = nL p_m.$$

7.2.2 Mutation rate values

The mutation probability stands for a parameter of the canonical genetic algorithm. Small values of p_m ($p_m \in [0.001, 0.01]$) were traditionally recommended for canonical genetic algorithms.

New results have demonstrated the benefits of emphasizing the role of mutation.

According to Mühlenbein (1992), Smith and Fogarty (1996), and Bäck (1993, 1996), the lower bound p_0 for the optimal mutation probability is

$$p_0 = \frac{1}{L},$$

where L is the chromosome length.

The value p_0 is almost optimal for a (1+1) genetic algorithm (a single parent generates a single offspring by mutation) and a specific simple ('counting ones') objective function (Mühlenbein, 1992; Bäck, 1993).

However, the value p_0 may serve as a reasonable heuristics for large classes of objective functions.

Schaffer, Caruana, Eshelman, and Das (1989) obtained an empirical value

$$p_m \approx \frac{1.75}{L^{\frac{1}{2}} n},$$

where n is the population size.

Some parameter control strategies including *variable* and *self-adaptive* mutation probability will be considered in the following.

7.3 Strong and weak mutation operators

There are different variants of the mutation operator. In what follows, we will describe some of them.

In the *strong form* of the mutation operator, the position selected for mutation automatically changes its value.

In the *weak form*, there is a certain probability of changing the value of the selected position.

The mutation operators typically used in canonical genetic algorithms are discussed next.

7.3.1 Selecting a position for mutation

Let p_m be the mutation rate.

Positions that undergo mutation are determined by a uniform random choice.

For each gene of the chromosome population, a uniform random number q is generated.

If, for the ith gene, the condition

$$q < p_m$$

is fulfilled, that gene is *selected* for mutation.

Within the weak mutation operator, a probability of inverting each selected gene value is also considered.

7.3.2 Strong mutation operator

This variant of mutation operator allows a selected gene to assume the new value when the condition

$$q < p_m$$

is fulfilled.

Within the strong mutation operator, the mutated value x_i' of the gene i is computed according to the rule:

$$x_i' = \begin{cases} 1-x_i, & \text{if } q < p_m \\ x_i, & \text{if } q \geq p_m \end{cases},$$

where x_i is the old gene value. The strong mutation procedure may be outlined as below.

STRONG MUTATION PROCEDURE

P1. For each chromosome of the current population and for each position of the chromosome do:

P1.1. Generate a random number q in the interval $[0,1]$.

q is the realization of a uniform random variable.

P1.2. If

$$q < p_m,$$

then the corresponding position is inverted

(replacing 0 with 1, and 1 with 0).

If

$$q \geq p_m,$$

the respective position does not change.

7.3.3 Weak mutation operator

There are implementations for which the condition

$$q < p_m$$

does not automatically trigger change of the position being taken into account.

We can think of a mechanism in which the new value of the position that fulfills the mutation condition is randomly generated. The resulting value may coincide with the old one (in this case, no real change takes place).

In such a case, step P1.2. from the previous algorithm is replaced with step P′1.2. :

P′1.2. If

$$q < p_m,$$

then one of the values 0 or 1 is chosen at random. The value selected is assigned to the current position.

If

$$q \geq p_m,$$

then the current position does not change.

7.3.4 Mutation within a unique chromosome

In this variant of the mutation operator, each application of the operator affects one gene (or, possibly, more genes) from a single chromosome (that has been selected for mutation).

7.4 Non-uniform mutation

As the search process approaches a good solution (the population begins adapting to the problem), the mutation operator is more likely to disrupt good solutions rather than improve them. To prevent this tendency, we may consider a mutation probability depending on the generation index.

At the first generations, the mutation probability may be high, decreasing over time. In this way, high mutation rates occur in the first stages of the search. This strategy ensures the search progress in the initial phase.

Decreasing the mutation probability in the advanced stages of the search generates smaller changes. This fact allows a more effective local search. In other words, in the neighborhood of the optimum point, the search becomes more discrete.

This is an example of the way in which, by using a single operator, the global search of the initial stages is replaced by local exploitation of the identified solutions toward the end of the search.

7.4.1 Time-dependent mutation rate

Non-uniform mutation may be achieved if we allow the mutation probability to decrease with time according to the law:

$$p_m(t) = p_m e^{-\beta t},$$

where

- p_m is the mutation probability at the first generation,

- t is the time (generation index), $t \geq 0$,

- $\beta \geq 1$ is a real parameter of the method.

Remarks

(i) The greater the value of the parameter β, the more rapidly the mutation probability decreases.

(ii) The operator described may be regarded as a non-uniform mutation operator because of the mutation rate's dependence on the population age t.

Hesser and Männer (1991, 1992) considered a similar expression of time-varying mutation rate including population size n and string length L. In this approach, the mutation rate is expressed as

$$p_m(t) = \left(\frac{\alpha}{\delta}\right)^{1/2} \frac{e^{-\beta t/2}}{L^{1/2} n},$$

where α, β and δ are real-valued positive parameters.

The parameters are problem dependent and no general heuristics is available to estimate them.

Bäck and Schütz (1996) assumed that the mutation rate decreases according to the function

$$p_m(t)=\frac{1}{2+\dfrac{L-2}{T}t},$$

where

- $0 \leq t \leq T$, and

- T is the maximal number of generations.

Within this scheme, we have

$$p_m(0)=0.5,$$

and the minimum value of the mutation rate is

$$p_m(T)=\frac{1}{L}.$$

7.4.1.1 Fitness-dependent mutation rate

Bäck (1992) suggested a mutation rate that is a function of the individual's fitness.

The mutation rate $p_m(x)$ of the individual x in the populaton $P(t)$ is expressed as

$$p_m(x)=\frac{1}{2[f(x)+1]-L}.$$

7.5 Adaptive non-uniform mutation

Let us suppose the search space is $[a,b] \subset \mathbf{R}$. Assume that a chromosome encodes a real-valued solution as a binary string.

Binary encoding may introduce an asymmetry in the action of the mutation operator. If a gene is placed at the beginning of a chromosome, then its change induces a significant modification of the chromosome.

The solutions corresponding to the two chromosomes (the initial one and the one containing the altered gene) will be extremely different.

On the contrary, the mutation of the genes situated near the end of the chromosome will introduce a much smaller change.

Allowing the mutation probability to depend on the generation and the position within the chromosome, we can accomplish a global search in the first stages and a local search in the last phase of the iterative process. For this, it is sufficient to let the mutation probability of the first (last) positions decrease (increase) as the generation index increases.

One may notice that this operator contains two kinds of non-uniformity: one generated by the dependence on the population age and the other linked to the position within the chromosome.

7.6 Self-adaptation of mutation rate

In this section, self-adaptation schemes of the mutation rate are considered.

The mutation rate is included in the genotype and self-adapts each time the genotype undergoes mutation.

7.6.1 Self-adaptation mechanism

Bäck and Schütz (1996) considered a self-adaptation mechanism for the mutation probability p_m.

The parameter p_m representing the mutation rate is incorporated into the genotype of the individuals.

7.6.1.1 Mutation rate modification

A genotype c will assume the form

$$c = (x, p_m),$$

where

- $x \in \{0, 1\}^L$ is the search vector, and

- $p_m \in [0, 1]$.

The current mutation probability p_m yields a new mutation probability p_m' given by

$$p_m' = \frac{1}{1 + \dfrac{1 - p_m}{p_m} e^{-\gamma N(0,1)}}, \qquad (7.1)$$

where

- $N(0,1)$ denotes a realization of a (one-dimensional) normal distributed random variable with expectation zero and standard deviation one,

- γ is a learning rate (the proposed value is $\gamma = 0.2$).

7.6.1.2 Transformed genotype

By mutation, the genotype (x, p_m) is transformed into the genotype (x', p_m'), i.e., we have

$$(x', p_m') = M(x, p_m),$$

where M denotes the mutation operator.

The mutation of the object variables x_j, $j = 1, ..., L$, is given by

$$x_j' = \begin{cases} x_j & \text{if } q \geq p_m' \\ 1 - x_j & \text{if } q < p_m' \end{cases}$$

where

- q is a realization of a uniform random variable sampled anew for each position j,

- p_m' is the new mutation rate calculated according to (7.1).

7.6.2 Local mutation probabilities

The previous scheme may be generalized by including a vector p of mutation strategy parameters.

Each component x_j of the search vector is allowed to have its own mutation probability p_j.

In this situation

$$p = (p_1, ..., p_L).$$

A genotype c will assume the form

$$c = (x, p).$$

The mutation rate parameters are updated as follows:

$$p_j' = \frac{1}{1 + \frac{1-p_j}{p_j} e^{-\gamma N_j(0,1)}}, \quad j=1,...,L,$$

where

- p_j is the old mutation rate of the component x_j of the search vector x,

- p_j' is the *updated value* of the mutation rate.

7.7 Crossover vs. mutation

In a simple genetic algorithm, the task of *global search* in the problem space is ascribed to the crossover operator. Progress within the search space is possible due to the combination of the building blocks existing in the population.

The role of the mutation operator is to prevent an irreparable loss of diversity. Let us suppose that the first gene has the same value for all the individuals of a population. Using only crossover in the absence of the mutation operator, this gene value could not be changed for any individuals.

Therefore, the mutation operator forestalls the premature convergence, generating a supplementary diversity in a population. This diversity allows the exploration of larger regions of the search space.

Some experimental and theoretical results underlined the importance of the mutation operator.

The results obtained by Grefenstette (1986), and Schaffer, Caruana, Eshelman, and Das (1989) indicate a modified perspective of the relation between the crossover and mutation operators.

The recent results demonstrate the benefits of emphasizing the role of mutation as a search operator in genetic algorithms.

Some of the important conclusions may be summarized as below:

(i)   The role of mutation is more important than admitted traditionally (in early researches on evolutionary algorithms).

(ii)   Evolutionary search strategies based only on selection and mutation might be powerful search procedures, even without using crossover. This fact is obvious not only in the case of evolution strategies, evolutionary programming, or real encoding-based GAs, but also for canonical genetic algorithms.

(iii)   The use of mutation probability decreasing over time allows maintenance of population diversity and ensures the fine tuning of the search process.

7.8 The inversion operator

Crossover, mutation, and inversion have been the genetic operators considered from the outset (Holland, 1975). Current implementations of genetic algorithms pre-eminently use the first two operators (crossover and mutation) and very seldom the third one.

The *inversion* operator acts on a single chromosome. It inverts the values between two positions of a chromosome. The two positions are chosen at random. The inversion operator was inspired by biological processes.

It was noted that the inversion operator is generally considered of little use in the practice of evolutionary algorithms. It is usually admitted that this operator would be useful if we had chromosomes at least one order of magnitude longer than the ones used in current implementations.

7.9 Selection vs. variation operators

In the case of genetic algorithms, the balance between the exploitation and exploration processes is achieved through the operators used.

Selection accomplishes the exploitation of the current population (solutions), making many copies of the most successful individuals.

Crossover, mutation, and inversion operators are responsible for exploring the search space looking for better solutions. The effectiveness of a genetic algorithm depends, therefore, on establishing an equilibrium between selection and search genetic operators.

If the most successful individuals have too many copies in the intermediate population (too many selections), then the population diversity decreases. The range in which the search can be extended by using the crossover, mutation, and inversion operators is reduced. It follows that genetic algorithms should be designed so that the balance between exploration and exploitation is ensured.

Within certain classes of problems, for given crossover probability and selection pressure, relationships that guarantee the maintenance of the equilibrium have been established (Goldberg, Deb and Thierens, 1993; Thierens and Goldberg, 1993).

7.10 Simple genetic algorithm revisited

We are now able to indicate more exactly the way in which a genetic algorithm works. The genetic operators considered are crossover and mutation.

By $P(0)$ we denote an initial population made up of n individuals (chromosomes) of length L.

The basic variant of a simple genetic algorithm with crossover and mutation is given below:

CANONICAL GENETIC ALGORITHM

(WITH CROSSOVER AND MUTATION)

P1.   Set $t = 0$.

The population $P(0)$ is initialized at random.

A selection mechanism is chosen and, if necessary, a scaling mechanism.

P2.   The chromosomes of the population $P(t)$ are evaluated using the fitness function.

The most successful individual from $P(t)$ is kept.

P3.   The selection operator is applied n times.

The selected chromosomes make up an intermediate population P^1 (having n members as well) representing candidates for the mating pool.

Some chromosomes from $P(t)$ may have more copies in P^1, while others may have none.

P4.   The crossover operator is applied to the chromosomes from the mating pool.

The newly generated chromosomes form a population P^2.

The parents of the chromosomes obtained through crossover are discarded from the intermediate population P^1.

The chromosomes that remained in P^1 become members of the population P^2.

P5.   The mutation operator is applied to the population P^2. The outcome is the new generation $P(t + 1)$.

P6.   Set $t = t + 1$.

If $t < M$, where M is the maximum number of generations, then go to step P2.

Otherwise stop.

Remarks

(i)   The solution to the problem is given by the best member of the last population or by the best individual in all generations.

(ii)   This algorithm may be slightly modified so as to include the inversion operator and other types of operators.

References and bibliography

Bäck, T., (1992), The interaction of mutation rate, selection and self-adaptation within a genetic algorithm, *Proc. 2nd Conf. on Parallel Problem Solving from Nature*, R. Männer, B. Manderick (Eds.), North-Holland, Amsterdam, 85-94.

Bäck, T., (1993), Optimal mutation rates in genetic search, *Proc. 5th Int. Conf. on Genetic Algorithms*, S. Forrest (Ed.), Morgan Kaufmann, San Mateo, CA, 2-8.

Bäck, T., (1996), *Evolutionary Algorithms in Theory and Practice*, Oxford University Press, New York.

Bäck, T., Schütz, M., (1996), Intelligent mutation rate control in canonical genetic algorithms, *Foundations of Intelligent Systems,* Lectures Notes in Artificial Intelligence, 1079, Z.W. Ras, M. Michalewicz (Eds.), Springer, Berlin, 158-167.

Booker, L.B., (1987), Improving search in genetic algorithms, *Genetic Algorithms and Simulated Annealing*, L. Davis (Ed.), Morgan Kaufmann, San Mateo, CA.

Caporale, L.H., (1999), Chance favors the prepared genome, *Molecular Strategies in Biological Evolution*, L.H. Caporale (Ed.), The New York Academy of Science, New York, 23-35.

Goldberg, D.E., (1989), *Genetic Algorithms in Search, Optimization and Machine Learning*, Addison-Wesley, New York.

Goldberg, D.E., Deb, K., Thierens, D., (1993), Toward a better understanding of mixing in genetic algorithms, *J. Soc. Instrum. Control Eng.*, 32 (1), 10-16.

Grefenstette, J., (1986), Optimization of control parameters for genetic algorithms, *IEEE Trans. on Systems, Man and Cybernetics*, 16, 122-128.

Hesser, J., Männer, R., (1991), Towards an optimal mutation probability in genetic algorithms, *Parallel Problem Solving from Nature*, 1, H.-P. Schwefel, R. Männer (Eds.), Springer, Berlin, 23-32.

Hesser, J., Männer, R., (1992), Investigation of m-heuristic for optimal mutation probabilities, *Parallel Problem Solving from Nature*, 2, R. Männer, B. Manderick (Eds.), Elsevier, Amsterdam, 115-124.

Holland, J.H., (1975), *Adaptation in Natural and Artificial Systems*, University of Michigan Press, Ann Arbor (Second edition: MIT Press, 1992).

Manderick, B., Weger, M., Spienssens, P., (1991), The genetic algorithms and the structure of the fitness landscape, *Proc. 4th Int. Conf. on Genetic Algorithms*, R.K. Belew, L.B. Booker (Eds.), Morgan Kaufmann, CA, 143-150.

Mühlenbein, H., (1992), How genetic algorithms really work. Part I: Mutation and hillclimbing, *Parallel Problem Solving from Nature*, 2, R. Männer, B. Manderick (Eds.), Elsevier, Amsterdam, 15-25.

Schaffer, J.D., Caruana, R.A., Eshelman, L.J., Das, R., (1989), A study of control parameters affecting online performance of genetic algorithms for function optimization, *Proc. 3rd Int. Conf. on Genetic Algorithms*, J.D. Schaffer (Ed.), Morgan Kaufmann Publishers, Los Altos, CA, 51-60.

Schraudolph, N.N., Belew, R.K., (1990), Dynamic parameter encoding for genetic algorithms, CSE Technical Report, CS90-175, University of San Diego, La Jolla.

Schraudolph, N.N., Belew, R.K., (1992), Dynamic parameter encoding for genetic algorithms, *Machine Learning*, 9, 9-21.

Shaefer, C.G., (1987), The ARGOT strategy: adaptive representation genetic optimizer technique, *Proc. 2nd Int. Conf. on Genetic Algorithms*, J.J. Grefenstette (Ed.), Erlbaum, Hillsdale, NJ, 50-58.

Smith, J.E., Fogarty, T.C., (1996), Self-adaptation of mutation rates in a steady-state genetic algorithm, *Proc. 3rd IEEE Conf. on Evolutionary Computation*, IEEE Press, Piscataway, NJ, 318-323.

Smith, J.E., Fogarty, T.C., (1997), Operator and parameter adaptation in genetic algorithms, *Soft Computing*, 1, 81-87.

Thierens, D., Goldberg, D.E., (1993), Mixing in genetic algorithms, *Proc. 5th Int. Conf. on Genetic Algorithms*, S. Forrest (Ed.), Morgan Kaufmann, San Mateo, CA, 38-45.

8

Schema theorem, building blocks, and related topics

8.1 Introduction

This chapter introduces some mathematical results pertaining to standard genetic algorithms. These results point out the mechanisms on which working of genetic algorithms is based. However, we do not intend to develop a general theory. We will focus on a simple (canonical) model of genetic algorithm.

Binary encoding and the traditional genetic algorithm (with proportional selection, one-point crossover, and mutation) will be considered.

We will show that, in this case, the number of instances (representatives) of the above-average schemata increases exponentially with time (with the generation index) in successive generations. Meanwhile, the number of schemata with a performance below the average decreases.

This result, known as the *schema theorem,* assures that the search process carried out by a genetic algorithm develops in the direction of the proliferation of the most successful schemata, concomitantly with destroying unsuccessful schemata.

The schema theorem (Holland, 1975) represents the fundamental theoretic result regarding standard genetic algorithms. The importance of this result surpasses the frame of the simple model for which it has been established.

However, we are entitled to conjecture that a similar mechanism acts on genetic algorithms in real codification. This mechanism allows the proliferation of the most successful structures.

To demonstrate a result of this kind some technical problems have to be solved, such as suitably defining some information structures that here would play the part the schemata played within binary encoding.

Such a mechanism would also be applicable to evolution strategies, due to their similitude with the genetic algorithms that use real representation.

The schema theorem does not exhaust all problems connected with the behavior of genetic algorithms. The *building block hypothesis* explains the way in which the proliferation of successful schemata eventually leads to the optimum solution.

According to this hypothesis, building blocks, or the successful schemata with reduced order and defining length, combine in order to form (within chromosomes) substrings of greater and greater length and success.

Another interesting matter is to establish some sets of problems (or objective functions) for which standard genetic algorithms do not lead to a global optimum.

Such *deceptive problems* (or *deceptive functions*) are important because they may suggest new means of improving genetic algorithms and new ways of understanding the intricate mechanisms that generate their behavior.

8.2 Elements characterizing schemata

In order to express the schema theorem we need to recall the definitions of the two measures specific to schemata, i.e., the *order* and *defining length*.

Definition

The *order* of a schema S, denoted by $O(S)$, represents the number of well-defined (i.e., 0 or 1) symbols within schema S.

Example

We have, for instance,

$$O(*010)=3$$

$$O(***)=0.$$

Definition

The *defining length* of a schema S, noted $\delta(S)$, is a number equal to the difference between the last and the first specific (i.e., non-asterisk) positions of the schema.

If a schema has no specified position, its defining length is zero.

Example

$$\delta(*010)=4-2$$

$$\delta(***)=0$$

$$\delta(*1*0)=4-2.$$

Definition

We say that a chromosome x is an *instance* (or a *representative*) of the schema S if all the well-defined symbols of S coincide with the values of the corresponding positions of x.

Remark

We may also assume that the instance x is a *copy* of the schema S.

Let $n(S,t)$ denote the number of representatives of a schema S in the generation $P(t)$.

Definition

The *average fitness* of the representatives of the schema S in the population $P(t)$ is denoted by $f(S,t)$ and is expressed as follows:

$$f(S,t)=\frac{\sum f(x)}{n(S,t)},$$

where the sum is considered with respect to all the representatives of S in the population $P(t)$.

Remark

We may interpret $f(S,t)$ as being *the fitness of the schema S* in the generation $P(t)$.

Definition

The *average performance* (or *average fitness*) of the entire population $P(t)$ is denoted by $F(t)$ and is expressed as

$$F(t) = \frac{\sum\limits_{x \in P(t)} f(x)}{N},$$

where N is the number of individuals belonging to the population $P(t)$.

8.3 Schema dynamics

In what follows, we intend to study the mechanism that ensures the functioning and success of genetic algorithms. We will limit ourselves to the simple genetic algorithm model.

We consider a standard (canonical) genetic algorithm that has the following features:

- binary encoding,

- proportional selection,

- one-point crossover,

- strong mutation.

Analyzing the effect of selection and search operators on this genetic algorithm, we will deduce the *schema theorem* (or *fundamental theo-*

rem of genetic algorithms), which describes the growth of the schemata with fitness above the average.

Let S be a schema present in the generation $P(t)$. We wish to find how the number of representatives of the schema S evolves.

In this respect, we first have to identify a relationship between the numbers of representatives of the schema S in the populations $P(t)$ and $P(t + 1)$, respectively.

This leads to establish a functional dependence of the type:

$$n(S,t+1)=g(n(S,t)).$$

The function g expresses the *dynamics* of the schema S.

In order to find the schema dynamics, we will consider separately the effects of genetic operators. These effects will be integrated afterward in the schema theorem.

8.4   Effect of selection on schema dynamics

In this section, we consider the effect of proportional selection on schema dynamics in a simple genetic algorithm.

8.4.1   Schema dynamics within selection

Assume that, at each generation t, the size of the population $P(t)$ is N.

Let $n(S,t)$ be the number of instances of the schema S in the population $P(t)$.

According to proportional selection, the selection probability of the chromosome x^i is

$$p_i = \frac{f(x^i)}{\sum\limits_{j=1}^{N} f(x^j)} .$$

To turn the generation $P(t)$ into $P(t+1)$, the selection operator is applied N times. Each time, any of the $n(S,t)$ representatives of the schema S may be selected.

In N applications of the selection operator, the individual x^i is expected to be selected n_i times.

So we have the expected number of selections (descendants):

$$n_i = N \frac{f(x^i)}{\sum\limits_{j=1}^{N} f(x^j)} .$$

Without loss of generality, we may suppose that the representatives of the schema S are numbered $1, 2, \ldots, n(S,t)$.

Summing the expected number of descendants, we find that, at time $(t+1)$, the expected number of representatives of the schema S is the number $n(S,t+1)$ given by

$$n(S,t+1) = \sum\limits_{i=1}^{n(S,t)} n_i .$$

If, in this equality, we replace n_i with its previously found expression, we obtain

$$n(S,t+1)=N\sum_{i=1}^{n(S,t)}\frac{f(x^i)}{\sum_{j=1}^{N}f(x^j)},$$

which may also be expressed as

$$n(S,t+1)=\frac{N}{\sum_{j=1}^{N}f(x^j)}\,n(S,t)\,\frac{\sum_{i=1}^{n(S,t)}f(x^i)}{n(S,t)}.$$

Taking into account the expression of $F(t)$, i.e., the average fitness of the entire population, and of $f(S,t)$, i.e., the average fitness of the schema S, we have

$$n(S,t+1)=n(S,t)\frac{f(S,t)}{F(t)}.$$

This result concerns the dynamics of the schema S when subject to selection.

The previous result may be expressed in the form of the following proposition (Holland, 1975).

Proposition

Consider a genetic algorithm in which only proportional selection is used. If the schema S has $n(S,t)$ representatives in the generation $P(t)$, the expected number of representatives of schema S in the next generation is

$$n(S,t+1)=n(S,t)\frac{f(S,t)}{F(t)}.$$

8.4.2 Dynamics of above/below-average schema

Let us suppose that S is a schema whose fitness at generation t is above the average fitness $F(t)$ of the population $P(t)$.

This is expressed by the inequality

$$f(S,t)>F(t),$$

from which we deduce that

$$n(S,t+1)>n(S,t).$$

Therefore, a schema whose fitness is above the average will increase; that is, it will have more representatives in the next generations.

Remark

Similarly, one may notice that a below-average schema tends to disappear in the next generations (it has fewer and fewer representatives).

Let us assume that, at each generation, the schema S is superior to the average for a fraction α of $F(t)$.

Then we can write

$$f(S,t)=F(t)+\alpha F(t),$$

where α is a positive constant.

If, in the equation describing the schema dynamics, we use

$$\frac{f(S,t)}{F(t)} = (1+\alpha),$$

we obtain

$$n(S,t+1) = (1+\alpha)\, n(S,t).$$

If we set

$$t = 0,$$

from the above equality we get

$$n(S,1) = (1+\alpha)\, n(S,0).$$

Then it follows that

$$n(S,2) = (1+\alpha)\, n(S,1)$$
$$= (1+\alpha)^2\, n(S,0).$$

The following equality has been found by induction:

$$n(S,t+1) = (1+\alpha)^{t+1}\, n(S,0).$$

This equality allows formulation of the following results.

Proposition

The number of representatives of an above-average schema increases exponentially if proportional selection is used.

A dual result for below-average schemata is given by the next proposition.

Proposition

The number of representatives of a below-average schema decreases exponentially if proportional selection is used.

8.5 Effect of recombination on schema dynamics

In what follows, we limit ourselves to the case of one-point crossover.

Applying crossover to long schemata tends to disrupt the schemata. A short schema is more likely to survive a crossover operation than a long schema.

8.5.1 Schema disruption probability

Let S be a schema of length r and of defining length $\delta(S)$. For this schema there are $(r - 1)$ crossover points. There is a great probability that the schema will be disrupted if the crossover point falls between two well-defined symbols.

The result is that there are $\delta(S)$ crossover points that lead (with great probability) to schema disruption.

Assuming that a crossover point is chosen uniformly, the probability P that the crossover operation disrupts the schema S may be approximated by the ratio between the number of crossover points that destroy the schema, and the total number of possible crossover points:

$$p = \frac{\delta(S)}{r-1}.$$

Remarks

(i)   Let us note that p is actually an upper bound of the disruption probability, since we have not taken into consideration the effect of the probability with which the crossover is applied.

(ii)   The second parent schema in the crossover operation may restore the initial schema through crossover, even if the crossover point lies between two specific positions.

Example

Let us consider the following schemata:

$$S = 1*****0$$

and

$$S_1 = 0*****0.$$

According to the established formula of p, the probability that S is disrupted by crossover is

$$p = \frac{7-1}{7-1}$$

$$= 1.$$

Involving the schemata S and S_1 in any kind of crossover (be it one- or multiple-point crossover), we still obtain S and S_1.

So neither S nor S_1 is destroyed. Obviously, this is a particular situation that points out the limits of the established formula.

8.5.2 Actual disruption probability

The actual probability p_1 that the crossover operation disrupts the schema S is smaller than p.

Hence, we have

$$p_1 \le \frac{\delta(S)}{r-1}.$$

This formula corresponds to the situation in which crossover is applied with probability 1 on schema S.

Now, let us consider the fact that, actually, the crossover operator is applied to the schema S (and to any other schema) with a sub-unitary probability $p_{c,s}$.

Selecting the schema S for crossover does not influence the choice of the crossover point.

Therefore, the selection for crossover and the choice of the crossover point are independent events.

It follows that the probability p_2 that the schema will be destroyed is the product of the probabilities p and $p_{c,s}$.

So we have

$$p_2 = p_{c,s} \frac{\delta(S)}{r-1}.$$

The reasons invoked above (in connection with the possibility of re-storing the schema S through a convenient crossover) lead us to the conclusion that the actual probability p_d that the schema S will be destroyed is smaller than the probability p_2 calculated above.

Hence, we have

$$p_d' \leq p_{c,s} \frac{\delta(S)}{r-1}.$$

8.5.3 Survival probability

The probability that the schema S will survive application of the crossover operator with a probability $p_{c,s}$ is

$$p_s = 1 - p_d.$$

We denote by p_s the *survival probability* of the schema S.

Taking the previous inequality into account, we obtain

$$p_s \geq 1 - p_{c,s} \frac{\delta(S)}{r-1}. \tag{8.1}$$

8.6 Combined effect of selection and recombination on schema dynamics

In this section, the combined effect of selection and recombination on schema dynamics is studied. Some interesting qualitative results are established.

8.6.1 Schema dynamics within selection and crossover

In the case of selection, we have established the equality

$$n(S,t+1)=n(S,t)\frac{f(S,t)}{F(t)}, \tag{8.2}$$

which expresses the evolution undergone by the number of representatives of the schema S.

We wonder how the evolution equation will change if we also consider recombination.

One may notice that, after recombination, the population $P(t+1)$ does not contain all the representatives of S given by the evolution equation (8.2).

With $n_{s,c}(S,t+1)$ we denote the number of representatives of the schema S in $P(t+1)$ that result from selection followed by crossover.

We may consider that the probability of survival p_s represents the ratio between the number $n_{s,c}(S,t+1)$ of representatives of the schema in the generation $P(t+1)$ (obtained by applying crossover) and the number $n(S,t+1)$ of representatives in the absence of crossover.

Then we have

$$p_s=\frac{n_{s,c}(S,t+1)}{n(S,t+1)}.$$

The evolution equation is obtained from this equality:

$$n_{s,c}(S,t+1)=p_s n(S,t+1).$$

Taking into account inequality (8.1) established for p_s and the form of $n(S,t+1)$ given by (8.2), we find the inequality

$$n_{s,c}(S,t+1) \geq \left(1 - p_{c,s}\frac{\delta(S)}{r-1}\right)\frac{f(S,t)}{F(t)}n(S,t). \tag{8.3}$$

The established result lets us express the following proposition.

Proposition

Let us consider a genetic algorithm with proportional selection and one-point crossover. Let $p_{c,s}$ be the crossover probability. The number $ns_{s,c}(S,t+1)$ of representatives of the schema S in the generation $P(t+1)$ satisfies the inequality

$$n_{s,c}(S,t+1) \geq \left(1 - p_{c,s}\frac{\delta(S)}{r-1}\right)\frac{f(S,t)}{F(t)}n(S,t),$$

where $n(S,t)$ is the number of representatives of the schema in the generation $P(t)$, r is the schema length, and $\delta(S)$ its defining length.

Remark

The result established here is a slightly modified version of the one obtained by Holland, 1975 (the parameter $p_{c,s}$ is replaced by p_c).

Remark

In order to simplify matters, we will delete the indexes s and c, and we write $n(S,t+1)$ instead of $n_{s,c}(S,t+1)$.

8.6.2 Qualitative results concerning schema dynamics

The inequality

$$\frac{n(S,t+1)}{n(S,t)} \geq \frac{f(S,t)}{F(t)}\left(1 - p_{c,s}\frac{\delta(S)}{r-1}\right)$$

points out that the evolution of the number of representatives of the schema S depends on two factors:

(i)   the ratio between the fitness $f(S,t)$ of the schema S and the average fitness $F(t)$ of the generation t,

(ii)   the defining length of the schema.

The bigger the fitness of a schema as compared to the average fitness of generation t, the more representatives it will have in the next generation $(t+1)$.

Therefore, evolution favors the survival of the fittest (most successful, above-average) schemata. This evolution is due to selection, as we have seen above.

The second factor suggests that, for two schemata having the same fitness, the schema with a shorter defining length will have more representatives in the next generation.

Hence, the following qualitative result has been established:

The frequency of schemata having above-average fitness and short defining length will increase in the next generation.

The schemata that fulfill these conditions play an essential part in the evolution of the search process toward a global optimum.

The increase (decrease) of the number of representatives of the above-average (below-average) schemata is exponential (see the reasoning regarding the effect of selection).

This result, associated with the *implicit parallelism* of genetic search, accounts for the speed of the search process.

8.7 Effect of mutation on schema dynamics

We will consider now the schema dynamics when the mutation operator is applied. In this case, the survival probability of the schema depends on the mutation probability and the order of the schema.

In order for a schema S to outlive the action of the mutation operator, all its specific positions have to survive. We will consider here the *strong version* of the mutation operator, i.e., the variant in which the value of a gene is automatically transformed as a result of mutation.

The mutation probability p_m is the probability that a certain position (a gene) will change its value. It follows that the probability that a certain position of the schema will survive the action of mutation is $(1 - p_m)$.

Let us assume now that there is a schema S without specific positions (i.e., a schema with zero defining length). Applying the mutation operator does not modify this schema; that is, its survival probability is one.

If the schema has one specific position, then its probability of surviving is $(1 - p_m)$.

These observations can be generalized for a schema with a number $O(S) > 1$ of specific positions.

We may, therefore, formulate the following result.

Proposition

Le S be a schema of order $O(S)$. The probability that the schema S will survive the application of the mutation operator is

$$q_m = (1 - p_m)^{O(S)}. \tag{8.4}$$

Proof. We will proceed by induction with respect to the length of the schema. We have seen that for

$$O(S) = 0$$

we have

$$q_m = (1 - p_m)^0$$
$$= 1.$$

For

$$O(S) = 1$$

we have established the equality

$$q_m = 1 - p_m.$$

We suppose now that for a schema of order k we have

$$q_m = (1 - p_m)^k.$$

Let S be a schema of order $(k+1)$.

According to the assumption made, the probability that the first k specific positions of the schema will survive mutation is

$$q = (1 - p_m)^k.$$

The survival probability of the last specific position is $(1 - p_m)$.

The mutation of the other (unspecific) positions of the schema does not affect the schema survival.

Let us recall that if A and B are two independent events, then the probability that these events occur simultaneously is the product of their respective probabilities, i.e.,

$$P(A \cap B) = P(A)P(B).$$

The mutation of each position is an event independent of all the other mutations. It follows that the mutation of the last specific position is independent from the mutation of the first k specific positions.

Consequently, the survival probability of a schema of order $(k+1)$ will be

$$q_{m+1} = q(1 - p_m)$$
$$= (1 - p_m)^{k+1}.$$

This completes the proof. $\square$

Remarks

(i)   As the mutation probability is small ($p_m \ll 1$), we may write:

$$q_m = (1-p_m)^{O(S)}$$
$$\approx 1 - p_m \, O(S).$$

(8.5)

(ii)   This result is obtained retaining only the first (linear) term in Taylor expansion of q_m as a function of $O(S)$.

We may therefore approximate the probability that the schema S will survive mutation as follows:

$$q_m' = 1 - p_m \, O(S).$$

8.8 Schema theorem

This section focuses on the combined effect of selection, recombination, and mutation on schema dynamics. These three operators act independently.

8.8.1 Schema dynamics within selection and search operators

The survival probability of a schema under the effect of selection, crossover, and mutation is the product of the respective survival probabilities.

Using (8.3), we obtain that the expected number of instances of the schema S will change in a generation according to

$$n(S,t+1) \geq n(S,t) \frac{f(S,t)}{F(t)} \left(1 - p_{c,s} \frac{\delta(S)}{r-1} \right) p_m.$$

(8.6)

From (8.4) and (8.6), we obtain the following inequality for the expected number of instances of the schema S:

$$n(S,t+1) \geq n(S,t)\frac{f(S,t)}{F(t)}\left(1-p_{c,s}\frac{\delta(S)}{r-1}\right)(1-p_m). \quad (8.7)$$

Therefore we established the following proposition:

Proposition

The dynamics of the expected number of representatives of the schema S will satisfy the inequality

$$n(S,t+1) \geq n(S,t)\frac{f(S,t)}{F(t)}\left(1-p_{c,s}\frac{\delta(S)}{r-1}\right)\left[(1-p_m)^{O(S)}\right].$$

8.8.2 Approximating schema dynamics

If we consider in (8.7) the established approximation (8.5) for mutation survival probability, we obtain the following result:

$$n(S,t+1) \geq n(S,t)\frac{f(S,t)}{F(t)}\left(1-p_{c,s}\frac{\delta(S)}{r-1}\right)\left[1-p_m O(S)\right].$$

If we disregard the (small) product term

$$p_{c,s}\, p_m \frac{\delta(S)}{r-1} O(S),$$

from the previous inequality, we obtain the following result, which represents the fundamental theorem of genetic algorithms (Holland, 1975):

$$n(S,t+1) \geq n(S,t) \frac{f(S,t)}{F(t)} \left(1 - p_{c,s} \frac{\delta(S)}{r-1} - p_m O(S) \right). \tag{8.8}$$

8.8.3 Fundamental theorem

Using the established inequality (8.8), we may now state the schema theorem as follows.

Schema theorem

(Fundamental theorem of genetic algorithms)

Consider a simple genetic algorithm that uses binary encoding, proportional selection, one-point crossover, and strong mutation.

The dynamics of the number of instances of a schema S is characterized by the inequality:

$$n(S,t+1) \geq n(S,t) \frac{f(S,t)}{F(t)} \left(1 - p_{c,s} \frac{\delta(S)}{r-1} - p_m O(S) \right).$$

Remarks

(i)   One may notice that the smaller the order of a schema, the more copies it will have in the next generation.

(ii)   The global result obtained points out that the frequency of schemata with above-average fitness (i.e., short schemata of low order) tends to increase in the next generations.

The growth is exponential. This result stands for a theoretical basis of trust in the potential of standard genetic algorithms.

8.9 Building block

In this section, a non-formal definition of the building block concept is considered.

Definition

Short, low-order, high-performance schemata are called *building blocks.*

Remarks

(i)   According to the schema theorem, building blocks are those schemata that proliferate throughout generations, while the search process goes on.

(ii) Let us notice that sometimes in the definition of building blocks either the defining length or the order of schemata is used.

Usually, there is a concordance between these two measures, but they do not coincide.

Example

Let us consider the schema

$$S = (0 \underbrace{** ... *}_{99 \text{ times}} 1)$$

having length

$$r = 101.$$

This schema has the following features:

$$O(S) = 2,$$
$$\delta(S) = 101 - 1$$
$$= 100.$$

We may notice that the order and the defining length of the considered schema S differ by two magnitude orders.

8.10 Building block hypothesis and linkage problem

When the search operators of a genetic algorithm act on a certain population, several *building* blocks are created. The specific positions of building blocks are usually well clustered, a fact that ensures a reduced defining length.

Therefore, different building blocks correspond to substrings having various positions in the strings that represent the chromosomes.

Example

For a population made up of strings of length

$$r = 7,$$

the following schemata may represent building blocks:

$$S_1 = (10*****),$$
$$S_2 = (***11**),$$
$$S_3 = (****1*0).$$

We may admit that, due to the action of genetic algorithms, building blocks combine in order to form greater and greater building blocks with better and better performances.

Eventually, this process of combination converges toward the optimum solution. This model is known as the *building block hypothesis*.

In the absence of a rigorous demonstration of the convergence of genetic algorithms, the schema theorem and the building block hypothesis provide an intuitive explanation of the success of genetic algorithms. For this reason, in the case of binary-encoded genetic algorithms, the building blocks are considered to be the basic processing units.

8.10.1 Schema linkage

Let us suppose that S is a schema with a very good fitness, which is extremely useful in the search process. It would be helpful, therefore, to ensure the survival of this schema in the next generations. If we could reduce the order and the defining length of this schema, then its occurrence in the next generations would increase.

The degree of compactness of a schema, relative to its order, is referred to as its *linkage*.

We notice that the order and the defining length of a schema are not symmetrical measures. Further, by no means can we decrease the order without bringing about disruption of the schema.

The defining length is a measure related to the topology of the schema. The question that arises is how the typology could be changed without altering the meaning of the schema.

The simplest idea is to associate with each gene an index indicating the gene location within the schema. Then we can subject the genes to any kind of permutation without altering the essence of the schema. Thus the schema would become invariant to any permutations of its positions (be they specific positions or not).

By successive permutations, all the specific positions will be clustered, i.e., not separated by unspecific positions (identified by the symbol *). Such a transformation minimizes the defining length of a schema and increases its chances to survive.

A long, loosely linked schema may be transformed into a tightly linked equivalent schema. This idea has led to considering a special class of genetic algorithms called *messy genetic algorithms*.

8.10.2 Concluding remarks

Summarizing, we may underline the main conclusions obtained from the schema theorem:

(i)   According to the schema theorem, the building blocks (short, low-order, above-average schemata) will grow exponentially throughout the following generations.

(ii)   The number of representatives of a below-average schema decreases exponentially in further generations.

(iii)   The building blocks and their combinations, used for constructing longer and longer useful substrings stand for the genetic algorithms' most important processing mechanism (building block hypothesis).

(iv) Binary encoding points out the great number of schemata processed in parallel by a genetic algorithm. This intrinsic parallelism may be connected with the effectiveness of the search and the speed of convergence.

8.11 Generalizations of schema theorem

Several generalizations of the schema theorem have been proposed; for example, the possibility of creating a new building block from parents that are not building blocks.

By adding new terms, the schema theorem can be turned from an inequality to an equality expression (Bridges and Goldberg, 1987; Nix and Vose, 1991). Nix and Vose (1991) developed an approach based on the exact transition matrix describing the expected new generation.

Radcliffe (1991), and Radcliffe and Surry (1994) considered a more general formalism known as *forma analysis*. This formalism provides a general framework allowing results to be transferred between different representation spaces with different variation operators.

The notion of schema is generalized from binary strings to arbitrary representations (search spaces). The new notion is called *forma*.

Representation-independent recombination operators are also considered. These operators have features claimed to be helpful for evolutionary search.

The basic properties of representation-independent operators are the following:

•   *respect*

      (each offspring contains all the alleles common to its parents),

- *assortment*

  (it is possible to produce any solution that contains only alleles present in the parents),

- *transmission*

  (each allele in every offspring is present in at least one of its parents).

The resulting approach may be considered as an attempt toward a general, representation-independent theory of evolutionary algorithms.

Several attempts have also been made to generalize the schema theorem to genetic programming.

A dual approach of the schema theorem is to study the convergence in probability of the solution sequence.

Davis and Principe (1991) proved that the solution sequence generated by a simple genetic algorithm converges in probability to a global optimum solution.

This result, having a simulated annealing convergence flavor, is not very surprising or of very high practical importance. Convergence in probability is a weak one and many algorithms reputed as inefficient satisfy this type of convergence.

8.12 Deceptive functions

The schema theorem and the building block hypothesis supply a model of the processes that govern the dynamics of genetic algorithms. However, we do not have theoretical results that could indicate what conditions a criterion function should satisfy in order for the standard genetic algorithm to lead to the global optimum.

Reciprocally, we do not know which variant of genetic algorithm gives the best results for a given class of objective functions.

For these reasons we are interested in understanding those problems for which the genetic algorithms (or other evolutive algorithms) lead to erroneous results. Such problems can be called *deceptive problems*.

Thus, we are lead to search for certain functions or classes of functions, called *deceptive functions*, for which genetic algorithms fail.

In deceptive problems, the average fitness values of the schemata provide misleading information. For theoretical reasons, such problems are constructed to mislead the simple genetic algorithms.

Deceptive functions may or may not be difficult for other classes of (evolutionary) algorithms (Goldberg, 1987; Whitley, 1991; Grefenstette, 1993).

The search for deceptive functions and for methods of solving deceptive problems has allowed a better understanding of the genetic algorithm mechanisms.

The first papers in this field are due to Bethke (1980) and Goldberg (1987).

For a survey of some early results see Goldberg (1992).

Despite their apparent simplicity, genetic algorithms are complex probabilistic systems characterized by non-linearity, large dimension, and multiple facets. This is why genetic algorithms can interact with problems in numberless ways.

Usually, genetic algorithms combine short, low-order, above-average schemata in order to make up building blocks of greater order. The selection operator will favor the building blocks of low order while the recombination operator combines these building blocks in larger blocks.

If in a problem the building blocks of low order are instances of the global optimum, then the standard genetic algorithms converge toward this global optimum.

If, on the contrary, the low-order schemata are not instances of the optimal global solution, then it is possible that the algorithm does not converge toward the global solution, but rather toward a sub-optimal solution (a local optimum). The corresponding objective functions may be regarded as deceptive functions.

The condition for a problem to be deceptive is that the low-order schemata are unsatisfactory and do not combine in building blocks of greater order.

Usually, a deceptive function has a global optimum and several local optima. In the extreme case, as the low-order schemata correspond to a sub-optimal solution (local optimum), their fitness is greater than that of other schemata. It follows that, in this situation, the low-order combinations (schemata) tend to favor the complements of great-order combinations that are necessary to reach the global optimum.

It is obvious that, in the case of deceptive functions, the canonical genetic operators with standard selection and variation operators, as considered in the schema theorem, do not lead to satisfactory results (i.e., do not achieve the global optimum).

Various methods to solve deceptive problems have been considered. Some of these methods consider new search operators (like inversion or problem-specific operators) and more sophisticated population models.

Other methods introduce a more flexible chromosome encoding (like messy genetic algorithms or some virus-evolutionary genetic algorithms).

Messy genetic algorithms use position-independent encoding and allow for over-specification and under-specification (see Chapter 11).

References and bibliography

Bethke, A.D., (1980), Genetic Algorithms as Function Optimizers, Ph.D. Thesis, University of Michigan.

Bridges, C., Goldberg, D.E., (1987), An analysis of reproduction and crossover in a binary-coded genetic algorithm, *Proc. 2nd Int. Conf. on Genetic Algorithms*, J.J. Grefenstette (Ed.), Erlbaum, Hillsdale, NJ, 9-13.

Davis, T.E., Principe, J.C., (1991), A simulated annealing-like convergence theory for a simple genetic algorithm, *Proc 4th Int. Conf. on Genetic Algorithms*, R.K. Belew, L.B. Booker (Eds.) Morgan Kaufmann, San Mateo, CA, 174-181.

Goldberg, D.E., (1987), Simple genetic algorithms and the minimal, deceptive problem, in *Genetic Algorithms and Simulated Annealing*, L. Davis (Ed.), Pitman, London, 74-88.

Goldberg, D.E., (1989), *Genetic Algorithms in Search, Optimization, and Machine Learning*, Addison-Wesley, New York.

Goldberg, D.E., (1992), Construction of high-order deceptive functions using low-order Walsh coefficients, *Annals of Mathematics and Artificial Intelligence*, 5, 35-48.

Goldberg, D.E., Deb, K., Horn, J., (1992), Massive multimodality, deception and genetic algorithms, *Parallel Problem Solving from Nature*, 2, R. Männer, B. Manderick (Eds.), Elsevier Publ., 37-46.

Grefenstette, J., (1993), Deception considered harmful, *Foundations of Genetic Algorithms*, 2, D. Whitley (Ed.), Morgan Kaufmann, San Mateo, CA, 75-91.

Holland, J.H., (1975), *Adaptation in Natural and Artificial Systems*, University of Michigan Press, Ann Arbor (Second edition: MIT Press, 1992).

Nix, A.E., Vose, M.D., (1991), Modeling genetic algorithms with Markov chains, *Annals of Mathematics and Artificial Intelligence*, 5, 79-88.

Radcliffe, N.J., (1991), Forma analysis and random respectful recombination, *Proc. 4th Int. Conf. on Genetic Algorithms*, R.K. Belew, L.B. Booker (Eds.), Morgan Kaufmann, San Mateo, CA, 222-229.

Radcliffe, N.J., Surry, P.D., (1994), Fitness variance of formae and performance prediction, *Foundation of Genetic Algorithms*, 3, L.D. Whitley, M.D. Vose (Eds.), Morgan Kaufmann, San Mateo, CA, 51-72.

Whitley, D., (1991), Fundamental principles of deception in genetic search, *Foundations of Genetic Algorithms*, G.J.E. Rawlins (Ed.), Morgan Kaufmann, San Mateo, CA, 221-241.

9

Real-valued encoding

9.1 Introduction

This chapter presents the basic aspects of real-valued encoding. The basic evolutionary operators using this coding are presented and several variants of these operators are considered.

The main topics of the chapter are

- discrete and continuous recombination,

- multi-parent recombination,

- SBX recombination operator,

- fitness-based recombination,

- uniform and non-uniform mutation,

187

- normal and Cauchy mutations.

9.2 Real-valued vectors

Various particular problems that use specific encoding require the development of some special genetic algorithms. One of the most usual encoding technique is the one that considers *real numbers* for representing the values of the genes.

In this case, we say that we have a *real-valued encoding* of the search space elements.

Real-valued encoding is suitable especially for solving some optimization problems in which the variables take values in a continuous domain.

In what follows, we will present the real-valued encoding and the main operators associated with it.

In *real-valued encoding*, each solution is represented (encoded) as a real-valued search vector. Therefore the system uses real-valued component vectors as chromosomes.

The dimension of the chromosomes is constant and equal to the dimension of the solution vectors.

The main aim of this approach is to make encoding closer to the solution space of the problem.

Let

$$x = (x_1, x_2, \ldots, x_s)$$

be the encoding of a solution.

The ith position of this encoding represents the value of the ith gene in the chromosome x.

In real-valued encoding, $x_i \in \mathbf{R}$, so x belongs to the Euclidean space $\mathbf{R}^s$. Each gene corresponds to a parameter (or a variable) of the function to be optimized.

The values of the ith gene in different chromosomes stand for values of the parameter corresponding to the gene.

Each parameter (variable) assumes values in a fixed domain and genetic operators have to maintain the values in the respective domains.

Remarks

(i)   Sometimes, for the sake of simplicity, we identify a gene with its value.

(ii)   In order to create new solutions using crossover and mutation operators, it is necessary to consider new search strategies. Real-valued encoding requires defining some specific genetic operators.

In what follows, we will consider the main operators acting on real-valued vectors.

9.3   Recombination operators for real-valued encoding

The crossover operator with one or more crossover points is easy to apply. Unfortunately, in the case of real-valued encoding, this operator is not suitable. Indeed, it cannot perform the search with respect to each variable. This search would rely entirely on the mutation operator. Because of this, it is necessary to reconsider the crossover operator.

In real-valued encoding, there are more possibilities to redefine the crossover (recombination) operator. We introduce the most familiar variants of this operator below.

9.3.1 Discrete recombination

Discrete crossover is analogous to uniform crossover within binary encoding.

For each position i of the first offspring, we choose (with a fixed probability p) the parent whose ith gene will be transmitted to this descendant.

The respective position of the second offspring will be completed with the value of the corresponding gene from the other parent.

If

$$p = 0.5,$$

the role of the two parents is symmetrical.

Example

Let us consider the chromosomes:

$$x = (x_1, x_2, x_3, x_4, x_5)$$

and

$$y = (y_1, y_2, y_3, y_4, y_5).$$

Discrete crossover with

$$p = 0.5$$

may lead, for instance, to the following descendants:

$$x_1 = (x_1, x_2, y_3, x_4, y_5)$$

and

$$y_1 = (y_1, y_2, x_3, y_4, x_5).$$

9.3.2 Continuous recombination

Within the *continuous crossover* operator (also called *average crossover* operator), some positions are chosen at random. Each position may be selected with a fixed probability.

The corresponding genes in the descendants represent the arithmetical average of the corresponding genes in the parents.

Example

Consider the two chromosomes from the preceding example. Let us suppose that the genes 3 and 5 have been selected.

In these conditions, the descendants obtained through continuous crossover are the following:

$$x_1 = (x_1, x_2, (x_3 + y_3)/2, x_4, (x_5 + y_5)/2)$$

and

$$y_1 = (y_1, y_2, (x_3 + y_3)/2, y_4, (x_5 + y_5)/2).$$

It is quite easy to design other types of crossover. Several possibilities are outlined below.

9.3.3 Complete continuous recombination

Complete continuous recombination produces a single descendant. The offspring's genes represent the arithmetic mean of the values of the genes that occupy the same positions in its two parents.

The ith gene of the descendant will have the form:

$$z_i = \frac{1}{2}(x_i + y_i), \quad i=1, ..., s.$$

9.3.4 Convex (intermediate) recombination

In *convex* (or *intermediate*) recombination, the offspring is (are) expressed as a convex combination of two or more parents. Several situations are considered in the following.

9.3.4.1 One offspring

Let us consider a more general situation in which the parents do not have the same weight in producing the offspring.

In this case, the genes of the descendant may be given by a convex combination of its parents' genes.

The gene occupying the position i of the unique descendant will have the value:

$$z_i = \alpha \, x_i + \beta \, y_i,$$

where $\alpha, \beta \in [0,1]$ are two parameters that satisfy the convexity condition

$$\alpha + \beta = 1.$$

Remark

If α and β reflect the quality (fitness) of the parents, then this type of crossover favors the better parent.

9.3.4.2 Two offspring

We can set up a convex crossover mechanism that generates two descendants. The chromosomes x and y will produce the descendants u and v whose genes are of the form:

$$u_i = \alpha \, x_i + (1-\alpha) \, y_i, \quad i=1, \, ..., \, s \, ,$$

$$v_i = \alpha \, y_i + (1-\alpha) \, x_i, \quad i=1, \, ..., \, s.$$

In this case, it is not useful to relate the parameter α to the performance of the parent chromosomes.

If the parameter α is constant for all generations, then we have *uniform convex crossover*.

Remark

We can design a mechanism that would allow α to depend on generation (on the age of population). In this case, we have a *non-uniform convex crossover* operator.

9.3.4.3 Random coefficient

It is also possible to introduce a random element into convex crossover. If only one descendant is considered, its genes may be expressed as follows:

$$z_i = \alpha \, x_i + (1-\alpha) \, y_i, \quad i = 1, \, ..., \, s,$$

where α is a random number from the interval $[0,1]$.

If we have two descendants, the value of their genes will be calculated with the formulas:

$$u_i = \alpha \, x_i + (1-\alpha) \, y_i, \quad i = 1, ..., s,$$

and

$$v_i = \alpha \, y_i + (1-\alpha) \, x_i, \quad i = 1, ..., s.$$

The number α may be the same for all generations or may be chosen anew for each generation.

9.3.4.4 Local crossover

If we let the parameter α change its value for each gene, then we obtain a special kind of crossover, called *local crossover*.

Local crossover is a combination of crossover and mutation.

If a unique descendant is considered, its genes are

$$z_i = \alpha_i x_i + (1 - \alpha_i) y_i.$$

When two offspring are produced, their genes are

$$u_i = \alpha_i x_i + (1 - \alpha_i) y_i,$$

$$v_i = \alpha_i y_i + (1 - \alpha_i) x_i,$$

where $\alpha_i \in [0,1]$.

9.3.5 SBX operator

Deb (1996) described an operator, called SBX (*simulated binary crossover*) that simulates the action of the one-point crossover operator within binary encoding.

The SBX operator respects the continuity of the search space.

The process of producing offspring is based on the use of a continuous probability distribution $P(\alpha,\beta)$.

The parameter β is a non-negative real number that imposes the form of the probability distribution.

The probability distribution has the form

$$P(\alpha,\beta) = \begin{cases} \dfrac{\alpha+1}{2}\beta^{n}, & \text{if } 0 \le \beta \le 1 \\[2ex] \dfrac{\alpha+1}{2}\dfrac{1}{\beta^{n+2}}, & \text{if } \beta > 1. \end{cases}$$

We now outline the generative mechanism of the SBX operator.

Let x_1 and x_2 be the parent chromosomes. The descendants y_1 and y_2 are produced using the following algorithm:

SBX ALGORITHM

P1. A random number $u \in [0,1]$ is generated.

P2. A parameter δ is determined so that

$$\int_{0}^{\delta} P(\alpha,\beta)\, d\beta = u.$$

P3. The calculated value of δ is used to obtain the descendants y_1 and y_2 via the formulas:

$$y_1 = \frac{1}{2}\left(x_1 + x_2 - \delta|x_1 - x_2|\right),$$

$$y_2 = \frac{1}{2}\left(x_1 + x_2 + \delta|x_1 - x_2|\right).$$

Remark

The advantage of a parameterized probability distribution lies in getting descendants similar to their parents.

More precisely, if the parents are similar, the descendant solutions cannot be very far from the parent solutions.

On the other hand, if the parents are very dissimilar, then new solutions, distant from the parent solutions, may be obtained.

9.3.6 Multiple-parent recombination

Other recombination scenarios are also possible. We can, for instance, combine not only two, but more parents and build offspring taking the quality of the parents into account.

The *diagonal multi-parent crossover* (Eiben, Raué, and Ruttkay, 1994) creates p offspring from p parents.

A number of $N \geq 1$ crossover points are chosen.

The first offspring contains the ith segment from the parent i, $i = 1, ..., p$.

The other offspring are constructed from a rotation of segments of the parents.

9.3.7 Fitness-based recombination

Employing the fitness values in order to guide recombination accelerates the search. Mechanisms centered on local exploitation of the search space may be used for crossover. These mechanisms are different from the classical rules based mainly on chance.

The need for establishing a compromise between exploration and exploitation appears again. We may safely say that the ideal solution to this compromise depends on the particular problem being considered, since a global approach is rather difficult.

9.3.7.1 Fitness-based scan

Eiben, Raué, and Ruttkay (1994) considered fitness-based multi-parent recombination. A unique offspring is obtained from $p \geq 2$ parents.

Each component (gene) of the offspring is selected from one of the parents with a probability corresponding to the parent's relative fitness.

The probability of selecting each component from the parent x^i is

$$p_i = \frac{f(x^i)}{\sum_{j=1}^{k} f(x^j)},$$

where

• f is the fitness function,

• k is the parent population size.

9.3.7.2 Heuristic crossover

The heuristic crossover operator of Wright (1994) produces a unique offspring z from the parents x and y.

Let us suppose y is not worse than x, i.e.,

$$f(y) \geq f(x).$$

Recall that a maximization optimization/search problem is considered.

In this case, the offspring is

$$z = y + u(y - x),$$

where u is a uniform random variable over $[0,1]$.

The heuristic crossover operator uses local information to determine a direction of search.

Remark

We may observe that this operator may be considered as a random variant of the *steepest descent* optimization procedure.

9.3.7.3 Simplex crossover

Simplex crossover of Renders and Bersini (1994) may be viewed as a multiple-parent non-random variant of heuristic crossover.

The operator selects $p > 2$ parents and determines the best and worst of them (say x and y, respectively).

The mass center m of the parent group without y is computed.

The offspring z has the expression

$$z = m + (m - y).$$

9.3.7.4 Random simplex crossover

Simplex crossover may be generalized to allow random variations. The search direction $(m - y)$ will be randomly perturbed.

Using the previous notations, the offspring has the expression

$$z = m + u(m - y),$$

where u is a uniform random variable over $[0,1]$.

9.4 Mutation operators for real-valued encoding

Let us consider a chromosome that encodes s parameters (it contains s genes). The values of the parameters are expressed as real numbers and for each parameter the domain of possible values is specified.

We may consider different forms of the mutation algorithm. Generally, we may speak about *uniform* and *non-uniform mutation operators*.

The action of a non-uniform operator depends on the generation (on the age of population).

9.4.1 Uniform mutation

The action of uniform mutation operators is independent of the population age (generation index).

In this section, some simple uniform mutation operators are considered.

9.4.1.1   One-position mutation operator

The action of the mutation operator M generates a unique offspring x' from x, i.e.,

$$x' = M(x).$$

This variant of the mutation operator replaces a single chromosome gene with a real number generated at random within the domain of the corresponding parameter.

The value of each gene may be changed with a fixed probability. Usually, it is assumed that all genes have the same mutation probability.

Let

$$x = (x_1, x_2, \ldots, x_s)$$

be a chromosome.

The action of the mutation operator generates a chromosome of the form

$$x' = (x_1, x_2, \ldots, x_i', \ldots, x_s), \quad 1 \le i \le s,$$

where x_i' is a random value from the domain of the ith parameter.

The position i that will undergo mutation is randomly generated.

The mutated gene value x_i' may represent a (normal) perturbation of the allele x_i.

9.4.1.2 All-positions mutation operator

We may assume that all the components of the vector x are perturbed in a similar way. There are different methods to achieve mutation.

We may consider, for instance, an additive normal mutation. In this case, we may write

$$x_i' = x_i + \alpha_i N(0, \sigma_i), \quad i = 1, ..., s,$$

where

- α_i is a real parameter, and

- $N(0, \sigma_i)$ is the realization of a normal random variable (with zero mean and standard deviation σ_i).

An important particular case corresponds to equal standard deviations for all chromosome components, i.e.,

$$\sigma_i = \sigma, \quad i = 1, ..., s.$$

We may also consider

$$\alpha_i = \alpha, \quad i = 1, ..., s.$$

A usual value is

$$\alpha = 1.$$

A multiplicative mutation may be written as

$$x_i' = x_i N(0, \sigma_i), \quad i = 1, ..., s.$$

A multiplicative lognormal perturbation may sometimes be more interesting.

In this case, we have

$$x_i' = x_i\, e^{\beta N(0,\sigma_i)}, \quad i=1, ..., s,$$

where β is a real parameter.

9.4.2 Non-uniform mutation

The non-uniform variant of the mutation operator is inspired by the *Metropolis algorithm* for establishing thermodynamic equilibrium, and the *simulated annealing* algorithm (for details regarding these algorithms, see van Laarhoven and Aarts, 1987).

9.4.2.1 A non-uniform mutation operator

In this approach, the genes undergo significant modifications in the first generations. Then modifications decrease gradually. Thus, in the initial stage of the search process, important progress is achieved, and a refinement, or *fine control*, of the search process takes place in the last phases.

Two parameters are randomly generated at each generation t. The first parameter, p, indicates the nature of the change, that is, the increase or decrease of the value of a gene.

The value

$$p = 1$$

indicates an increase of the value, whereas

$$p = -1$$

indicates a decrease.

The second parameter, r, determines the amplitude of the change. The parameter r is a random number from the interval $[0,1]$, following a uniform distribution.

Let

$$x = (x_1, x_2, \ldots, x_s)$$

be a chromosome and x_i the gene chosen for mutation.

The new value x_i' of the ith gene is given (according to Janikow and Michalewicz, 1991) by

$$x_i' = x_i + (x_{\max} - x_i)\left[1 - r^{\left(1-\frac{t}{T}\right)}\right], \quad \text{if } p = 1,$$

or

$$x_i' = x_i - (x_i - x_{\min})\left[1 - r^{\left(1-\frac{t}{T}\right)}\right], \quad \text{if } p = -1,$$

where

- r is a random parameter in $[0,1]$,

- x_{min} and x_{max} stand for the lower and upper bounds of x_i (the ith parameter value), respectively,

- T is the index of the generation for which the amplitude of the mutation is annihilated (that is, the subsequent generations will not undergo any mutations whatsoever).

Remarks

(i)   In certain implementations, T indicates the maximum number of generations of the evolutionary algorithm.

(ii)   The chromosome obtained by the action of the mutation operator will be

$$(x_1, x_2, \ldots, x_i', \ldots, x_s).$$

(iii)   We may also consider a version allowing all positions x_i, $i = 1, \ldots, s$, in a chromosome to be mutated as shown above.

The mutated chromosome will be

$$(x_1', x_2', \ldots, x_s').$$

9.4.2.2   Generalized non-uniform mutation

We can give a more general expression of the modifications undergone by x_i. Let us consider a function h:

$$h : \{0, 1, \ldots, T\} \to [0,1]$$

that has the properties:

(a) h is decreasing,

(b) $h(T) = 0$.

Remark

In this case, T is the maximum number of generations of the algorithm.

A usual expression of h is

$$h(t) = 1 - r^{\left(1 - \frac{t}{T}\right)^b},$$

where

- r is the realization of a uniform random variable on $[0,1]$,

- b is a system parameter that determines the non-uniformity degree.

Remarks

(i)   We usually consider $b \geq 1$.

(ii)   If, in the expression of h, we set

$$b = 1,$$

then we obtain the initial form of the modification undergone by the value occupying the ith position.

(iii)   If T is the index of the generation for which the mutation amplitude is annihilated, then h is a function

$$h : \mathbb{N} \to [0,1],$$

that satisfies the axioms (a) and (b) given above.

If we use the function h, the modification of the ith gene is written

$$x_i' = x_i + (x_{max} - x_i) h(t), \qquad \text{if } p = 1,$$

or

$$x_i' = x_i - (x_i - x_{min}) h(t), \qquad \text{if } p = -1.$$

Remarks

(i)   Let us note that a non-uniform operator realizes a zero-mean mutation.

(ii)   For the first generations, the mutation operator that we have described so far accomplishes a uniform exploration of the search space.

(iii)   For the last generations, as the variations are small, the exploitation becomes local and the search process is subject to fine control.

9.4.3 Normal perturbation-induced mutation

Several mutation mechanisms may be designed. As already mentioned, one possibility is to modify all the positions of a chromosome at one step. This mechanism may be applied to all types of mutation operators.

In this section, mutation operators induced by normal perturbations are considered. The standard deviation of the perturbation is included in the genotype and is modified by a self-adaptive process.

Mutation is the main operator in evolution strategies and evolutionary programming. Real-valued encoding may also use mutation operators specific to these methods of search/optimization.

9.4.3.1 Multiplicative self-adaptation procedure

Within evolution strategies, a genotype (chromosome) is a pair (x, σ), where x denotes the object variable (phenotype) and σ represents the vector of the strategy parameters.

The strategy parameters may be updated by using a *lognormal multiplicative* procedure.

A lognormal multiplicative mutation procedure for self-adaptation of strategy parameters may be expressed as

$$\sigma_i' = \sigma_i e^{aN(0,1)+bN_i(0,1)},$$

where a and b are real-valued parameters of the method.

The object variables may be mutated according to the normal additive rule

$$x_i' = x_i + N(0, \sigma_i').$$

In this case, the mutated strategy parameters are used.

Another possibility is to mutate the strategy parameters after the mutation of object variables.

Thus, the object variables are

$$x_i' = x_i + N(0, \sigma_i).$$

9.4.3.2 Additive self-adaptation procedure

An *additive* normal mutation procedure for self-adaptation of strategy parameters may also be used.

In this case, we may write

$$\sigma_i' = \sigma_i + \alpha_i N(0, \sigma_i),$$

where α_i is a parameter of the method.

The parameter α_i is computed anew for each component σ_i.

9.4.3.3 Other self-adaptation procedures

It is possible to consider normal mutations having non-zero expectation, as in the approach of Ostermeier (1992).

In such a self-adaptation process, the expectation values as well as the standard deviations may be updated.

A different interesting idea is to generate offspring by perturbing the parent in a random direction (Bremermann and Rogson, 1964).

In this case, a constant perturbation amplitude (or step size) is usually considered.

For difficult, highly nonlinear problems a variable perturbation amplitude could lead to better search progress.

Other *self-adaptation procedures* based on real-valued encoding have been proposed (see, e.g., Spears, 1995).

Such procedures consider mechanisms to adapt search operators including crossover and mutation.

9.4.4 Cauchy perturbation

The Gaussian distribution is the usual choice for a mutation distribution. Other distributions may also be considered. A good candidate is *Cauchy distribution*.

The normal and Cauchy distributions are stable in the sense that the distribution of the sum of two independent random variables having distributions of type T is also of type T.

Therefore, the Cauchy distribution may be considered as a limit law describing the cumulative effect of independent random perturbations.

The one-dimensional Cauchy density function centred in μ is

$$f_c(x) = \frac{1}{\pi} \frac{t}{t^2 + (x-\mu)},$$

where $t > 0$ is a scale parameter.

A multivariate version of the Cauchy distribution may be obtained by drawing a univariate standard Cauchy random number independently for each entry of the random vector.

The Cauchy distribution with independent univariate Cauchy random variables in each dimension is not the unique one. Another variant is the *spherically symmetric Cauchy distribution* (see Rudolph, 1997).

Experimental results (Yao, Liu and Lin, 1999) indicate that evolutionary algorithms with Cauchy mutations perform better than those using normal mutations for multimodal functions with many local optima.

Cauchy mutations seem to be useful for searches in a large region. Normal mutations perform better searches in a small local region.

9.5 Concluding remarks

In what follows, some qualitative remarks on real-valued encoding are made.

These remarks emphasize the importance and advantages of real-valued encoding for large classes of problems.

(i)   Experimental results (Michalewicz, 1992) pointed out that real-valued representation allows a better average convergence than binary encoding.

(ii)   Real-valued encoding permits a greater degree of precision. This fact is obvious mostly in those situations in which binary encoding requires vectors of very great dimensions.

(iii)   The performance of real-valued encoding also increases because of the use of specific operators that have a greater degree of accuracy than binary operators.

(iv)   Real-valued encoding is more natural, being generally closer to the problem space.

          Chromosomes may even stand for points in the solution space of the problem (in the case of optimization problems, for instance).

          This feature facilitates the introduction of special operators that incorporate knowledge specific to the problem domain.

(v)   Since a gene represents a variable (a dimension of the search space or a parameter) the intuitive nature of this type of encoding becomes more evident.

          Moreover, real-valued encoding ensures a certain contiguity of the representation space. Two close chromosomes (in the representation space) will correspond to close points in the problem space.

          This is not achieved in binary encoding, where the distance between chromosomes is usually given by the Hamming distance.

(vi)   Real-valued encoding ensures a better balance between the initial global search and the local exploitation of the solutions already found. Due to this, it may be successfully used for the fine tuning of the search process.

(vii)   Real-valued encoding establishes a bridge between genetic algorithms and the other classes of evolutive methods (evolution strategies and evolutionary programming).

References and bibliography

Bremermann H.J., Rogson M., (1964), An evolution-type search method for convex sets, ONR Technical Report, Contracts 222(85) and 365(58), Berkeley, CA.

Davis, L., (Ed.), (1991), *Handbook of Genetic Algorithms*, Van Nostrand Reinhold, New York.

Deb, K., (1996), Genetic algorithms for function optimization, *Genetic Algorithms for Soft Computing*, F. Herrera, J.L. Verdegay (Eds.), Physica Verlag, Heidelberg, 3-29.

Eiben, A.E., Raué, P.-E., Ruttkay, Zs., (1994), Genetic algorithms with multi-parent recombination, *Parallel Problem Solving from Nature*, 3, Yu Davidor, H.-P. Schwefel, R. Männer (Eds.), Springer, Berlin, 78-87.

Janikow, C.Z., Michalewicz, Z., (1991), An experimental comparison of binary and floating point representation in genetic algorithms, *Proc. 4th Int. Conf. on Genetic Algorithms*, B. Belew, L.B. Booker (Eds.), Morgan Kaufmann, San Mateo, CA, 31-36.

Michalewicz, Z., (1992), *Genetic Algorithms + Data Structures = Evolution Programs*, Springer-Verlag, Berlin.

Ostermeier, A., (1992), An evolution strategy with momentum adaptation of the random number distribution, *Parallel Problem Solving from Nature*, 2, R. Männer, B.K. Manderick (Eds.), North Holland, Amsterdam, 197-206.

Rawlins, G.J.E. (Ed.), (1991), *Foundations of Genetic Algorithms*, Morgan Kaufmann Publishers, San Mateo, CA.

Renders, J.M., (1995), *Algorithmes Génétiques et Réseaux de Neurones*, Hermes, Paris.

Renders, J.M., Bersini, H., (1994), Hybridizing genetic algorithms with hill-climbing methods for global optimization: two possible ways, *Proc. 1st IEEE Conf. on Evolutionary Computation*, IEEE, Piscataway, NJ, 312-317.

Rudolph, G., (1997), Local convergence rate of simple evolutionary algorithms with Cauchy mutations, *IEEE Trans. on Evolutionary Computation*, 1, 249-258.

Spears, W.M., (1995), Adapting crossover in evolutionary algorithms, *Proc. 4th Ann. Conf. on Evolutionary Programming*, J.R. McDonnell, R.G. Reynolds, D.B. Fogel (Eds.), MIT Press, Cambridge, MA, 367-384.

van Laarhoven, P.J.M., Aarts, E.H.L., (1987), *Simulated Annealing: Theory and Applications*, D. Reidel Publishers, Dordrecht.

Whitley, D., (Ed.), (1993), *Foundations of Genetic Algorithms*, 2, Morgan Kaufmann, San Mateo, CA.

Wright, A.H., (1994), Genetic algorithms for real parameter optimization, *Foundations of Genetic Algorithms*, G.J.E. Rawlins (Ed.), Morgan Kaufmann, San Mateo, CA, 205-218.

Yao, X., Liu, Y., (1996), Fast evolutionary programming, *Proc. 5th Conf. on Evolutionary Programming*, L.J., Fogel, P.J., Angeline, T. Bäck (Eds.), MIT Press, Cambridge, MA, 451-460.

Yao, X., Liu, Y., Lin, G., (1999), Evolutionary programming made faster, *IEEE Trans. on Evolutionary Computation*, 3, 82-102.

10

Hybridization, parameter setting, and adaptation

10.1 Introduction

This chapter considers several techniques to improve evolutionary algorithms by using hybridization and representation adaptation. The problems of evolutionary algorithm parameter setting and adaptation are also addressed.

Hybridization is an attempt to incorporate some general optimization heuristics into evolutionary algorithms. To do this, a more natural representation (usually real-valued encoding) has to be used.

Actually, the hybridization approach expresses the current tendency to rely on more flexible representation (like real-valued representa-

213

tion) instead of using a general, but somehow artificial, representation (binary encoding).

Parameter setting is a very important matter for all evolutionary algorithms.

In the previous chapters, various techniques to adapt control parameters of evolutionary algorithms (like crossover probability and mutation rate) have been considered.

In this chapter, some general methods for parameter setting and adaptation are reviewed.

10.2 Specialized representation and hybridization within GAs

Binary encoding was the most popular encoding technique in early GA works. It is easy to create and handle. Moreover, this modality of representation makes it possible to obtain interesting theoretical results, such as the schema theorem.

Binary encoding confers *robustness* to genetic algorithms, ensuring their success for different classes of problems. Binary representation can encode almost any situation, and the operators do not include pieces of knowledge about the problem domain.

These are the reasons why a genetic algorithm can be applied to solve very different problems.

10.2.1 Specific representation

In certain situations, it is necessary to use the *'natural'* encoding of a problem, instead of the standard binary representation. Thus we are led to modified versions of genetic algorithms. Such variants may work directly with the parameters to be optimized.

The recent trend in the actual applications of genetic algorithms is to abandon the standard binary representation scheme and to rely on more specific and flexible representations.

The need to replace binary encoding appears, for instance, when we wish to combine an evolutionary algorithm with another algorithm.

Let us suppose that we know an algorithm, not necessarily an optimal one, for solving the problem at hand. We will name this non-optimal algorithm the *current algorithm*.

10.2.2 Hybridization

The combination of the evolutionary algorithm techniques and the current algorithm is called *hybridization*. Hybridization has to incorporate the best part of the current algorithm into the evolutionary algorithm itself. The result is a *hybrid* evolutionary algorithm.

Hybridization may be done keeping the following aspects in mind (Davis, 1991):

(i)   *Use a specific encoding scheme as close as possible to the natural representation suggested by the problem.*

This implies that the method used for encoding the current algorithm is also employed in the hybrid algorithm. The advantages are the preservation of the domain expertise embodied in the specific encoding, and a high acceptance by the user.

(ii)   *Achievement of hybridization wherever possible.*

The two techniques are combined and the most promising features of the current algorithm are integrated within the hybrid procedure.

If the current algorithm is fast, we may add its solutions to the initial population of the hybrid evolutionary algorithm.

An elitist selection mechanism is usually considered in this context.

Associating doping of the initial population with good solutions and elitism may cause premature convergence. A ranking selection mechanism may be used to avoid premature convergence.

(iii)   *Adaptation of genetic operators.*

New genetic operators, adapted to the new encoding, should be created. This entails developing standard search operators (recombination and mutation) able to work with the new, specific encoding.

(iv)   *Use of domain heuristics.*

Certain heuristics of the domain may be integrated as distinct operators.

10.2.3 Use of specific encoding and hybridization

The use of specific encoding offers certain advantages. This encoding guarantees, for instance, to easily transfer the expertise of the problem domain into the algorithm.

Due to the encoding used and the knowledge of the way in which the current algorithm works, the hybrid algorithm may be perceived by the user as being more 'natural'.

Specific, real-valued encoding is more suitable for solving continuous numerical and combinatorial optimization problems.

Moreover, real-valued encoding allows research to incorporate classical computational methods into various evolutionary procedures.

The hybrid versions of evolutionary algorithms are sometimes closer to the needs and habits of the problem domain experts. That is why, for instance, hybrid methods are used more often than standard genetic algorithms for solving real problems that appear in engineering.

Hybridization techniques may incorporate problem-specific knowledge, local search operators, gradient-based methods, *simulated annealing* techniques (van Laarhoven and Aarts, 1987), and elements of *tabu search* (Glover and Laguna, 1997). Evolutionary algorithms may also be combined with *fuzzy systems* and *neural networks*.

Specific encoding may be used even in the absence of any hybridization. In such a case, we obtain an evolutionary algorithm that acts directly on the search space associated with the problem parameters. The use of specific encoding often leads to better results than the ones obtained by using binary encoding.

Specialized representation, whether it uses hybridization or not, relies on the following ideas:

(i)   it uses specific data structures,

(ii)   it considers new appropriate genetic operators if needed,

(iii)   it ensures that genotypes encode feasible solutions,

(iv)   it ensures that search operators preserve feasibility.

It is also useful to represent solutions by using orthogonal genes, i.e., genes whose semantics are independent of other genes. The orthogonal property avoids some undesirable interactions among genes like *epistasis*.

Epistasis occurs when the expression of a gene suppresses the expression (i.e., masks the phenotypic effects) of another.

10.3 Parameter setting and adaptive GAs

Evolutionary algorithms are procedures very sensitive to parameter values. A slight modification of parameters may completely change the results.

Several methods for setting and controlling parameters have been proposed.

Controlling the parameter values of an evolutionary algorithm allows adjustment of the search process.

10.3.1 Parameter setting in GAs

Several general parameter setting procedures have already been considered. Some robust methods dealing with parameter setting for genetic algorithms with a fixed population are outlined below:

- *hand optimization,*

- *brute force search,*

- *encoding parameters in the genetic algorithm and using the search mechanism to evolve parameters,*

- *using a metalevel GA for parameter adaptation,*

- *using adaptive parameter fitness,*

- *parameter control using rule-based fuzzy controllers.*

According to Eiben, Hinterding and Michalewicz (1999), parameter setting may be classified as one of the following categories:

- *blind parameter control,*

- *adaptive parameter control,*

- *self-adaptive parameter control.*

In *blind control*, the parameters are altered by some well-defined rules. Usually, a time-varying schedule is used for parameter modifications.

Adaptive control uses a feedback related to the progress of the search process to determine the change of the parameters.

In *self-adaptive control*, parameters are encoded into the genotype and are evolved during the search process. Parameter self-adaptation is thus obtained by the effect of search operators.

Remark

Eiben, Hinterding and Michalewicz (1999) used 'deterministic control' instead of 'blind control'. But since the parameter control strategies sometimes imply stochastic procedures, we consider 'blind control' to be more appropriate.

10.3.2 Parameter setting and representation adaptation

Evolving parameters encoded in the chromosome is a very early adaptation method.

Unfortunately this natural and appealing method does not give satisfactory results when used in a simple, 'naive' form.

Another important aspect is representation adaptation. This means that shape and size of individuals may be adapted during the search process.

In this section, some approaches dealing with adaptive representations and parameter adaptation strategies are reviewed.

Grefenstette (1986) uses a *metalevel genetic algorithm* to tune the parameters of a current genetic algorithm.

Delta coding (Whitley, Mathias and Fitzhorn, 1991) is also a model using two levels: a *search* level and a *perturbation* level.

ARGOT system (Shaefer, 1987) is a model using an *adapting representation*. A flexible mapping from the object variables to the genes is considered.

Messy genetic algorithms use variable chromosomes by allowing the representation to be unspecified or over-specified.

Adaptive representations involving *introns* (noncoding sequences of a genotype) may be very appealing. Wu and Lindsay (1995) considered such an approach that explicitly defines introns in the individual representation.

One of the earliest methods of self-adaptive control is the dominance mechanism of the diploid representation. This mechanism, as well as delta coding and messy genetic algorithms, will be considered in Chapter 11.

Grefenstette (1995) and Manderick, Weger, and Spiessens (1991) considered methods to estimate search operator performance. Fitness correlation coefficients for different operators are computed for several problems.

Altenberg (1994) considered a *transmission function in the fitness domain* to evaluate the operator quality.

Julstrom (1995) proposed the concept of an *operator tree* and an adaptive mechanism to regulate the ratio between the number of crossover and mutation applications.

The new mechanism is used to enhance an operator if it produces high-fit offspring. Both operators are used independently.

An operator tree is associated with each individual in the population. The nodes of the operator tree contain the operators used to generate the individual as well as all its ancestors.

Let us suppose that an offspring is superior to the population average fitness. The corresponding operator tree is visited to compute the *credit* due to recombination and mutation.

The credit of one individual may be defined as the sum of the credits of the operators that generated that individual.

Possibly, we may consider only the tree of the recent contributions to reward the search operators.

The credits of the most recent individuals are recorded. This information is used to update recombination and mutation probabilities.

Several adaptive strategies for recombination operators have been proposed by Schaffer and Morishima (1987), Levenick (1995), Angeline (1996), Hong, Kahng and Moon (1995).

10.3.3 Adaptive fitness of a search operator

Davis (1991) proposes an adaptation mechanism based on the modification of the application probability of the search operators.

The main idea is to alter the application probability of an operator as the result of its observed performance.

Intuitively, an operator performance may be defined as the number of improvements (e.g., the number of offspring better than the best individual in the population) for which the operator is responsible divided by the number of all offspring the operator created.

All operators that take part in creating a successful individual (e.g., an offspring better than the fittest individual in the population) are rewarded by increasing their *fitness*.

A *credit* value is assigned to each individual. The operator performance is measured using the credits of the offspring it produces.

In particular, let us consider an offspring better than the best individual already existing in the population. This offspring is rewarded by
increasing its credit by a value equal to the amount that its evaluation
(fitness) exceeds the best evaluation.

The parents of the rewarded offspring receive a portion of the credit
gained by the offspring. The rate of the credit passed to the parents is
a parameter of the algorithm.

The adaptation mechanism uses the credit assignment procedure to
update the search operator probabilities after a number G of generations.

Let S be the sum of the credits associated with all the offspring the
operator has produced in G generations.

The *performance P* of the search operator is defined as follows:

$$P = \frac{S}{N},$$

where N is the number of offspring the operator produces in G generations.

The operator probability is updated according to the rule:

$$P_{new} = (1-s)\,P_{old} + sP,$$

where s is a real parameter between 0 and 1.

The *evaluation window G*, i.e., the number of generations within
which the adaptation takes place, is also a parameter of the procedure.

Remarks

(i) Adaptive parameter setting procedures may be considered as instances of adaptive genetic algorithms.

(ii) The considered methods are not restricted to simple genetic algorithms or to binary-encoded evolutionary algorithms.

10.4 Adaptive GAs

The possibility of improving standard GAs by endowing them with some adaptation mechanism is a very appealing approach.

In this section, we briefly review some adaptation mechanisms.

10.4.1 Adaptation problem

Adaptive GAs (AGAs) may be considered in order to improve the performance of the simple genetic algorithm.

The main goals of AGAs are

- *maintaining diversity in the population,*

- *improving GA convergence and avoiding premature convergence,*

- *avoiding schemata disruption due to the crossover operator.*

Adaptation may be achieved by taking into account the elements of a genetic algorithm.

More precisely, according to (Herrera and Lozano, 1996), an AGA includes

- *adaptive parameter setting,*

(i.e., adapting crossover probability, mutation probability, genotype length, and population size),

- *adaptive fitness function,*

- *adaptive selection operator,*

- *adaptive search (variation) operators,*

- *adaptive representation.*

The adaptation mechanism may be completely separate from the GA search mechanism. This *uncoupled* situation seems not to be very appealing because it implies a central control unit, superimposed on the GA search mechanism.

Another possibility is that the GA search mechanism is partially used for the adaptive mechanism. In this case, GA and the adaptive mechanism are said to be *loosely coupled.*

If the adaptation is driven by the internal forces of the evolutionary search we may speak about a *tightly coupled* situation. In this case, a coupling of two search spaces (namely, the solution space and the parameter space) arises (Spears, 1992).

Messy GAs represent examples of tightly coupled systems using adaptive chromosome length.

Remark

The previous considerations, concepts, and methods regarding genetic algorithms may be extended without difficulty to *adaptive evolutionary algorithms.*

10.4.2 Adaptive techniques based on fuzzy logic control

Fuzzy logic controllers are used intensively as GA adaptive methods (see Herrera and Lozono, 1996, for a review of early work in the field).

The integration of GAs and fuzzy controllers is focused on the following topics:

- choose GA control parameters (before the GA run),

- tune control parameters on-line to adapt to new situations,

- assist the user in detecting the emergent useful solutions, in monitoring the evolution process in order to avoid the premature convergence, and in designing GAs for a given task.

It is interesting to remark here that, in turn, evolutionary algorithms are intensively used as optimization procedures in designing fuzzy controllers.

References and bibliography

Ackley, D.H., (1987), *A Connectionist Machine for Genetic Hill Climbing*, Kluwer, Boston, MA.

Altenberg, L., (1994), Evolving better representations through selective genome growth, *Proc. 1st IEEE Conf. on Evolutionary Computation*, Part 1 (Piscataway, NJ: IEEE), Orlando, FL, 182-187.

Altenberg, L., (1995), The schema theorem and the Price's theorem, *Foundations of Genetic Algorithms*, 3, M.D. Vose, L.D. Whitley (Eds.), Morgan Kaufmann, San Mateo, CA, 23-49.

Angeline, P., (1996), Two self-adaptive crossover operators for genetic programming, *Advances in Genetic Programming*, 2, P.J. Angeline, K.E. Kinnear, Jr. (Eds.), MIT Press, Cambridge, MA, 89-109.

Bäck, T., (1993), Optimal mutation rates in genetic search, *Proc. 5th Int. Conf. on Genetic Algorithms*, S. Forrest (Ed.), Morgan Kaufmann, San Mateo, CA, 2-8.

Bäck, T., Schütz, M., (1996), Intelligent mutation rate control in canonical genetic algorithms, *Foundations of Intelligent Systems*, Lectures Notes in Artificial Intelligence, 1079, Z.W. Ras, M. Michalewicz (Eds.), Springer, Berlin, 158-167.

Booker, L.B., (1987), Improving search in genetic algorithms, *Genetic Algorithms and Simulated Annealing*, L. Davis (Ed.), Morgan Kaufmann, San Mateo, CA, 61-73.

Booker, L.B., (1993), Recombination distributions for genetic algorithms, *Foundations of Genetic Algorithms*, 2, L.D. Whitley (Ed.), Morgan Kaufmann, San Mateo, CA.

Davis, L. (Ed.), (1991), *Handbook of Genetic Algorithms*, Van Nostrand Reinhold, New York.

Eiben, A.E., Hinterding, R., Michalewicz, Z., (1999), Parameter control in evolutionary algorithms, *IEEE Trans. on Evolutionary Computation*, 3, 124-139.

Eshelman, L.J., Caruana, R.A., Schaffer, J.D., (1989), Biases in the crossover landscape, *Proc. 3rd Int. Conf. on Genetic Algorithms*, J.D. Schaffer (Ed.), Morgan Kaufmann Publishers, Los Altos, CA, 10-19.

Furuya, H., Haftka, R.T., (1993), Genetic algorithms for placing actuators on space structures, *Proc. 5th Int. Conf. on Genetic Algorithms*, S. Forrest (Ed.), Morgan Kaufmann, San Mateo, CA, 536-542.

Glover, F., Laguna, M., (1997), *Tabu Search*, Kluwer Academic Publishers, Boston.

Goldberg, D.E., (1989), *Genetic Algorithms in Search, Optimization, and Machine Learning*, Addison-Wesley, New York.

Goldberg, D.E., Deb, K., Thierens, D., (1993), Toward a better understanding of mixing in genetic algorithms, *J. Soc. Instrum. Control Eng.*, 32 (1), 10-16.

Goldberg, D.E., Richardson, J., (1987), Genetic algorithms with sharing for multimodal function optimization, *Proc. 2nd Int. Conf. on Genetic Algorithms*, J.J. Grefenstette (Ed.), Lawrence Erlbaum Associates, Hillsdale, New York, 41-49.

Grefenstette, J., (1986), Optimization of control parameters for genetic algorithms, *IEEE Trans. on Systems, Man and Cybernetics*, 16, 122-128.

Grefenstette, J., (1995), Virtual Genetic Algorithms: First Results, Navy Center for Applied Research in AI, Report AIC-95-013.

Herrera, F., Lozano, M., (1996), Adaptation of genetic algorithm parameters based on fuzzy logic controllers, F. Herrera and J.L. Verdegay (Eds.), *Genetic Algorithms and Soft Computing*, Physica-Verlag, Heidelberg, 95-125.

Holland, J.H., (1975), *Adaptation in Natural and Artificial Systems*, University of Michigan Press, Ann Arbor (Second edition: MIT Press, 1992).

Hong, I., Kahng, A., Moon, B., (1995), Exploiting synergies of multiple crossover: initial studies, *Proc. IEEE Int. Conf. on Evolutionary Computation*.

Janikow, C.Z., Michalewicz, Z., (1991), An experimental comparison of binary and floating point representation in genetic algorithms, *Proc. 4th Int. Conf. on Genetic Algorithms*, B. Belew, L.B. Booker (Eds.), Morgan Kaufmann, San Mateo, CA, 31-36.

Julstrom, B.A., (1995), What have you done for me lately? Adapting operator probabilities in a steady-state genetic algorithm, *Proc. 6th*

Int. Conf. on Genetic Algorithms, L.J. Eshelman (Ed.), Morgan Kaufmann, San Mateo, CA, 81-87.

Levenick, J. (1995), Metabits: generic endogenous crossover control, *Proc. 6th Int. Conf. on Genetic Algorithms*, L.J. Eshelman (Ed.), Morgan Kaufmann, San Francisco, CA, 88-95.

Manderick, B., Weger, M., Spiessens, P., (1991), The genetic algorithms and the structure of the fitness landscape, *Proc. 4th Int. Conf. on Genetic Algorithms*, R.K. Belew, L.B. Booker (Eds.), Morgan Kaufmann, CA, 143-150.

Schaffer, J., Caruana, R., Eshelman, L., Das, R., (1989), A study of control parameters affecting online performance of genetic algorithms for function optimization, *Proc. 3rd Int. Conf. on Genetic Algorithms*, J.D. Schaffer (Ed.), Morgan Kaufmann Publishers, Los Altos, CA, 51-60.

Schaffer, J.D., Morishima, A., (1987), An adaptive crossover distribution mechanism for genetic algorithms, *Proc. 2nd Int. Conf. on Genetic Algorithms*, J.J. Grefenstette (Ed.), Lawrence Erlbaum Associates, Hillsdale, NJ, 36-40.

Schraudolph, N.N., Belew, R.K., (1990), Dynamic parameter encoding for genetic algorithms, CSE Technical Report, CS90-175, University of San Diego, La Jolla.

Schraudolph, N.N., Belew, R.K., (1992), Dynamic parameter encoding for genetic algorithms, *Machine Learning*, 9, 9-21.

Shaefer, C.G., (1987), The ARGOT strategy: adaptive representation genetic optimizer technique, *Proc. 2nd Int. Conf. on Genetic Algorithms*, J.J. Grefenstette (Ed.), Erlbaum, Hillsdale, NJ, 50-58.

Spears, W.M., De Jong, K.A., (1991), On the virtues of parameterized uniform crossover, *Proc. 4th Int. Conf. on Genetic Algorithms*, R.K. Belew, L.B. Booker (Eds.), Morgan Kaufmann Publishers, San Mateo, CA, 230-236.

Spears, W.M., (1992), Adapting crossover in a genetic algorithm, Report AIC-92-025, Navy Center for Applied Research in Artificial Intelligence, USA.

Syswerda, G., (1989), Uniform crossover in genetic algorithms, *Proc. 3rd Int. Conf. on Genetic Algorithms*, J.D. Schaffer (Ed.), Morgan Kaufmann Publishers, San Mateo, CA, 2-9.

Thierens, D., Goldberg, D.E., (1993), Mixing in genetic algorithms, *Proc. 5th Int. Conf. on Genetic Algorithms*, S. Forrest (Ed.), Morgan Kaufmann, San Mateo, CA, 38-45.

van Laarhoven, P.J.M., Aarts, E.M.L., (1987), *Simulated Annealing: Theory and Applications*, D. Reidel Publishers, Dordrecht.

Vose, M.D., Liepins, G.E., (1991), Schema disruption, *Proc. 4th Int. Conf. on Genetic Algorithms*, R.K. Belew, L.B. Booker (Eds.), Morgan Kaufmann Publishers, 237-242.

Whitley, D., Mathias, K., Fitzhorn, P., (1991), Delta Coding: An iterative search strategy for genetic algorithms, *Proc. 4th Int. Conf. on Genetic Algorithms*, R.K. Belew, L.B. Booker (Eds.), Morgan Kaufmann Publishers, San Mateo, CA, 77-84.

Wu, A., Lindsay, R.K., (1995), Empirical studies of genetic algorithms with noncoding segments, *Evolutionary Computation*, 3(2).

11

Adaptive representations: messy genetic algorithms, delta coding, and diploidic representation

11.1 Introduction

Evolutionary computation literature contains several approaches that regard the modification of certain essential aspects of genetic algorithms with the aim to improve their performance. This chapter presents some techniques to obtain adaptive representations.

Messy genetic algorithms (introduced by Goldberg, Korb and Deb, 1989) use a variable-length binary encoding of chromosomes. This representation allows for under-specification and over-specification.

Each gene of the chromosome is represented by a pair (position, value). This flexible representation ensures the adaptation to a larger variety of situations (for instance, the use of incomplete or contradictory information).

Moreover, this representation forestalls the problems triggered by the disruption of certain useful blocks as a consequence of recombination (the problem of linking important variables (see Section 11.2.2)).

A messy genetic algorithm adapts its representation to the problem being solved.

If more than one gene specifies the same position, the first gene is used. If some gene values are missing, the corresponding locations are filled by using the so-called *competitive templates*.

The operators used by messy genetic algorithms are generalizations of standard genetic operators (within binary encoding). Algorithms using variable-length encoding may be generalized for both real encoding and evolution strategies.

Delta coding uses an adaptation mechanism that is distinct from the search mechanism. Thus, there is a two-level process. The first level is that of potential solutions, while at the second level (the delta level) the optimal modification to the current solution is determined.

This chapter also deals with the problem of *recessive genes*, i.e., the genes that, although present in the chromosome, do not become manifest (are not expressed). We can talk about recessive genes in the case in which the genotype of one individual contains two or more chromosomes (the diploidy phenomenon).

Similar genes in a genotype refer to the same function, but only one of them controls the corresponding phenotypic trait (i.e., only one gene is expressed or is dominating).

Diploidy stands for a supplementary adaptation mechanism. A feature may disappear when the environmental conditions require it, and may reappear when the changes in the environment make it useful again.

Genetic algorithms based on diploidy are suitable for dealing with difficult problems, such as the non-stationary optimum problems.

Other topics of the chapter are

- generalized messy GAs,

- a short review of adaptive representation approaches,

- real-valued delta coding,

- triallelic and quadrallelic diploidic representations,

- evolving dominance map.

11.2 Principles of messy genetic algorithms

In this section, the basic aspects of messy genetic algorithms are considered.

11.2.1 Variable-length encoding

The main objection against binary fixed-length representation is that it lacks dynamic variability. By limiting the string length, the search space itself is limited and consequently the system's learning abilities are drastically limited.

In order to overcome this restriction a variable-length representation may be used. Variable-length encoding also allows encoding to deal with partial information, or to use contradictory information.

Messy genetic algorithms consider variable-length representation, using position-independent encoding and allowing for under-specification and over-specification of the strings that represent solutions.

11.2.2 Linkage problem

The linkage problem of important variables within fixed-length binary encoding is considered.

11.2.2.1 Linkage within binary encoding

As we have seen, building blocks represent the main tool that can help us to explain the successes and failures of simple genetic algorithms.

Intuitively, we may consider that a building block is a combination of genes (bits) that is important for solving a particular problem. In order for such a combination to preserve itself through recombination processes, the genes must be represented compactly. Therefore, genetic algorithms are efficient if the building blocks are encoded compactly within the chromosome.

By the action of the recombination operator, useful combinations can grow, generating solutions that are closer and closer to the global optimum. However, growth of building blocks takes place only if the links between the genes that compose them are sufficiently strong to prevent recombination from splitting the useful combinations.

This difficulty represents the *linkage* problem of important variables. The closer the specific positions of the combination, the stronger the linking strength is.

Therefore, the clustering of the positions of a schema is a measure of the linking strength (or of the internal cohesion of the schema).

We may point out two situations in which canonical genetic algorithms do not lead to the optimal solutions:

- The linkage between the components of a useful combination (building block) is not sufficiently strong; so the combinations may be destroyed through recombination. Let us note that the linkage problem is actually a question of coding. Better coding may increase the cohesion of useful combinations.

- The objective function is a deceptive one.

We may observe that the linkage and deception problems are correlated.

11.2.2.2 Solutions to the linkage problem

Various remedies to the linkage problem and to deception have been proposed. We recall three of them:

(i)   introduce a new inversion operator that makes the gene semantics non-positional;

(ii)   use the objective function to build a new, non-deceptive encoding;

(iii)   use an encoding scheme able to deal with under-specification and over-specification of a chromosome.

Holland (1975) suggested that the use of *reordering* operators (such as the inversion operator) may solve the linkage problem by generating certain useful combinations that are sufficiently compact. It has been proved, however, that such operators are not strong enough to surpass inadequate encoding.

In what follows, we consider a new type of evolutionary algorithm capable of bypassing the difficulties mentioned above. The important point is to obtain better and better solutions by cutting and pasting together the partial solutions.

These operations are analogous to the ones specific to canonical genetic algorithms, but they are more general. Thus, for instance, fragmenting a chromosome and reordering the obtained segments are allowed.

11.2.3 Messy encoding

As we remarked, it is difficult to maintain the building blocks in a population under the action of the recombination operator (linkage problem).

In order to solve the linkage problem, Goldberg, Korb and Deb (1989) proposed a generalization of genetic algorithms known as *messy genetic algorithms*.

In the messy GA approach, a particular encoding scheme is considered. Chromosome length is variable, and genes may be arranged in any order. It is the last characteristic that has given the name to these algorithms.

Each gene is represented by a pair of numbers. The first component is a natural number that encodes the gene location. The second number represents the gene value. Usually the gene value is either 0 or 1.

Example

Let us consider the binary-encoded chromosome

$$x = (01101).$$

This chromosome can be transformed into the following sequence of pairs:

$$x' = \big((1,0),(2,1),(3,1),(4,0),(5,1)\big).$$

In the messy genetic algorithm paradigm, the string x' represents an individual (a chromosome). The meaning of this chromosome does not change if the pairs are arranged in a different order.

For instance, the above chromosome x' is equivalent to the following chromosome:

$$x'' = \big((3,1),(2,1),(1,0),(5,1),(4,0)\big).$$

Remarks

(i)   Since the gene location is also encoded, the chance of disruption of important building blocks due to recombination is reduced.

(ii)   While in standard GAs the manipulation of building blocks is implicit, messy genetic algorithms manipulate the building blocks explicitly.

11.2.4 Incompleteness and ambiguity

As chromosomes have a flexible structure, we may consider a string missing one or more genes (*under-specified* string). This possibility corresponds to the ability to encode and deal with incomplete information.

The opposite situation is *over-specification*. It occurs whenever a string contains multiple pairs for the same gene (redundant or even contradictory genes).

Example

For instance, the chromosome

$$x = \big((1,0),(2,1),(3,0),(4,1),(3,1)\big)$$

has two genes 3 (these are (3,0) and (3,1)) with the values 0 and 1 contradicting each other.

11.2.4.1 Dealing with over-specification

Over-specification may be correlated with the capacity of genetic algorithms to code and handle ambiguous and contradictory information. The conflict generated by the presence of contradictory genes may be resolved using a tie-breaking mechanism.

A simple mechanism to solve ambiguity may be developed on the basis of a first-come, first-served rule.

According to this rule, only the first (the leftmost) occurrence of the gene is taken into consideration.

11.2.4.2 Dealing with under-specification

Due to their ability to evaluate (though partially) under-specified chromosomes, messy genetic algorithms can deal with under-specification problems.

The fitness of an under-specified chromosome can be determined in different ways. One possibility is to try to approximate the absent value or to identify the probability p that the missing gene has the value 1 (obviously, the probability of the value 0 will be $(1 - p)$).

Another idea is to look for the complete chromosome that is the closest to the under-specified string. The fitness of the latter can be approximated by the fitness of the complete string.

Under-specified strings may also be completed by filling the missing genes using a *competitive template*.

The template may be considered a locally optimal string. The values of the missing genes will be the corresponding gene values in the template.

A local optimum is defined as a string that cannot be improved by changing a single bit at a time.

The local optimum is found by using a *binary hill-climbing* technique (by comparing the strings obtained by changing one bit at a time).

11.3   Recombination within messy genetic operators

The operators used by messy genetic algorithms are generalizations of classical operators. The differences between operators are negligible. Major dissimilarities appear in the case of the recombination operator. Selection for recombination is based on the fitness evaluation.

11.3.1 Recombination

In messy genetic algorithms, classical recombination is replaced with the *cut-and-splice* operator.

The cut-and-splice operator acts much like one-point crossover. We have to consider that strings are of variable length and may be under-specified or over-specified.

Two parents are cut in two and the resulting substrings are recombined. The position of the crossover point is chosen with a probability that is uniform with respect to the string length.

The difference from the classical case consists of the fact that the crossover points are independent in the two parents.

The *splice* operation concatenates the substrings obtained through cutting. There is no restriction regarding the way in which substrings are combined.

We may obtain an offspring by combining substrings that come either from two parents or from a single one. Therefore, substrings can be spliced in any order or combination.

The first-come, first-served rule and the competitive template (or a different mechanism) are used to handle over-specified and under-specified strings generated by the splice operator.

11.3.2 Examples

Let us consider the chromosomes

$$x = (a, b)$$

and

$$y = (c, d).$$

With a and b we denote the substrings of the chromosome x, and with c and d the substrings of y, respectively.

Let us suppose that these chromosomes are represented as below:

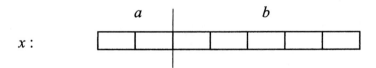

x :

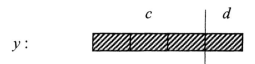

$$y:$$

We assume that, for the first chromosome, the crossover point is

$$t = 2,$$

and, for the second chromosome, the crossover point is

$$t' = 3.$$

Below we give a list of the chromosomes obtainable through recombination (cut and splice):

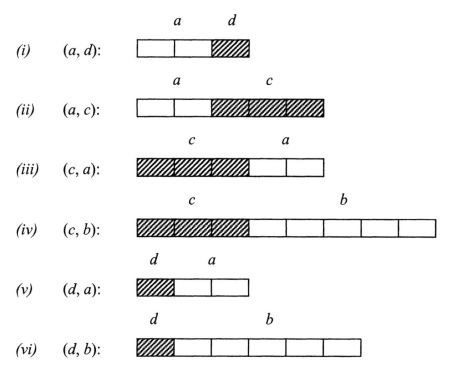

(i)   *(a, d)*:

(ii)   *(a, c)*:

(iii)   *(c, a)*:

(iv)   *(c, b)*:

(v)   *(d, a)*:

(vi)   *(d, b)*:

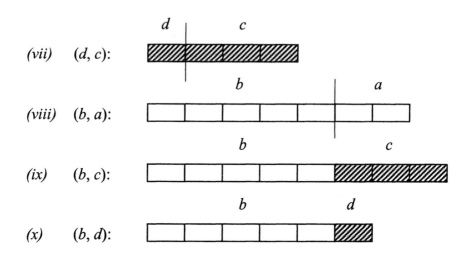

Remarks

(a) Let us notice that the considered (cut-and-splice) version of the recombination operator also includes an *inversion*-type operation. This fact is manifest in the case in which both substrings come from the same chromosome (the chromosomes (b, a) and (d, c) from the above illustration).

(b) Compared with the classical crossover, examples *(v)*, *(vi)*, *(ix)* and *(x)* also imply an inversion.

(c) The recombination operator may be generalized in order to allow the existence of multiple crossover points.

11.4 Mutation

Messy genetic algorithms may operate without mutation. If the mutation operator is used, it acts as the classical case of binary encoding.

Mutation affects only the value of a gene, not its meaning (position).

The mutation probability p_m is generally represented by a small number. Usually, $p_m \in [10^{-3}, 10^{-2}]$.

As in the classical case, the standard mutation operator may assume a strong form or a weak form.

The *strong form* always changes the value of the gene selected for mutation. Thus, for instance, the gene (3,0) is transformed into the gene (3,1).

In the *weak form* of the mutation operator, there is a fixed probability (usually $p = 0.5$) that the selected gene changes its value.

Any version of the mutation operator may be used, including non-uniform, adaptive, or self-adaptive procedures.

11.5 Computational models

The messy genetic procedure finds a local optimum (a competitive template) at the beginning of a run. Each under-specified string is completed by filling the missing bits from the template. The resulting strings are evaluated by using the fitness function.

Messy GAs have three phases:

Initialization phase.

The initial population of strings of a messy GA is created.

Primordial phase.

A tournament selection mechanism is applied to the population; the population size is reduced, using selection by eliminating poor individuals.

Juxtapositional phase.

Partial solutions found in the primordial phase are mixed together.

Reproduction operators are used to evolve the population.

The competitive templates are used for filling the missing values.

Messy genetic algorithms have given satisfactory results for some difficult problems (Goldberg, Deb and Korb, 1990). The method was applied to deceptive binary problems specially built to mislead simple genetic algorithms.

In the case of deceptive functions, messy genetic algorithms perform better than simple GAs and usually find the best solution.

One important computational problem within messy genetic algorithms is the dimension of the search space. Since large chromosomes may appear, this dimension could be very high.

The search space size is polynomial (it increases polynomially) with respect to the number of variables of the search space.

In parallel implementations, the search time is reduced and it is logarithmic with respect to the number of variables of the search space.

11.6 Generalizations of messy GAs

Goldberg, Deb, Kargupta, and Harik (1993) proposed a modified version of messy genetic algorithms. The proposed version considers a *probabilistically complete initialization* procedure based on stepwise filtering and selection.

By *filtering*, some genes in the strings are discarded. The shortened strings are evaluated using the *competitive template*.

This modified version of messy genetic algorithms is very effective for solving deceptive problems of varying degrees of complexity.

Messy genetic algorithms use binary encoding of chromosomes. However, the messy model may be extended so as to allow real-valued encoding.

For real-valued encoding, there are several variants of the recombination operator. Therefore, we can do this generalization without the effort of considering new operators. Obviously, new operators may be defined.

It would be of great interest, for instance, to define some continuous variants of the recombination operator based on cut and splice.

Another possibility of generalization consists of considering genotypes of the form $(x^i, \theta^{\,i})$, where $x^i \in \mathbf{R}^{k_i}, 1 \le k_i \le s,$ and $\theta^{\,i}$ is the vector of the control parameters.

If, for an individual, we have $k_i < s$, it means that the corresponding individual lacks certain object variables. From a biological point of view, this may signify that certain characteristics are not relevant for such an individual.

This representation may lead to *messy evolution strategies* or to *messy evolutionary programming.*

11.7 Other adaptive representation approaches

Several systems have been proposed to allow genetic algorithms to adapt their representation. Some well-known approaches are the adaptive representation used in the ARGOT system, dynamic parameter encoding, and delta coding.

11.7.1 ARGOT system

The ARGOT system (Shaefer, 1987) contains a parameterized representation procedure.

A flexible mapping from the object variables to the genes is adopted. The number of bits used to represent an object parameter is variable and may be adapted.

The binary strings are mapped into real target intervals from $\mathbf{R}^s$. The range of the target intervals and the averages of the map values are also adaptive parameters.

Representation and mapping adaptation are based on some statistics about projection scattering. The standard deviation of the gene projections is taken into account. Other parameters are the distance of the gene projections from the current range boundaries, and the convergence of these projection values.

Some heuristics use these statistics to shift the mapping ranges and to increase or decrease the resolution (i.e., the minimum distance between two gene projections).

11.7.2 Dynamic parameter encoding

Similar ideas regarding dynamic encoding of parameters can be found in Schraudolph and Belew (1990, 1992).

The *dynamic parameter encoding* technique considers a mapping of the genes to their phenotypic values. The adaptation is realized by modifying this mapping.

11.8 Delta coding

Delta coding (Whitley, Mathias and Fitzhorn, 1991) represents an interesting modification of genetic algorithms. Delta coding also contains the idea of *adaptive representation*.

A genetic algorithm with multiple restarts is considered within delta coding. The first run is used to obtain an intermediate solution.

At convergence, the representation is remapped so that the parameter ranges are centered around the best values found.

The procedure is restarted with the new (renormalized) population. In this way, the search space may be expanded or contracted at each restart.

Delta coding was initially developed for binary representation of individuals. Despite this, the mechanism seems to be very suitable for the case of real-valued representation.

Delta coding is not only natural and simple, but it also allows improvement of time and precision performances.

Mathias and Whitley (1993) proposed a variant of delta coding able to cope with deceptive problems.

11.8.1 Real-valued delta coding

Let us assume that the potential solutions are represented by vectors $x \in \mathbf{R}^s$. Let $\delta \in \mathbf{R}^s$ be the vector of the perturbations (small changes) that can improve the current solution.

Delta coding acts on a population of solutions and on a population of perturbations of these solutions.

We can talk about a search (or learning) mechanism with two levels:

- *the level of the potential solutions of the problem*

  (this is called the *level x*),

- *the level of the delta perturbations*

  (this is called the *level δ*).

Remarks

(i)   A similar learning system is typical of *evolution strategies* (ESs), in which we have a solution level and a control parameter level.

(ii)   However, in evolution strategies, the two levels are less separated though they may be recognized at each iteration. The separation and hierarchy of the two levels are more clear-cut in delta coding.

(iii) In the case of delta coding, the communication between the two levels is achieved by means of the evaluation function.

11.8.2 Real-valued delta coding procedure

The mechanism of real-valued delta coding can be described as follows.

Initialization

A population $P(0) = \{x^1, x^2, ..., x^n\}$, $x^i \in \mathbf{R}^s$, of potential solutions is initialized at random.

Level x

An evolutionary algorithm is applied to the initial population $P(0)$ using a fitness function f.

Let x^* be the solution supplied by the evolutionary algorithm.

Level δ

A population $Q(0) = \{\delta^1, \delta^2, ..., \delta^n\}$ of perturbations is randomly initialized.

An evolutionary algorithm is applied having $Q(0)$ as the initial population.

The quality $g(\delta)$ of the individual (perturbation) δ is considered as being

$$g(\delta) = f(x^* + \delta),$$

where f is the fitness function.

Let δ^* be the best individual obtained as a result of the evolutionary algorithm.

Updating

The best perturbation δ^* serves to update the solution x^* found so far, by setting

$$x^* = x^* + \delta^*.$$

Iteration

The operations corresponding to the levels x and δ are repeated.

At the level x, the population $P(t)$ obtained at the end of the previous iteration is considered as the initial population.

At the level δ, the population is reinitialized at random at each new iteration.

The procedure stops when the established number of iterations is reached or when another stopping condition is fulfilled.

Remarks

(i)   The population at the level δ is reinitialized at each iteration. For this reason, we could give up mutation at the level x (Michalewicz, 1992).

         We are entitled to do this in the case of binary encoding, where the role played by mutation is rather reduced.

(ii)   In real coding, however, mutation plays a much greater part in bringing about progress of the search. This is why the role of mutation is essential at both levels of delta coding.

11.8.3 The algorithm

Delta coding may be described in the form of the following algorithm. Real-valued representation is again considered.

DELTA CODING ALGORITHM

P1. Set $t = 0$.

A population $P(t)$ of potential solutions is randomly initialized.

P2. **while** (termination-condition not satisfied) **do**

P2.1.   Apply an evolutionary algorithm (denoted EA1) in order to obtain a solution x^* at convergence.

P2.2.   A population of random perturbations is initialized.

P2.3.   An evolutionary algorithm (denoted EA2) is applied in order to obtain, at convergence, the optimum perturbation δ^*.

P2.4. The solution is updated by adding the optimum perturbation that has been calculated:

$$x^* = x^* + \delta^*.$$

P2.5. The solution x^* is compared with the preceding solution and the fitter is kept.

end while

Remarks

(i)   Usually, the evolutionary algorithm EA1 used at step P2.1 is identical to the algorithm EA2 at step P2.3.

In certain situations, it may be more advantageous to use different algorithms.

(ii)   Usually EA1 and EA2 are genetic algorithms.

Different variations may occur if we combine evolutionary procedures, such as the sequences GA+ES, ES+GA, or ES+ES.

(iii)   It may seem out of place to consider an evolution strategy in place of EA2. Indeed, due to this replacement, a relatively complicated perturbation method would be needed to calculate a δ perturbation.

Actually, it is the advancement of search that matters, not the way in which this progress is achieved. The use of evolution strategies in delta coding seems to be both a justified and promising approach.

11.9 Diploidy and dominance

In this section, a different adaptive representation technique based on the presence of recessive genes is considered.

The method relies on a powerful biological mechanism that we briefly recall in the following.

11.9.1 Haploid and diploid chromosome structures revisited

So far we have generally considered that an individual is represented by a single *haploid* chromosome. Although most approaches to evolutionary algorithms use this convention, it is not fully concordant with biological facts.

Usually, the genotype of a species contains more chromosomes. In somatic cells, the number of chromosomes is generally double if compared to the number of chromosomes in germinative cells.

Doubling the number of chromosomes is called *diploidy*. Most complex organisms have diploid or polyploid chromosomes.

In *diploid* organisms, the cells contain two sets of chromosomes, i.e., the genotype of diploid organisms contains a pair of *homologous* chromosomes.

The homologous chromosomes that make up a pair in a diploid genotype bear similar or identical genes. Similar (homologous) genes have the same positions in the two chromosomes and carry information about the same function.

Only one of the two homologous genes is phenotypically expressed.

Remarks

(i)   In certain somatic tissues apart from diploid cells, there are also tetraploid, hexaploid, octaploid, etc. cells.

(ii)   In what follows, we deal only with diploid structures.

Homologous chromosomes encode the same set of individual features, but the values of some characteristics may be different (the corresponding alleles are different).

The question that arises is which of the contradictory features are transmitted to descendants (i.e., are actualized in the phenotype) or, stated otherwise, which genes are *expressed*. Obviously, we did not encounter this problem in the case of the genotype made of a single chromosome.

11.9.2 Dominance

The conflict resolution mechanism deciding which allele (gene value) is expressed in the phenotype is called *dominance*.

We may describe dominance as a function from the set of homologous genes to the set of expressed genes (or to the set of alleles).

Let us consider two genes having the same locus (position) in two homologous chromosomes. In a phenotype, only one of the two genes is expressed (or the corresponding allele value is actualized). The expressed gene controls the corresponding feature (the color of eyes, for instance).

The expressed gene is called *dominant*. The other, unexpressed, gene is called *recessive*.

In nature, the dominance is not fixed, but evolves. The dominance *shift* operator provides a switching mechanism allowing a recessive gene to become dominant and making a dominant gene recessive.

In this way, the diploid representation conserves some qualities that have been useful in the species evolution. In a changing environment these qualities could be useful again.

Diploidy and dominance represent a supplementary adaptation mechanism and may be considered as a long-term genetic memory for previously successful alleles. The recessive alleles are kept as a reserve for further environment challenges. The effects of diploidy are emphasized in a non-stationary environment.

11.9.3 Diploidic representation

Within evolutionary algorithms, diploidic representations include multiple allele values for each position in the genome.

Some cyclic environmental changes can be modeled using a diploidic representation.

The diploidic representation provides a mechanism for solving the conflict appearing between contradictory allele values. This mechanism is used for determining which allele value for a gene will be expressed when the allele values are different.

Some dominance methods have been proposed to deal with diploidic representations in evolutionary computation.

11.9.4 Triallelic representation

A *dominance relation* between allele values may be considered by using a ternary alphabet.

The triallelic Hollstein-Holland representation is described as follows.

(a)   The alphabet symbols are 0, 1 and 1_0.

(b)   The symbols 1 and 1_0 both correspond to the allele value 1.

(c)   The value 1 corresponds to a *dominant* allele value and the symbol 1_0 to a recessive one.

(d)   We admit that

    (d.1) 1 dominates 0, and

    (d.2) 0 dominates 1_0.

Therefore, the dominance of 1 over 0 could be altered via mutation (by altering the value 1 to 1_0).

Remarks

(i)   The considered triallelic representation combines dominance and allele information in a single position.

(ii)   Let us assume that the allele value b dominates the value a. In this case, we write

$$a < b.$$

With this notation, the dominance relation in Hollstein-Holland triallelic representation is expressed (Goldberg, 1989) as

$$1_0 < 0 < 1.$$

Example

Let us consider the genotype (x, y) with the chromosomes

$$x = (0, 1_0, 1, 1_0),$$

and

$$y = (1_0, 1_0, 0, 1).$$

According to the considered dominance relation, the corresponding phenotype will be

$$(0, 1, 1, 1).$$

11.9.5 Quadrallelic representation

Ng and Wong (1995) considered a fourth value for recessive 0. We may denote 0_0 as this new value.

The dominance relation is now expressed as

(i)   1 dominates 0 and 0_0;

(ii)   0 dominates 1_0 and 0_0.

A random element is introduced in the dominance computation. When both allele values for a gene are dominant (or recessive), the dominant value is chosen randomly.

11.9.6 Evolving dominance map

The self-adaptive control of the dominance mechanism may be achieved by encoding dominance information in a separated vector. This vector (called *dominance map vector*) will be used as a *dominance function* during evolution.

We may assume that the dominance map vector is allowed to change during the search process. It may be mutated and may recombine with other dominance vectors. In this way, we may describe natural dominance dynamics more adequately.

In Bagley (1967) approach, the gene with the highest dominance value is dominant.

Green (1997) considered a different approach. The chromosome with the highest fitness is considered as the dominant one.

An evolving dominance map allows a faster adaptation to environment changes than a representation using a fixed dominance mapping.

11.9.7 Use of diploidy

Diploidic representations in EC are important for treating non-stationary optimization problems.

Using a diploidic representation for stationary optimization/search problems we do not observe a significant increase in performance.

To apply recombination, the following procedure may be considered:

(i)   two pairs of homologous chromosomes are selected (using the fitness function),

(ii)   each pair produces two *gametes* (intermediary chromosomes),

(iii)   using gametes, crossover generates two offspring.

References and bibliography

Bagley, J.D., (1967), The behaviour of adaptive systems which employ genetic and correlation algorithms, Ph.D. Thesis, University of Michigan, Ann Arbor.

Deb, K., (1991), Binary and Floating-point Function Optimization using Messy Genetic Algorithms, Ph.D. Thesis, University of Alabama, Illinois.

Goldberg, D.E., (1989), *Genetic Algorithms in Search, Optimization, and Machine Learning*, Addison-Wesley, Reading, MA.

Goldberg, D.E., Korb, B., Deb, K., (1989), Messy genetic algorithms: Motivation, analysis and first results, *Complex Systems*, 3, 493-530.

Goldberg, D.E., Deb, K., Korb, B., (1990), Messy genetic algorithms revisited: nonuniform size and scale, *Complex Systems*, 4, 415-444.

Goldberg, D.E., Deb, K., Korb, B., (1991), Don't worry, be messy, *Proc. 4th Int. Conf. on Genetic Algorithms*, R.K. Belew, L.B. Booker (Eds.), Morgan Kaufmann, San Mateo, CA, 24-30.

Goldberg, D.E., Deb, K., Kargupta, H., Harik, G., (1993), Rapid, accurate optimization of difficult problems using fast messy genetic algorithms, *Proc. 5th Int. Conf. on Genetic Algorithms*, S. Forrest (Ed.), Morgan Kaufmann, San Mateo, CA, 56-64.

Greene, F., (1997), Performance of diploid dominance with genetically synthesized signal processing network, *Proc. 7th Int. Conf. on Genetic Algorithms*, T. Bäck (Ed.), Morgan Kaufmann, San Mateo, CA, 615-622.

Holland, J.H., (1975), *Adaptation in Natural and Artificial Systems*, University of Michigan Press, Ann Arbor.

Hollstein, R.B., (1971), Artificial Genetic Adaptation in Computer Control Systems, Ph.D. Thesis, Univ. of Michigan.

Mathias, K.E., Whitley, L.D., (1993), Remapping hyperspace during genetic search: Canonical delta folding, *Foundations of Genetic Algorithms*, 2, L.D. Whitley (ED.), Morgan Kaufmann, San Mateo, CA, 167-186.

Michalewicz, Z., (1992), *Genetic Algorithms + Data Structures = Evolution Programs*, Springer-Verlag, Berlin.

Ng, K.P., Wong, K.C., (1995), A new diploid scheme and dominance change mechanism for non-stationary function optimization, *Proc. 6th Int. Conf. on Genetic Algorithms*, L.J. Eshelman (Ed.), Morgan Kaufmann, San Francisco, CA, 159-166.

Schraudolph, N.N., Belew, R.K., (1990), Dynamic parameter encoding for genetic algorithms, CSE Technical Report, CS90-175, University of San Diego, La Jolla.

Schraudolph, N.N., Belew, R.K., (1992), Dynamic parameter encoding for genetic algorithms, *Machine Learning*, 9, 9-21.

Shaefer, C.G., (1987), The ARGOT strategy: adaptive representation genetic optimizer technique, *Proc. 2nd Int. Conf. on Genetic Algorithms*, J.J. Grefenstette (Ed.), Erlbaum, Hillsdale, NJ, 50-58.

Whitley, D., Mathias, K., Fitzhorn, P., (1991), Delta Coding: An iterative search strategy for genetic algorithms, *Proc. 4th Int. Conf. on Genetic Algorithms*, R.K. Belew, L.B. Booker (Eds.), Morgan Kaufmann Publishers, San Mateo, CA, 77-84.

12

Evolution strategies and evolutionary programming

12.1 Introduction

In this chapter, we present the basic aspects of two main streams of evolutionary algorithms: evolution strategies and evolutionary programming.

12.2 Evolution strategies

Evolution strategies (ESs) (Rechenberg, 1973; Schwefel, 1981) represent one of the main paradigms of evolutionary computation. The starting point was the necessity for building systems that are able to solve difficult optimization and search problems involving real-valued parameters.

The first applications were related to solving several optimization problems of fluid dynamics. Later, evolution strategies were extended to solve optimization problems with discrete parameters.

A specific part of evolution strategies is the representation of individuals as real-component vectors. The main operator is the *mutation* operator.

For advanced evolution strategies, the strategy control parameters are included in the representation of individuals (genotypes). These parameters are mainly related to the perturbation amplitude generated by the mutation operator.

In the (1+1) evolution strategy, the first and simplest ES model, the collective learning aspect in a population is lacking. The changes are aimed at adapting a unique individual, which is modified by the action of the mutation operator.

The mutations are normal perturbations with an amplitude given by the standard deviation vector σ. In this simple model, the change is uniform for all search directions (the components of σ being equal).

The convergence rate of the (1+1) strategy has been studied for two distinct model functions (Rechenberg, 1973). These functions allow establishment of an empirical rule (known as Rechenberg's 1/5 success rule) for the control of the standard deviation parameter.

The limits of the (1+1) model have led to the search of mechanisms dealing with the evolution of several individuals.

In the (μ+1) strategy, μ parents generate one descendant, using the *recombination* and the *mutation* operators.

In the case of modern models (namely, the ($\mu+\lambda$) and (μ,λ) strategies), the number of descendants is $\lambda \geq 1$. The main characteristic of these models is the incorporation of the strategy parameters into the individual's representation.

This characteristic allows the *self-adaptation* of the strategy parameters. We may consider this as a two-level learning process.

The first level corresponds to the changes of the state vector as a response to the local characteristics of the fitness function (the search surface).

The second level corresponds to the self-adaptation of the control parameters associated with the strategy. The possibility of changing the strategy parameters can be interpreted as a self-tuning of the search process, without the intervention of any process-monitoring mechanism.

The self-adaptation of the strategy parameters supplies one of the sources of success of evolution strategies.

The search in the object variable space and the search in the strategy parameter space are accomplished simultaneously by using the evolutionary search principles.

12.3 (1+1) strategy

Within the (1+1) evolution strategy, an individual is usually represented as a pair

$$v = (x, \sigma).$$

The vector x corresponds to a point in the search space (an object variable vector), while σ is the standard deviation vector.

If the search space is $\mathbf{R}^n$ (or a subset of $\mathbf{R}^n$), then x and σ are real n-component vectors.

We may consider the vector x as the *phenotype* associated with the *genotype* (x, σ).

The evolution (or mutation or perturbation) law can be written as

$$x(t)=x(t)+N(0,\sigma(t+1)),$$

where $N(0,\sigma(t+1))$ denotes a realization of a normal n-dimensional random variable with zero mean and standard deviation $\sigma(t+1)$.

The standard deviation σ may be interpreted as the *mutation step size*.

The better of $x(t)$ and $x(t+1)$ is selected to become the parent of the next generation, while the other one is discarded.

12.3.1 1/5 success rule

Rechenberg's '*1/5 success rule*' incorporates feedback from the search process.

The 1/5 success rule states that

- *The ratio of successful mutations to all mutations should be 1/5.*

- *If this ratio is greater than 1/5, then the standard deviation should be increased.*

- *If the ratio is lower than 1/5, the mutation dispersion should be decreased.*

The use of the 1/5 success rule increases the convergence speed. The intuitive idea behind the rule is the improvement of the search efficiency.

If the vectors obtained during k consecutive generations are better than their predecessors, then the search step can be increased in order to accelerate the convergence. Otherwise, the search step should be decreased.

The 1/5 success rule modifies the standard deviation every k trials, where k is a parameter of the method.

Usually k is given by

$$k = 10\,n,$$

where n is the dimension of the search space.

The mutation of the search vector $x(t)$ is thus realized by replacing its components according to the following correction rule:

$$x_i(t) = x_i(t) + N(0, \sigma(t+1)), \quad i=1,\dots,n.$$

The same value $\sigma(t+1)$ is used for all variables of each vector.

12.3.2 Standard deviation adaptation

Let us denote by $p(k)$ the frequency of successful mutations for the last k generations:

$$p(k) = \frac{s(k)}{k},$$

where $s(k)$ is the number of successful mutations in the last k trials.

The standard deviation is adapted at each generation, using the following version of the 1/5 success rule:

$$\sigma(t+1) = mu_\sigma(\sigma(t))$$

$$= \begin{cases} c_i\sigma(t), & \text{if } p(k) > \dfrac{1}{5} \\[2mm] c_d\sigma(t), & \text{if } p(k) < \dfrac{1}{5} \\[2mm] \sigma(t), & \text{if } p(k) = \dfrac{1}{5}, \end{cases}$$

where mu_σ is the mutation operator of the strategy parameter σ.

The coefficients c_i and c_d of the 1/5 success rule have the meaning of learning rates.

Usually, it is assumed that the two coefficients are inversely proportional, i.e.,

$$c_i c_d = 1.$$

12.3.3 Schwefel's version of the 1/5 success rule

Another version of the correction rule proposed by Schwefel (1995) consists in the updating of the standard deviation every n generations, with learning rates c and c^{-1}.

In this case, we have

$$\sigma(t+n) = \begin{cases} \dfrac{1}{c}\sigma(t), & \text{if } p(k) > \dfrac{1}{5} \\ c\,\sigma(t), & \text{if } p(k) < \dfrac{1}{5} \\ \sigma(t), & \text{if } p(k) = \dfrac{1}{5}, \end{cases}$$

where

- n is the search space dimension, and

- $k=10n$.

Remarks

(i)   The value of c is chosen in the range $[0.82, 1]$. This range has been obtained in a heuristic way.

(ii)   Usually, the value

$$c = 0.85$$

is adopted (Schwefel, 1981).

The 1/5 success rule with a period of

$$k = 10n$$

trials can be formulated as follows:

Every n trials the number of successful mutations during the previous 10n trials is computed.

If this number is lower than 2n (i.e., $p(k) < 1/5$), then the length of the current step size (the standard deviation) is multiplied by a factor c.

If the number of successful mutations is greater than 2n, the current step size is divided by c.

12.4 Multimembered evolution strategies

In the $(\mu+1)$ evolution strategy, where $\mu \geq 1$, μ parents may generate a unique descendant at a time. The search operators are recombination (crossover) and mutation. First, through recombination, we obtain an individual to whom the mutation operator is applied.

Then the least fit individual (which may be either the descendant or one of the parents) is discarded.

The representation of individuals in evolution strategies is similar to the real encoding for genetic algorithms. For this reason, the recombination types may be similar as well.

Recombination was initially applied to the state vectors only. Experience has proved that the strategy effectiveness is improved if the recombination is extended to the strategy parameters.

In what follows, we will treat the $(\mu+\lambda)$ and (μ,λ) evolution strategies (Schwefel, 1977).

In these strategies, the adaptation mechanism is transferred to the individuals, which are equipped with a set of control parameters. The model of this mechanism is a biological one: Biologists have emphasized the fact that the genotype incorporates a mechanism that controls its own mutability, through a mutation gene, for instance.

The $(\mu+\lambda)$ and (μ,λ) strategies use multiple populations of parents and descendants. The increase of the population sizes leads to an increase of the convergence rate.

In the $(\mu+\lambda)$ strategy, a number of $\mu \geq 1$ parents are used to generate λ descendants $(\lambda \geq \mu)$. All the $(\mu+\lambda)$ individuals of the intermediate population enter in competition for survival.

Remark

Most implementations consider $\lambda > \mu$.

The best μ individuals (from parents and offspring) are selected as parents of the new generation. The selection probability is the same for all individuals.

In the (μ,λ) evolution strategy, only the λ descendants compete for survival. The parents are entirely replaced at each generation. It follows that the lifetime of a solution is limited to one generation. For this reason the (μ,λ) evolution strategy is suitable for problems where the criterion function is affected by noise.

We may also consider the schemes (μ,λ) and $(\mu+\lambda)$ as two types of selections of the same strategy. In the (μ,λ) selection, the best λ descendants $(\mu \leq \lambda)$, selected through a deterministic procedure, replace the previous generation.

This choice allows the best member of generation $(t+1)$ to be less fit than the best member of generation t.

12.4.1 Representation of individuals

In the (μ,λ) and $(\mu+\lambda)$ evolution strategies, the individuals are characterized by a position (state) vector x, $x \in \mathbf{R}^n$, of the search space and by the *parameters of the strategy*.

The *self-adaptation* of the strategy parameters is thus ensured by including them in the representation of the individuals.

An individual (a genotype) is usually represented by a pair of vectors (x, σ), where $x \in \mathbf{R}^n$ is the position vector and σ is the standard deviation vector.

In this case, σ represents the control parameter of the strategy, i.e.,

$$\sigma = (\sigma_1, \sigma_2, ..., \sigma_n)^T,$$

where σ_i is the ith standard deviation (corresponding to the system coordinate i).

The vector σ indicates the way in which the vector x is transformed by mutation. As we already stated, the vector σ is subject to mutation, too.

It follows that the control parameter σ is neither constant, nor modified by a deterministic mechanism (like the 1/5 success rule), but is included in the structure of the individuals and is subject to the evolution process.

12.5 Standard mutation

In this section, some standard mutation operators for multimembered evolution strategies are considered.

12.5.1 Standard mutation of the control parameters

The standard mutation mechanism includes the standard deviation vector within the genotype structure, to ensure self-adaptation.

Let (x', σ') be the individual obtained through mutation of (x, σ):

$$(x', \sigma') = mu(x, \sigma),$$

where

- mu denotes the global mutation operator,
- σ is the mutation step size of the individual.

Let us consider the individual

$$(x, \sigma) = (x_i, ..., x_n, \sigma_1, ..., \sigma_n).$$

A typical, lognormal perturbation (mutation) of the standard deviation is

$$\sigma_i' = \sigma_i e^{N(0,m)}, \quad 1 = 1, ..., n,$$

where m is a parameter of the method.

The mutation of the solution vector may be described as

$$x_i' = x_i + N(0, \sigma_i').$$

A more general mutation mechanism for the standard deviation considers the perturbations

$$\sigma_i' = \sigma_i e^{\tau N(0,1) + \tau_1 N_i(0,1)}, \quad i = 1, 2, ..., n,$$

where

- $N_i(0,1)$ denotes a realization of a normal random variable having expectation zero and standard deviation one,
- τ and τ_1 are parameters of the method.

Remark

$N_i(0,1)$ is sampled anew for each index i.

To make clearer the interpretation of the standard deviation as the step size, the mutation of the object vector is written as

$$x_i' = x_i + \sigma_i' N_i(0,1), \quad i = 1, 2, ..., n,$$

where σ_i' is the updated step size.

12.6 Genotypes including covariance matrix. Correlated mutation

A more general mutation scheme considers the perturbation covariances. The covariance matrix is included in the genotype representation.

12.6.1 Covariance matrix for mutation

Let C denote the covariance matrix. The diagonal components of the matrix C are the variances

$$C_{ii} = \sigma_i^2, \quad i = 1, ..., n.$$

Let us consider the individual's representation where the genotype includes the object variable vector $x, x \in \mathbf{R}^n$.

The genotype is thus represented as (x, C).

The phenotype corresponding to the genotype (x, C) is the object variable vector x, and the strategy parameters correspond to the covariance matrix.

The strategy parameters are

(i) n standard deviations $\sigma_1, ..., \sigma_n$,

$$\sigma_i = \sqrt{C_{ii}}, \quad i = 1, 2, ..., n;$$

(ii) m covariances $C_{ij}, i \neq j$, where

$$m = \frac{n(n-1)}{2}.$$

An additive normal perturbation may be used to perturb the genotypes.

12.6.2 Correlated mutations

Schwefel (1981) pointed out that, applying independent normal perturbations to each object variable x_i, the mutation ellipsoids (surfaces of equal probability to place an offspring) have axes parallel to the axes of the coordinate system. Therefore, the preferred search directions lie along the system axes. But, in general, the best search directions do not have this particular orientation.

Schwefel (1981) proposed a method to perform rotations of the mutation ellipsoids. In this way, the search process may follow useful directions, thus preventing the trajectory of the population from zigzagging along the optimum search direction.

The vector of rotation angles is incorporated into the genotype and is modified by using normal perturbations.

12.7 Cauchy perturbations

The choice of a normal perturbation inducing mutation is quite arbitrary. Other probability distributions may be chosen. For instance, a Cauchy distribution has been proposed by Yao and Lin (1996); Rudolph (1997); and Yao, Liu and Lin (1999).

12.7.1 Cauchy distribution

The family of one-dimensional Cauchy density functions centered in μ is defined by

$$f_t(x) = \frac{1}{\pi} \frac{t}{t^2 + (x - \mu)^2},$$

where $t > 0$ is a scale parameter.

12.7.2 Cauchy perturbation-induced mutation

Let us assume that perturbations are generated by using a Cauchy random variable.

The components of the perturbed object variable vector may be written as

$$x_i' = x_i + \sigma_i' C_i(1,0), \quad i = 1, 2, ..., n,$$

where

- $C_i(1,0)$ is a Cauchy random variable with scale parameter $t = 1$, and $\mu = 0$,

- σ_i' is the current perturbation step size.

Remarks

(i)   The Cauchy perturbation may be considered for object variables as well as for strategy parameters.

(ii)   A combination of Cauchy and normal perturbations may be useful. The strategy parameters may be perturbed by using a normal distribution while, for the object variables, a Cauchy perturbation may be adopted.

12.8 Evolutionary programming

Evolutionary programming (EP) represents a class of paradigms for simulating evolution that utilizes the concepts of *Darwinian evolution* to iteratively generate appropriate solutions (organisms) within a static or dynamically changing environment.

Evolutionary programming (Fogel, 1962; Fogel, Owens and Walsh, 1966) appeared as the result of the effort to generate intelligent behavior of a machine, which is described by a deterministic finite-state automaton.

In this case, intelligent behavior is a prediction of the environment, which is described as a succession of input symbols of the automaton.

In order to find a machine capable to offer a better prediction, a randomly generated population of machines is considered. The different parts of the machines (states, transitions, output symbols) are modified by mutation.

The recombination of two automata does not seem to be a biologically motivated idea. That is why the only search operator is mutation.

The machines are compared by means of an evaluation function. The choice is strictly deterministic.

The ideas used in evolutionary programming surpassed the initial domain and were also applied to solve optimization and search problems (Fogel, 1992). The evolutionary programming optimization algorithm has many aspects in common with evolution strategies.

12.8.1 Sequential machine model

Initially, the main goal of evolutionary programming was to operate with sequential machines and with their discrete representations. The intention was to obtain predictions of the environment.

In this case, the intelligent behavior was seen as the ability of a machine to obtain reasonable predictions of its environment. These predictions are translated into responses regarding a domain.

The environment is described as the sequence of input symbols observed up to the current moment. The prediction realized by a machine is represented by the machine output symbol. The performance of the machine is measured using an evaluation (or error) function.

A set of machines representing a parent population is exposed to the environment. Each machine works as follows. When an input symbol is presented to the machine, the corresponding output symbol represents a prediction of the next state of the environment. The quality of the prediction can be evaluated by comparing the output symbol with the next input symbol.

The prediction quality is measured by using an appropriate evaluation (*payoff*) function (squared error, for instance). A payoff is thus associated with each prediction.

The fitness of the machine is calculated after the last input symbol is considered and the last prediction is made. The fitness is a function of the payoff for each symbol (an average symbol payoff, for instance).

The evolutionary programming paradigm uses a population of $\mu > 1$ parents. Each parent represents a sequential machine. From μ parents the mutation operator generates μ offspring.

Each parent produces a single offspring by mutation.

Mutation is achieved through random changes of the elements composing the parent machine.

There are five possible ways to perform mutation:

(i)   change an output symbol,

(ii)   change a state transition,

(iii)   add a new state,

(iv)   delete an existing state,

(v)   change the initial state.

The μ offspring obtained by mutation are evaluated with respect to the environment.

μ individuals are chosen among the parents and the offspring. They will be the parents of the new generation.

The selection is made in decreasing order of the quality. The used selection is of the type $(\mu + \mu)$ and is deterministic.

The process continues until an actual prediction of the next (not yet experienced) symbol of the environment is needed.

The best machine is selected to generate that prediction. The new symbol is added to the already explored environment, and the process continues.

12.8.2 Function optimization by evolutionary programming

D.B. Fogel (1992) extended evolutionary programming to optimize real-valued functions. The representation of individuals, the mutation operator, and self-adaptation of strategy parameters have many common aspects with the corresponding elements in evolution strategies.

Evolutionary programming is not supposed to use a recombination operator in this case either.

Mutation is typically achieved by replacing components of the solution vector x by

$$x_i' = x_i + \sigma_i N_i(0,1), \quad i = 1, 2, \ldots, n,$$

where

- $N_i(0,1)$ is a realization of a normal random variable with expectation zero and standard deviation one,

- σ_i is the standard deviation of the mutation amplitude.

Remark

σ_i represents the step size of the search process.

The parameter self-adaptation rule can be chosen as follows:

$$\sigma_i'^2 = \sigma_i^2 + \sigma_i \sqrt{\alpha} N_i(0,1),$$

where α is a parameter of the method.

12.9 Evolutionary programming using Cauchy perturbation

A faster search process may be achieved if Cauchy mutations are used instead of normal perturbations (Yao, Liu and Lin, 1999).

The perturbation of the solution vector x may be written as

$$x_i' = x_i + \sigma_i C_i(1,0), \quad i = 1, ..., n,$$

where

- σ_i is the search step size, and

- C_i is the realization of a Cauchy random variable.

The search step size parameter may be chosen as follows:

$$\sigma_i = [\beta_i f(x) + \gamma_i]^{\frac{1}{2}}, \quad i = 1, ..., n,$$

where β_i and γ_i are parameters of the method.

References and bibliography

Bäck, T., (1996), *Evolutionary Algorithms in Theory and Practice*, Oxford University Press, New York.

Bäck, T., Hammel, U., Schwefel, H.-P., (1997), Evolutionary computation: Comments on the history and current state, *IEEE Trans. on Evolutionary Computation*, 1(1), 3-17.

Bäck, T., Schwefel, H-P., (1993), An overview of evolutionary algorithms for parameter optimization, *Evolutionary Computation*, 1, 1-23.

Bäck, T., Schwefel, H.-P., (1996), Evolution computation: An overview, *Proc. 3rd IEEE Conf. on Evolutionary Computation 1996*, IEEE Press, Piscataway, NJ, 20-29.

Fogel, D.B., (1992), Evolving Artificial Intelligence, Ph.D. Thesis, University of California, San Diego.

Fogel, D.B., (1995), *Evolutionary Computation: Toward a New Philosophy of Machine Intelligence*, IEEE Press, Piscataway, NJ.

Fogel, L.J., (1962), Toward inductive inference automata, *Proc. Int. Federation for Information Processing Congress*, Munich, 395-399.

Fogel, L.J., Owens, A.J., Walsh, M.J., (1966), *Artificial Intelligence through Simulated Evolution*, John Wiley, New York.

Rechenberg, I., (1973), *Evolutionsstrategie: Optimierung Technischer Systeme nach Prinzipien der Biologischen Evolution*, Frommann-Holzboog Verlag, Stuttgart.

Rechenberg, I., (1994), *Evolutionsstrategie '94 Werkstatt Bionik und Evolutionstechnik*, Frommann-Holzboog, Stuttgart.

Rudolph, G., (1997), Local convergence rate of simple evolutionary algorithms with Cauchy mutations, *IEEE Trans. on Evolutionary Computation*, 1, 249-258.

Schwefel, H.-P., (1977), *Numerische Optimierung von Computer - Modellen mittels der Evolutionsstrategie*, Birkhäuser, Basel.

Schwefel, H.-P., (1981), *Numerical Optimization of Computer Models*, John Wiley, Chichester, UK.

Schwefel, H.-P., (1995), *Evolution and Optimum Seeking*, John Wiley, New York.

Yao, X., Liu, Y., (1996), Fast evolutionary programming, *Proc. 5th Conf. on Evolutionary Programming*, L.J. Fogel, P.J. Angeline, T. Bäck (Eds.), MIT Press, Cambridge, MA, 451-460.

Yao, X., Liu, Y., Lin, G., (1999), Evolutionary programming made faster, *IEEE Trans. on Evolutionary Computation*, 3, 82-102.

13

Population models and parallel implementations

13.1 Introduction

This chapter deals with several population models aimed at solving multiple optima detection problems.

In order to identify several optimum points, we have to endow an evolutionary algorithm with an additional mechanism that is intended to favor the appearance and maintenance of subpopulations related to the various optimum points.

A subpopulation (corresponding to a species) tends to occupy a certain area of the search space. Thus an analogy to the biological concept of a *niche* is induced.

Using niching methods (Goldberg and Richardson, 1987), evolutionary algorithms may be extended to solve problems requiring detection and maintenance of multiple solutions.

Multimodal function optimization is a typical application of niching evolutionary algorithms. Other applications are vectorial optimization, clustering, and machine learning.

13.2 Niching methods

Multiple optimal solutions in a multimodal optimization problem can be found simultaneously by forming subpopulations in the entire population. A subpopulation corresponds to a *niche*. Each niche is supposed to represent an optimum region of the search space.

To establish subpopulations containing the optimum points and to stabilize them, a niching method may be used. The focus of niching methods is to capture simultaneously, and to maintain, the solutions of interest.

The main niching methods are *sharing* (or *fitness sharing*) and *crowding*. These methods may extend genetic algorithms using binary or real-valued encoding, as well as other evolutionary algorithms.

13.3 Fitness sharing

In an evolutionary algorithm, the fact that the individuals belonging to one niche have to share the niche resources is translated into a modification of the fitness function.

Fitness sharing (Goldberg and Richardson, 1987) is a fitness scaling mechanism introduced to this end. It calculates the degree to which the resources should be shared among the individuals of an evolutionary algorithm population.

The idea is that similar individuals should share the resources to a larger extent because they are expected to belong to the same niche. It follows that similar individuals will have a significant degree of sharing. Conversely, remote individuals will have a low degree of sharing. Sharing may be combined with other scaling mechanisms.

The values of the sharing function will depend on the distance between individuals. The greater the distance between individuals, the smaller the value corresponding to the sharing function. The result is that the sharing function decreases with the increase of the distance between chromosomes.

Let us consider a multimodal optimization problem. Let f be the fitness function.

If similar individuals are required to share fitness, then the number of individuals that can lay in any region of the search space is limited by the fitness of that region. The number of individuals in the region of a peak (the attraction basin of that peak) depends on the height of that peak. By sharing, each individual's fitness decreases according to the presence of other similar, nearby individuals.

Sharing may be interpreted as the renormalization of each fitness value.

Renormalized (or shared) fitness of the individual x is given by its fitness $f(x)$ divided by the *niche count* of x.

The niche count of an individual x is the sum of the sharing function values between x and all individuals in the population, including x.

13.3.1 Sharing function

The sharing function may be defined as an application $s : \mathbf{R} \to [0,1]$. If two chromosomes are identical, then the corresponding sharing degree is maximal. The sharing degree tends to zero as the distance between chromosomes tends toward the infinite.

13.3.2 Niche count

A niche count is defined for each population individual using the sharing function. The calculated niche count is used to renormalize the fitness value.

Let us consider a population of size n.

For each individual x^i of the population a value m_i is calculated by the formula:

$$m_i = \sum_{j=1}^{n} s\left(d(x^i, x^j)\right),$$

where

- s is the sharing function, and

- d is an appropriate distance concept.

We interpret m_i as the *niche count* corresponding to x_i.

13.3.3 Shared fitness

The fitness function f will be modified by using the niche count m_i. As a result, we obtain a *shared fitness function* f^* whose expression is

$$f^*(x^i) = \frac{f(x^i)}{m_i}.$$

The renormalized individual's evaluation is therefore

$$eval(x^i) = f^*(x^i).$$

Sharing tends to spread the population over different optima proportional to the values of these optima.

13.4 Crowding

Crowding techniques (De Jong, 1975) are used to spread individuals among the most promising optimum points of the search space.

Optimum regions representing crossover attraction basins are considered. The number of individuals concentrated around an optimum point depends on the size of the attraction basin.

To maintain diversity of a population, crowding methods replace similar individuals. Usually, crowding replaces similar high-fit individuals

To measure similarity, an appropriate distance concept is used.

13.5 Island and stepping stone models

The *island model* (Cohoon, Hedge, Martin and Richardson, 1987) considers small disjoint subpopulations (called *islands* or *demes*) having isolated evolution.

Demes represent semi-independent (interbreeding) groups of individuals. One deme has a loose coupling to other neighboring demes.

The coupling takes the form of *migration* (or *diffusion*) of some individuals between demes.

The isolated evolution within subpopulations achieves the *exploitation* of the search space.

A small subpopulation strongly exploits the region of local optima connected to this subpopulation.

Migrations achieve the *exploration* of the search space by reinjecting diversity into subpopulations.

The overall population is partitioned into m subpopulations (demes) P_1, ..., P_m, where m is a parameter of the method. Usually the subpopulations have different sizes.

The individual migration is controlled by several parameters. The most important migration parameters are

- *Communication topology*

  defining the subpopulation interconnections.

- *Migration scheme*

  controlling which individuals (best, worst, random) from a deme migrate to another deme and which individuals are replaced (worst, random).

- *Migration rate*

  controlling how many individuals migrate.

- *Migration interval*

  determining the frequency of migrations.

Remarks

(i)   The communication topology specifies inter-deme communications.

(ii)   The communication topology and the frequency of interaction determine the degree of isolation/interaction among demes.

(iii)   When the migration is allowed between neighboring sub-populations only, the model is called *stepping stone model.*

13.6 Fine-grained and diffusion models

Fine-grained models consider many small demes. A typical example is the diffusion model.

The *diffusion model* (Mühlenbein, 1989) represents an intrinsic parallel model of evolutionary computation. The intuitive idea behind these models is that the individuals spread throughout the global population like molecules in a diffusion process. Diffusion models are also called *cellular models.*

Diffusion model parallel implementations assign a processor to each individual. Generally, the population size is constant. The processors are placed on a large grid. The grid is usually toroidal or bidimensional.

Recombination is restricted to a local neighborhood of each individual.

Remark

Although fine-grained models were conceived as parallel implementation models, they may also be considered as potentially useful population models.

13.7 Coevolution

In nature, populations interact with the physical environment and with other populations. Evolution is actually coevolution: a complex process of simultaneous coadaptation.

The *prey-predator* or *host-parasite* relationships are typical examples of coevolution. For instance, if a species evolves defenses against parasites, then parasites evolve counter-adaptive changes to circumvent the defenses. This kind of 'arms race' is responsible for many evolutionary changes in coevolving populations.

Coevolution concepts are appealing for creating more robust evolutionary algorithms. In previous chapters we have already indicated several applications of coevolution to fitness evaluation.

Coevolution approaches may be either *competitive* or *cooperative*.

13.7.1 Competitive models

In a competitive approach, two (or more) populations may evolve simultaneously but with conflicting goals.

Hillis (1992) proposed a competitive coevolutionary method for sorting lists of integers involving a minimum number of exchanges.

Two populations were considered. One population evolves programs that sort lists. The other population tries to evolve difficult sorting problems (i.e., lists of numbers that are difficult to sort).

13.7.2 Cooperative models

Potter and De Jong (1994) proposed a cooperative model where multiple subpopulations are evolved separately by a genetic algorithm.

Each subpopulation, corresponding to a species, represents some components of the global solution.

A *credit* is assigned to each species according to its importance in solving the global problem.

Selection favors cooperation rather than competition between subpopulations. To obtain global solutions, species are combined into full solutions and evaluated on the global task.

13.8 Baldwin effect

The Baldwin evolution model (Baldwin, 1896) suggests that individual learning can alter the course of evolution. According to this theory, the evolutionary pressure favors individuals having learning capabilities.

The individuals able to learn are less dependent on the genetically encoded traits. The frequency of the genes responsible for learning will increase in the subsequent generations.

Individuals able to learn a certain adaptation (allowing learning individuals to survive preferentially) will be more likely to produce offspring having this learning capability.

This implicit learning model is usually referred to as the *Baldwin effect*.

The Baldwin effect highlights an indirect mechanism allowing individual learning to influence the rate of evolutionary progress.

By increasing survival chances and genetic diversity, individual learning capabilities increase the probability that the population evolves genetically encoded traits that better fit a challenging environment.

13.9 Parallel implementation of evolutionary algorithms

Evolutionary algorithms are computationally intensive. The fitness calculation of individuals is the most time-consuming part of the algorithm.

The operation that is most commonly parallelized is therefore the fitness evaluation. Normally, the operation requires only the knowledge of the individual to be evaluated. Consequently, no processor communication is needed during this phase.

Parallelization is a natural approach to accelerate evolutionary algorithm convergence and, at the same time, to preserve population diversity.

There exist other problems which can be addressed with *parallel evolutionary algorithms* (PEAs). For instance, PEAs can achieve a parallel search in different regions of the solution space. In this way the search process may escape from a sub-optimal region of the search space.

Parallel implementations are very useful when the memory required to store each solution is considerable, or the problem needs a very large population.

Some parallel evolutionary computation models are considered in the following.

13.9.1 Subpopulations with migration

Each population structure has a built-in parallelization model. The demes are organized in a spatial structure that ensures the interaction among them. A deme is usually processed on a separate processor.

The most common processor interconnection topologies include two-dimensional and three-dimensional grids, hypercube, and torus.

Characteristics of some parallel implementation models are described next.

13.9.1.1 Island model

In the island model, a parallel system architecture that assigns each subpopulation (a deme) to a separate processor is used.

The subpopulation's isolation is alleviated by a (weak) migration between processors.

The role of migrations is to reinject diversity in subpopulations, thus preventing premature convergence.

13.9.1.2 Coarse-grained models

Coarse-grained algorithms deal with a relatively small number of demes. Each deme contains many individuals.

A relatively long time is required for processing a generation within each deme. Only occasional inter-deme communication for exchanging individuals is performed.

13.9.1.3 Fine-grained models

Fine-grained algorithms deal with a large number of small subpopulations. Inter-deme communication is achieved by means of a migration operator. Overlapping demes may also be considered.

The diffusion model may be viewed as an instance of the fine-grained family of parallel algorithms.

13.9.1.4 Diffusion model

Within the diffusion model, each individual is typically placed on a processor of a large processor array organized as a mesh or grid. The grid geometry induces a communication topology. The initial population is generated in parallel.

Each processor evolves the associated individual. A processor communicates with its neighbors (not necessarily with all).

Fitness evaluation is done simultaneously for all individuals. Selection, mating, and recombination are local.

Selection for recombination is a local version of a global selection technique. The recombination mate of an individual is chosen from its neighborhood.

13.9.1.5 Overlapping subpopulations without migration

For the models of this family, the absence of a migration operator is counterbalanced by the existence of *overlapping demes*.

Some individuals belong to several demes and may participate to multiple selection and recombination operations in various subpopulations.

References and bibliography

Anderson, R.W., (1997), The Baldwin effect, *Handbook of Evolutionary Computation*, T. Bäck, D.B. Fogel, Z. Michalewicz (Eds.), Institute of Physics Publishing Ltd., Bristol, and Oxford University Press, New York.

Angeline, P.J., Pollack, J.B., (1993), Competitive environments evolve better solutions for complex tasks, *Proc. 5th Int. Conf. on Ge-*

netic Algorithms, S. Forrest (Ed.), Morgan Kaufmann, San Mateo, CA, 264-270.

Baldwin, J.M., (1896), A new factor in evolution, *American Naturalist*, 30, 441-451, 536-553.

Belew, R., (1990), Evolution, learning and culture: Computational metaphors for adaptive algorithms, *Complex Systems*, 4, 11-49.

Booker, L.B., (1982), Intelligent Behaviour as an Adaptation to the Task Environment, Ph.D. Thesis, University of Michigan, Dissertations Abstracts Int. 43 469 B.

Cohoon, J.P., Hedge, S.U., Martin, W.N., Richardson, D.S., (1987), Punctuated equilibria: a parallel genetic algorithm, *Proc. 2nd Int. Conf. on Genetic Algorithms*, J.J. Grefenstette (Ed.), Lawrence Erlbaum, Hillsdale, NJ, 148-154.

Deb, K., (1989), Genetic Algorithms in Multimodal Function Optimization, Master's Thesis, University of Alabama, TCGA Report 89002.

De Jong, K.A., (1975), An Analysis of the Behaviour of a Class of Genetic Adaptive Systems, Ph.D. Thesis, University of Michigan, Ann Arbor.

Dumitrescu, D., Lazzerini, B., Jain, L.C., (2000), *Fuzzy Sets and their Application to Clustering and Training*, CRC Press, Boca Raton, FL.

Eldredge, N., Gould, S.J., (1972), Punctuated equilibria: an alternative to phyletic gradualism, *Models of Paleobiology*, T.J.M. Schopf (Ed.), Freeman, Cooper, San Francisco, 82-115.

Eldredge, N., (1989), Macro-evolutionary Dynamics: Species, Niches and Adaptive Peaks, McGraw-Hill, New York.

French, R., Messinger, A., (1994), Genes, phenes, and the Baldwin effect: Learning and evolution in a simulated population, *Artificial Life*, 4, R. Brooks, P. Maes (Eds.), MIT Press, Cambridge, MA.

Goldberg, D.E., (1989), *Genetic Algorithms in Search, Optimization, and Machine Learning*, Addison-Wesley, Reading, MA.

Goldberg, D.E., Richardson, J., (1987), Genetic algorithms with sharing for multimodal function optimization, *Proc 2nd Int. Conf. on Genetic algorithms*, J.J. Grefenstette (Ed.), Lawrence Erlbaum Associates, Hillsdale, New York, 41-49.

Harvey, I., (1993), The puzzle of the persistent question marks: A case study of genetic drift, *Proc. 5th Int. Conf. on Genetic Algorithms*, S. Forrest (Ed.), Morgan Kaufmann, San Mateo, CA.

Hillis, W.D., (1992), Co-evolving parasites improve simulated evolution as an optimization procedure, *Artificial Life*, 2, C.G. Langton, C. Taylor, J.D. Farmer, S. Rasmussen (Eds.), Addison-Wesley, Reading, MA, 313-324.

Husbands, P., (1993), An ecosystem model for integrated production planning, *Journal of Computer Integrated Manufacturing*, 6, 74-86.

Mahfoud, S.W., (1992), Crowding and preselection revisited, *Parallel Problems Solving From Nature*, 2, R. Männer, B. Manderick (Eds.), Elsevier, Amsterdam, 27-36.

Mitchell, M., (1996), *An Introduction to Genetic Algorithms*, MIT Press, Cambridge, MA.

Mitchell, M., (1997), *Machine Learning*, McGraw-Hill, New York.

Mühlenbein, H., (1989), Parallel genetic algorithms, population genetics and combinatorial optimization, *Proc. 3rd Int. Conf. on Genetic Algorithms*, J.D. Schaffer (Ed.), Morgan Kaufmann, San Mateo, CA, 416-421.

Nolfi, S., Elman, J.L., Parisi, D., (1994), Learning and evolution in neural networks, *Adaptive Behavior*, 3, 5-28.

Novostawski, M., (1998), Parallel Genetic Algorithms in Geometry Atomic Cluster Optimization and Other Applications, M.S. Thesis, School of Computer Science, University of Birmingham.

Novostawski, M., Poli, R., (1999), Parallel genetic algorithm taxonomy, *3rd Int. Conf. on Knowledge-Based Intelligent Information Engineering Systems*, Adelaide, Australia, 88-92.

Perry, Z.A., (1984), Experimental Study of Speciation in Ecological Niche Theory Using Genetic Algorithms, Ph.D. Thesis, University of Michigan, Dissertation Abstracts Int. 45 3870 B.

Pollack, J.B., Blain, A.D. (1996) Coevolution of a backgammon player, *Artificial Life*, 5, MIT Press, Cambridge, MA.

Potter, M. De Jong, K., (1994), A cooperative coevolutionary approach to function optimization, *Proc. 3rd Conf. on Parallel Problem Solving from Nature*, Y. Davidor, H.-P. Schwefel (Eds.), Lectures Notes in Computer Science, Vol. 866, Springer-Verlag, 249-257.

Reynolds, R.G., (1994), An introduction to cultural algorithms, *Proc. 3rd Annual Conference on Evolutionary Programming*, A.V. Sebald, L.J. Fogel (Eds.), World Scientific, Singapore, 131-139.

Shimojima, K., Kubota, N., Fukuda, T., (1996), Virus-evolutionary genetic algorithm for fuzzy controller optimization. *Genetic Algorithm and Soft Computing*, F. Herrera, J.L. Verdegay (Eds.), Physica-Verlag, Heidelberg, 369-388.

Sipper, M., (1998), Programming cellular machines by cellular programming, *Bio-Inspired Computing Machines*, D. Mange, M. Tomassini (Eds.), Press Polytechnique et Universitaires Romandes, Lausanne.

Spears, W.M., (1994), Simple subpopulation schemes, *Proc. 3rd Conf. on Evolutionary Programming*, World Scientific, Singapore, 296-307.

Spector, L., Luke, S., (1996), Culture enhances the evolvability of cognition, *Proc. 8th Annual Conference of the Cognitive Science Society*, G. Cotrell (Ed.), Lawrence Erlbaum Associates, Mahwah, NJ, 672-677.

Teller, A., (1993), Learning mental models. *Proc. 5th Workshop on Neural Networks*, San Francisco.

Teller, A., (1994), The evolution of mental models, *Advances in Genetic Programming*, K.E. Kinnear (Ed.), MIT Press, Cambridge, MA, 199-219.

Waddington, C.H., (1942), Canalization of development and the inheritance of acquired characters, *Nature*, 150, 563-565.

Yin, X., Germany, N., (1993), A fast genetic algorithm with sharing scheme using cluster analysis methods in multimodal function optimization, *Artificial Neural Nets and Genetic Algorithms*, R.F. Albrecht, C.R. Reeves, N.C. Steele (Eds.), Springer, Berlin, 450-457.

14

Genetic programming

14.1 Introduction

The genetic programming (GP) paradigm mainly deals with the problem of automatic programming. The structures undergoing adaptation (evolving individuals) are themselves computer programs.

Within genetic programming, the process of problem solving is regarded as a search in the space of computer programs.

Actually, genetic programming provides a method for searching for the fittest computer program with respect to a given problem.

Genetic programming may be considered a form of *program discovery* or *program induction*, i.e., induction of programs that solve a given task when a set of examples (training cases or input-output relations) is given.

The training examples specify the desired behavior of the solution program.

14.2 Early GP approaches

Turing (1950, 1953) considered 'genetic or evolutionary search' to automatically develop intelligent computer programs, like chess player programs and general-purpose intelligent machines.

The classifier system proposed by Smith (1980) to find a good poker-playing strategy uses variable-size strings to represent strategies. This approach may be considered an early genetic programming approach.

Cramer (1985) considered a tree structure as program representation in a genotype. The method uses tree structures and subtree crossover in the evolutionary process.

Hicklin (1986) and Fujiki and Dickinson (1987) considered methods for evolving programs in LISP.

Dickmanns, Schmidhuber and Winklhofer (1987) considered a method for evolving PROLOG programs.

Koza (1989, 1992) emphasized the importance of genetic programming as a general approach to program induction and its effectiveness for a variety of problems in a wide range of fields.

These fields included planning, optimal control, discovery of a game-playing strategy, symbolic regression, automatic programming, discovering molecular structures, and evolving emergent behavior.

14.3 Program-generating language

The individuals evolved from genetic programming are program structures of variable sizes. A syntax in prefix (or postfix) form may be used.

A *restricted*, user-defined, *language* with appropriate operators, variables, and constants may be defined for the particular problem to be solved. In this way, syntactically correct programs will be generated and the program search space limited to the feasible solutions.

The *functions* and *terminals* in the restricted language are user-defined primitives with which a program is built.

The terminals provide a value to the GP system; the functions process values already existing in the system.

14.3.1 Terminal and function sets

The *terminal set* consists of

- the *inputs to the program,*

- the *constants,*

- the *functions without argument*

   (but having side-effects on the system state).

Remarks

(i)   A terminal returns a numerical value (without having an input).

(ii)   The existing constants may be combined by the GP system into new constants.

The *function set* includes

- the *functions*,

- the *operators*,

- the *statements of the system*.

The function set may be application specific. It should be powerful enough to supply a representation of the problem solutions.

If a too large function set is used, the search space may become too wide and prohibitive time may be needed to find an acceptable solution.

The function set may include, for example,

(i)   arithmetic operators,

(ii)   real-valued functions,

(iii)   boolean operators,

(iv)   boolean functions,

(v)   conditional statements (or conditional operators)

           (e.g., if-then-else, switch, case),

(vi)   control transfer statements

           (e.g., goto, call, jump),

(vii)   loop statements (functions causing iteration)

           (e.g., for-do, while-do, repeat-until),

(viii)   subroutines.

Functions and terminals may be represented as the nodes of a tree. Other structures of interest are graph structures, linear structures, or even cellular automata.

14.3.2 Closure property

An important requirement of the function set is the *closure property*. According to this property, each function in the function set must be able to accept as argument any other function's output and any terminal in the terminal set.

The set of possible structures in a GP system is the set of all possible compositions of the functions that can be recursively formed from the function set and the terminal set of the system.

14.3.3 Problem language and implementation language

An important aspect is the choice of an appropriate language for a given task. The problem itself may sometimes suggest a reasonable choice for functions and terminals. Genetic programming is very creative in building new functions.

Self-adaptation and *coevolution* of functions and terminals may also be considered for finding an adequate language.

Another aspect is the programming language chosen for GP implementation. The LISP language was the original one. Any programming language that can represent programs as parse trees (like C, C++, Java) may be used for implementation.

14.4 GP program structures

The fundamental program structures considered in genetic programming are *tree structures, graph structures,* and *linear structures.* Tree structures are the most common.

14.4.1 Tree structures

In tree representation, the nodes correspond to function symbols and terminal symbols. The *prefix* or *postfix* order of execution can be chosen.

Within *postfix order*, the operators appear after the operands. For instance, the expression

$$a * b + c$$

in postfix order is written as

$$ab * c +.$$

The postfix order evaluates the first (leftmost) subtree for which all inputs are available. The last evaluated node is the root.

Within the *prefix order*, the root is the first node that is executed (evaluated). Then the first subtree (in prefix order) is evaluated. In this way, the nodes close to the root are executed before the terminal nodes.

In a tree-structured system, the memory is local. This means that each function node needs to know only the values of its immediate successors. This local memory makes the system very powerful and flexible.

14.4.2 Graph structures

In order to deal with loops and recursion, a graph may be used to represent the program structure. *Graph structures* are able to represent complex programs compactly (Teller and Veloso, 1995).

The graph nodes contain function symbols or constants. The execution order is determined by the directed edges in the graph. The system works using a local memory (implemented by a stack memory) and a global memory (an indexed memory).

14.4.3 Linear structures

A linear program representation uses a linear string of instructions that are executed sequentially. To associate arguments with a function, the linear genome may be rewritten as a two-address register machine (Nordin, 1994).

The instructions operate on memory registers, reading and writing values from and to registers. Each instruction may access any register. The memory is not local, each register containing a global memory value. The linear program (genome) may include control and loop instructions. Of course, jump instructions will perturb the sequential execution order.

14.5 Initialization of tree structures

There are two common methods for initializing tree structures. These basic methods are called *grow* and *full* (Koza, 1992). Within both methods, if a terminal is chosen as the label of a node, that node becomes an endpoint of the tree.

Definition

The *depth* $D(x)$ of a node x in a tree may be defined recursively as follows:

$$D(x)=\begin{cases} 1, & \text{if } x=root \\ D(parent\ of\ x)+1, & \text{otherwise.} \end{cases}$$

14.5.1 Grow method

The *grow* method generates trees of irregular shapes. The root label is selected from the function set. The other node labels are selected at random from the function set and the terminal set. A maximum node depth is specified. A branch ends if either the maximum depth has been reached or it contains a node with a terminal label.

14.5.2 Full method

In the full method, all paths from the root to a terminal point have the same length D_{max}. Within each path, the node labels are chosen from the function set until the node depth equals the value $(D_{max} - 1)$. The selection of the labels for the nodes at the maximum depth D_{max} is restricted to the terminal set.

In this way, the full method produces uniform trees.

Remark

A maximum number N of nodes in the tree may also be specified. In this case, the generating process stops when the tree reaches N nodes.

14.5.3 Ramped half-and-half method

To introduce diversity in the initial population, a mixture of the grow and full methods may be considered.

The *ramped half-and-half* method (Koza, 1992) creates $(D_{max} - 1)$ sub-populations that contain the same number of trees. These sub-populations are generated using a depth parameter d that ranges between 2 and D_{max}, i.e.,

$$d \in \{2, ..., D_{max}\}.$$

For each value of the parameter d, half of the trees are created via the full method and the other via the grow method.

We may introduce an asymmetry using a parameter M and allowing a percentage of M trees to be created via the full method, while the rest are generated via the grow method. M is a parameter of the method.

14.6 Fitness calculation

If an objective function to be optimized is available, then the fitness function may be obtained by a *scale transform* of the objective function.

For many problems it is not easy to define an objective function. In such a situation we may use a set of training examples and define the fitness as an *error-based* function.

The training examples describe the desired behavior of the system as a set of input–output relations.

Let us consider a training set consisting of k examples

$$(x_i, y_i), \quad i = 1, ..., k,$$

where x_i is the input of the ith example in the training set and y_i is the corresponding output.

We may interpret y_i as the *correct answer* (or *target output*) associated with the ith training example.

The k training examples may also be considered as *fitness cases*.

Of course, the training set should be sufficiently large to provide a basis for evaluating programs over a number of different significant situations.

Also, the training examples should be representative enough since they form a basis for generalization to the entire search space.

Let us denote by o_i the actual output produced by a program P on the ith training example.

The corresponding error e_i may be defined as the (squared) difference between the correct answer (or target output) y_i and the actual output o_i.

Therefore, we have

$$e_i = (y_i - o_i)^2.$$

The fitness $f(P)$ of the program P may be defined as the total sum of the squared errors.

In this case, we may write

$$f(P) = \sum_{i=1}^{k} e_i$$

$$= \sum_{i=1}^{k} (y_i - o_i)^2.$$

Let us observe that a squared error function has the property of decreasing the importance of small deviations from the target outputs.

The fitness function may be scaled. Some scaling functions may amplify the importance of small differences in the fitness function values (or of small deviations from the target outputs). In this case, as the search progresses and the population improves, greater emphasis is placed on the small differences between individuals.

Sometimes the error-based fitness may have a natural interpretation. For instance, in a classification problem, the fitness may be considered as the number of correctly classified examples in a sample set.

For problems difficult to solve, several optimality concepts may be combined into the fitness function. In this case, we may have multi-objective fitness functions; vectorial optimization methods are needed to solve the corresponding problems.

14.7 Recombination operators

In early genetic programming, recombination was typically adopted as the only search (variation) operator. However, it is not clear if re-combination-based GP systems outperform mutation-based GP systems.

14.7.1 Standard recombination operator

The form of the recombination operator depends on the representation of the individuals. Here, we restrict ourselves to the tree-structured representation.

An elegant and rather straightforward recombination operator acting on two parents swaps a subtree of one parent with a subtree of the other parent.

The action of the recombination operator may be described as follows:

1.   Choose two parent program trees using a specific mating selection procedure.

2.   Select a subtree in each parent randomly.

      A biased selection may be used so that subtrees representing terminals are chosen with lower probability than other subtrees.

3.   Swap the selected subtrees between the two parents, thus producing two offspring.

Remarks

(i)   A variant of this operator that creates a unique offspring may also be considered. In this case, the unique offspring is obtained from either parent by replacing the subtree selected from that parent with the subtree selected from the other parent.

(ii)   This recombination operator seems to be merely a form of macromutation.

14.7.2 Brood recombination

Recombination is a constructive force that may have disruptive effects. To balance these contradictory aspects and to emphasize the constructive strength, various recombination techniques have been considered. In what follows, we will consider brood recombination.

Brood recombination (Tackett, 1994) generates more offspring each time recombination is applied. These offspring represent a '*brood*'. Only the best two offspring of the brood will be selected. The remainder of the offspring will be discarded.

A *brood size* parameter K is considered. Two parents are selected for recombination. The brood recombination operator proceeds through the following steps:

BROOD RECOMBINATION ALGORITHM

S1.   Perform standard recombination on the two selected

parents K times.

Each time a pair of children is obtained.

S2.   Evaluate each offspring by computing its fitness

function value.

S3.   Select the two fittest offspring.

The selected offspring will survive, while the non-selected offspring will be discarded.

Remarks

(i)   To avoid a too slow evaluating process, the offspring may be evaluated only on a small subset of the training set. The offspring compete in a *tournament* to be selected.

(ii)   In this way, the selected offspring will not necessarily be the best ones but will be good enough.

14.7.3 Selecting crossover points

Iba and de Garis (1996) proposed a method to detect some regularities in the tree program structure and to use these regularities as guidance for the recombination operator.

The method assigns a *performance value* to a subtree.

The performance measure is used to select the crossover points. The recombination operator learns how to choose good sites for crossover.

A similar idea has been devised for graph program structures (within the PADO system) by Teller and Veloso (1995). The information about the execution path followed by the evolved program is used to guide recombination.

Zannoni and Reynolds (1996) considered a *cultural algorithm* to choose the crossover points.

14.7.4 Introns

A biological *intron* is a DNA sequence within a gene bearing no genetic information. Introns are not expressed as proteins (see Chapter 1).

Introns are noncoding regions; they do not affect the survival chances of an organism directly.

In a sequential representation, genotypes may be represented in the following form:

$$x_1 \mid \text{intron} \mid x_2 \mid \text{intron} \mid \dots \mid \text{intron} \mid x_s,$$

where x_1, x_2, ..., x_s are the s components of the solution (these components are called *exons*).

Within GA approaches, introns are used to enhance the chances for crossover to recombine building blocks (Angeline, 1994), thus reducing the disruptive effect of recombination.

Within GP, an intron may be an operation whose execution does not cause any change in the system state at all (e.g., the increment of a variable by the value 0).

Introns may be considered as emergents from the search process, and they do not affect the fitness of a solution directly.

Therefore, any subtree that emerges in a tree-structured program and does not affect the program fitness may be regarded as an intron.

There are several techniques to insert introns artificially into genetic programming systems. Unlike introns that emerge spontaneously, *artificially inserted introns* do not emerge from the evolutionary process.

An approach to introduce explicitly defined introns into genetic programming has been proposed by Nordin, Francone and Banzhaf, (1996) and by Angeline (1996).

A real value (a weight) is assigned to each (un-ordered) pair of nodes of the tree structure.

Let us note that only in a very particular case does a pair of nodes correspond to an edge of the tree. Generally the nodes of a pair are not adjacent.

The probability that a crossover point lies between the nodes of a pair is considered to be proportional to the pair weight.

The weights are allowed to evolve in order to identify useful subtrees in an individual as an evolutionary, intrinsic emergent phenomenon. In other words, weights are kept low inside a useful subtree, and high outside. The weights strongly influence the crossover points.

In Angeline's (1996) approach, only normal (Gaussian) mutations for weights are allowed.

As a result of using evolving weights, the search process is substantially improved by allowing the procedure to protect some potentially useful regions of the tree from recombination.

The protected regions may be interpreted as *building blocks* in tree-structured individuals.

14.8 Mutation

Within genetic programming, several mutation models have been adopted. In what follows, we will consider some of these models.

14.8.1 Mutation of tree-structured programs

Mutation is applied to a single program tree to generate an offspring. Various mutation techniques may be utilized.

14.8.1.1 Macromutation

The *macromutation* operator randomly chooses a *mutation point* inside the parent tree selected for mutation.

The mutation point may be internal (an element of the function set) or may be external (a terminal symbol).

The corresponding subtree (including the mutation point and whatever is below it) is replaced by a new subtree generated at random.

The new subtree is usually obtained by means of the procedure used to produce the initial population of program trees, and is subject to the same limitations.

Typically, the parameter that controls the maximum node depth of randomly generated subtrees has the same value as in the initial population.

14.8.1.2 Micromutation

A particular case of mutation alters a single node. This operator inserts a randomly chosen function (terminal) symbol into a randomly selected function (terminal) node of the tree.

This mutation technique may be considered as the action of a *micromutation* operator. It is also called *point mutation*.

14.8.2 Mutation of linearly represented programs

Mutation of linearly represented programs is also straightforward. The mutation operator selects an instruction from the individual chosen for mutation.

The selected instruction is randomly perturbed by changing some of its parts. For instance, an operator (or constant) is replaced by another operator (or constant).

Another possibility is to randomly choose a sequence of instructions and replace them with another randomly selected sequence of instructions.

14.8.3 Mutation strategies

The usual strategy is to complete the offspring population by recombination. On this population, mutation is applied with a specific mutation probability.

A different strategy considers a separate application of crossover and mutation. In this case mutation seems to be emphasized with respect to the previous, standard strategy.

The importance of mutation in the search process depends on the mutation probability. Comparable mutation and recombination probabilities usually indicate a comparable role of the two search operators.

14.9 Selection

Selection operators within genetic programming are not specific.

The problem under consideration may impose a particular choice.

14.9.1 Selection for recombination

The fitness of an individual induces a probability of selecting the individual for recombination.

As genetic programming does not require a special selection operator, all variants of the selection operators may be used.

The choice of the most appropriate selection operator is one of the most difficult problems. Generally this choice is problem dependent.

However, we may remark that the tournament selection is suitable for large problem classes.

14.9.2 Selection for replacement

All types of replacement (survival) selection strategies may be considered. Generational as well as steady-state strategies may be used.

14.10 Population models

Various population models may be used to evolve a population of programs. The emergent sub-population structure may be useful to solve some difficult tasks. A typical difficult task is the multimodal optimization problem.

All population models available for genetic algorithms may be used in the framework of genetic programming, no matter how the program is represented.

14.11 Parallel implementation

Genetic programming presents the same advantages as the other evolutionary algorithms when implemented on parallel architecture systems.

Island models or *parallel fitness evaluation models* may be very suitable to genetic programming parallel implementation.

The variable sizes and complexities of the individuals may cause some implementation difficulties. For instance, massively parallel SIMD (Single-Instruction Multiple-Data) architectures are not suitable for GP implementation (mainly because of the amount of local memory needed to store tree-structured individuals).

14.12 Basic GP algorithm

GP algorithms may be considered as instances of the general evolutionary algorithm.

The starting point is an arbitrary population of programs.

To obtain a subsequent generation, search operators and a replacement policy are used. A generational or a steady-state replacement approach may be considered.

14.12.1 GP procedure setting

The following actions must be performed before a GP run:

- define the function set,

- define the terminal set,

- define the evaluation procedure,

- define the GP procedure parameters (such as population size, maximum node depth, maximum individual size, crossover and mutation probabilities).

14.12.2 Generational algorithm

The generational GP algorithm may be outlined as follows:

GENERATIONAL GP ALGORITHM

S1. Set $t = 0$.

Initalize population $P(t)$.

S2. **while** (termination condition not satisfied) **do**

 begin

  S2.1. Evaluate the individuals in $P(t)$.

  S2.2. Select individuals in $P(t)$ using the selection algorithm.

  S2.3. Apply variation operators to the selected individuals.

  S2.4. Insert the obtained offspring into the new population.

  S2.5. Set $t = t + 1$.

 end

14.12.3 Steady-state GP algorithm

Within each cycle of the steady-state approach, one individual is selected for modification. The offspring may replace an existing individual in the same population.

The fitness values may be assigned to individuals by means of a *ranking* method. This could be, for instance, the *local tournament* method.

The offspring may replace the worst individual forming the tournament pool.

The tournament size is a parameter of the method.

Within a slight generalization of the previous scheme, more individuals are allowed to be replaced in the population.

The following steady-state GP algorithm with tournament selection considers this case.

STEADY-STATE GP ALGORITHM WITH TOURNAMENT SELECTION

S1. Initialize the population.

S2. **while** (termination condition not satisfied) **do**

   begin

   S2.1. Choose a tournament pool (a subset of the population to take part in competition).

   S2.2. Play the tournament with the selected competitors.

   S2.3. Select the winner(s) of the tournament.

S2.4. Modify the winner(s) using variation
(search) operators.

S2.5. Replace (some of) the losers of the
tournament with the offspring.

end

Remarks

(i)   Other selection schemes are possible. We may consider, for
instance, the next procedure:

1. m parents are selected (using proportional selection, a
ranking method or another procedure),

2. m offspring are generated,

3. the offspring replace the m worst members of the population.

(ii)   Another possibility is that the m offspring and the m worst
individuals compete to enter the new population. The competition may be realized as a tournament scheme.

References and bibliography

Angeline, P.J., (1994), Genetic programming and emergent intelligence, *Advances in Genetic Programming*, K.E. Kinnear, Jr. (Ed.),
MIT Press, Cambridge, MA, 75-98.

Angeline, P.J., (1996), Two self-adaptive crossover operators for genetic programming, *Advances in Genetic Programming*, 2, P.J. Angeline, K.E. Kinnear, Jr. (Eds.), MIT Press, Cambridge, MA, 89-110.

Banzhaf, W., Nordin, P., Keller, R.E., Francone, F.D., (1998), *Genetic Programming*, Morgan Kaufmann, San Francisco, CA, and dpunkt.verlag, Heidelberg.

Cramer, N.L., (1985), A representation for the adaptive generation of simple sequential programs, *Proc. Int. Conf. on Genetic Algorithms and Applications*, J.J. Greffenstette (Ed.), Carnegie-Mellon University, Pittsburgh, PA, 183-187.

Dickmanns, D., Schmidhuber, J., Winklhofer, A., (1987), *Der genetische Algorithms: Eine Implementierung in Prolog*, Project, Technical University of Munich.

Fujiki, C., Dickinson, J., (1987), Using the genetic algorithm to generate LISP source code to solve the prisoner's dilemma, *Proc. 2nd Int. Conf. on Genetic Algorithms*, J.J. Grefenstette (Ed.), Lawrence Erlbaum Associates, Hillsdale, NJ, 236-240.

Hicklin, J.F., (1986), Application of genetic algorithm to automatic program generation, Master's Thesis, Department of Computer Science, University of Idaho.

Iba, H., de Garis, H., (1996), Extending genetic programming with recombinative guidance, *Advances in Genetic Programming 2*, P.J. Angeline, K.E. Kinnear, Jr. (Eds.), MIT Press, Cambridge, MA, 69-88.

Koza, J.R., (1989), Hierarchical genetic algorithms operating on populations of computer programs, *Proc. 11th Int. Joint Conf. on Artificial Intelligence*, N.S. Sridharan (Ed.), Morgan Kaufmann, San Francisco, CA, Vol. 1, 768-774.

Koza, J.R., (1992), *Genetic Programming*, MIT Press, Cambridge, MA.

Koza, J.R., (1994), *Genetic Programming*, 2, MIT Press, Cambridge, MA.

Nordin, N., (1994), A compiling genetic programming system that directly manipulates the machine code, *Advances in Genetic Pro-

gramming, K.E. Kinnear, Jr. (Ed.), MIT Press, Cambridge, MA, 311-331.

Nordin, P., Francone, F., Banzhaf, W., (1996), Explicitely defined introns and destructive crossover in genetic programming, *Advances in Genetic Programming*, 2, P.J. Angeline, K.E. Kinnear, Jr. (Eds.), MIT Press, Cambridge, MA, 111-134.

Smith, S.F., (1980), A Learning System Based on Genetic Adaptive Algorithms, University of Pittsburgh, PA.

Tackett, W.A., (1994), Recombination, Selection, and the Genetic Construction of Computer Programs, Ph.D. Thesis, Department of Electrical Engineering Systems, University of Southern California.

Tackett, W.A., (1995), Mining the genetic program, *IEEE Expert*, 10, 28-38.

Teller, A., Veloso, M., (1995), PADO: Learning tree structured algorithms for orchestration into an object recognition system, Technical Report CMU-CS-95-101, Department of Computer Science, Carnegie Mellon University, Pittsburgh, PA.

Turing, A.M., (1950), Computing machinery and intelligence, *Mind*, 59, 433-460.

Turing, A.M., (1953), Digital computers applied to games, *Faster than Thought*, B.V. Bowden (Ed.), Pittman, London, 286-310.

Zannoni, E., Reynolds, R., (1996), Extracting design knowledge from genetic programs using cultural algorithms, *Proc. 5th Conf. on Evolutionary Programming*, L. Fogel, P.J. Angeline, T. Bäck (Eds.), MIT Press, Cambridge, MA.

15

Learning classifier systems

15.1 Introduction

A *learning classifier system* (or, in short, a *classifier system*) is a machine learning system that evolves rules in order to improve its performance in a changing environment. A classifier system may be considered as a variation of a standard AI *production system*.

Classifier systems use simple *if–then* rules, traditionally called *production rules*. Production rules are encoded in fixed-length binary strings. In classifier systems, the *rules* (or *productions*) have the same role as instructions in ordinary programs.

A rule is also called a *classifier*. The name 'classifier' comes from the rule's capability of classifying messages into arbitrary message sets.

A classifier system processes the rules in parallel. The rules are evolved on the basis of intermittent stimuli and reinforcement from the environment. Using a learning algorithm, the classifier system learns appropriate responses for a given set of stimuli.

The rules represent a population that is evolved by an appropriate evolutionary algorithm. Classifier systems may thus be considered as learning systems using evolutionary algorithms for rule discovery.

15.2 Michigan and Pittsburgh families of learning classifier systems

Two fundamental families of classifier systems have been proposed. These families differ in what they learn: individual rules or rule bases.

15.2.1 Michigan approach

Within the *Michigan approach* (Holland and Reitman, 1978), each member of the population represents a unique, distinct rule. The evolutionary algorithm evolves a population of rules. The rule set needed to solve a problem is given by the entire population.

The system's aim is not to find the best rule but the best set of rules. Therefore the system has to coevolve a set of cooperative rules that jointly are likely to supply a solution to the problem. The population of rules is modified via interactions with the environment.

The Michigan approach has to solve some difficult intrinsic learning problems.

The first problem is that of reinforcing or adapting the *weight* (or *strength* or *fitness*) of the rules already existing in the system as a response to infrequent or late payoff. This is known as the *credit assignment problem* (or the *apportionment of credit problem*).

Actually, the utility of a rule may be obvious only after a long time (game-playing programs are typical examples).

Let us suppose that the rule population is evolved by means of an ordinary evolutionary algorithm. In this case, the rule set tends to evolve toward a homogeneous population, but the problem solution generally requires distinct components that correspond to non-uniform rules.

Therefore, the *credit assignment system* has to preserve population diversity. To prevent a population from becoming uniform is an important facet of the credit assignment problem.

The second learning problem is to discover new rules to replace existing, inadequate rules.

The credit assignment system may solve these problems by adopting some heuristic method that assigns positive (negative) credit to the rules that cooperate to produce a desirable (undesirable) solution. The *bucket brigade algorithm* is such a method.

15.2.2 Pittsburgh approach

Within the *Pittsburgh* (or *Pitt*) *approach* (Smith, 1980), each individual represents an entire set of rules for the problem under consideration. A population of rule bases is evolved in an environment. In this respect, a standard evolutionary algorithm may be used.

Each individual represents a complete solution (a rule base) that may be evaluated independently. The evolutionary algorithm generates a new set of rule bases for the next generation.

Only minimal modifications to an evolutionary algorithm are needed to make it useful for the learning classifier problem.

The advantage of the Pittsburgh approach is that it avoids the delicate credit assignment problem. The individuals (complete solutions) compete on the basis of their global fitness (strength). Hence a single payoff-induced fitness value provides enough information to guide the search process.

15.3 Michigan classifier systems

In this section, a typical example of classifier system based on the Michigan approach is considered.

15.3.1 Structure of a Holland system

A *Holland system* is a particular instance of the Michigan family of classifier systems. We will illustrate the Michigan approach by considering the model of Holland systems.

The components of a Holland system are

- *a rule system,*

- *a message system,*

- *a credit assignment system,*

- *a rule discovery system.*

The Holland system is characterized by parallel rule-firing and internal communication based on messages.

The classifier system performs actions in, and communicates with the environment. The system also detects information on the environment state.

The environment state is encoded as a *message*. The *detectors* of the system receive a message from the environment, encode it, and place it on the *message list*. The messages activate the rules (classifiers).

When activated, a classifier places a message on the message list. The new message may activate other classifiers or may cause an action. In the latter case, a message is decoded by the *effectors*, which perform appropriate actions in the environment.

The environment evaluates the system actions and a *payoff* for these actions is returned to the system. Rule strengths are updated using the returned payoff, via the credit assignment system.

In a Holland classifier system, the credit assignment method is the *bucket brigade algorithm* (Holland, 1986) or a similar method.

The *learning* (or *rule discovery*) method is an evolutionary algorithm. Usually a genetic algorithm is adopted as the learning mechanism.

Michigan classifier systems combine the convenience of *if–then* rules used in symbolic AI systems with a neural-style credit assignment algorithm, and the efficient search of evolutionary algorithms.

15.3.2 Rules and messages

A *message* is represented as a fixed-length string over a finite alphabet.

A classifier (a rule) C is a pair consisting of a condition and an action:

$$C = (condition, action).$$

The messages are compared with the condition part of the classifiers. Therefore, the condition part is represented as a string having the same length as a message.

If a binary alphabet is used, a message is a string from the set $\{0, 1\}^k$. In this case, a *condition* is a string from the set $\{0, 1, *\}^k$, where $*$ is a *wild card* ('don't care') symbol.

An *action* is also represented as a string of the same length as a message and is from the set $\{0, 1, *\}^k$.

A message matches a condition if and only if all non-asterisk symbols in the corresponding strings coincide.

A matching message gives origin to an *output message* obtained by merging the original message with the action part of the classifier. That classifier becomes a candidate to place its message into the message list. This will occur depending on the classifier's strength value.

15.4 Bucket brigade algorithm

The *bucket brigade* algorithm is the typical method for solving the credit assignment problem in Holland classifier systems.

The strength of the rules is updated in parallel for a given population.

15.4.1 Principle of the algorithm

The associated genetic algorithm interprets the strength of a rule as the fitness value of that rule. In this way, the rule strength is responsible for the *long-term behavior* of the classifier system.

On the other hand, the rule strength determines which rules will fire. This is an aspect of the *short-term behavior* of the system.

The strength assignment problem is not simple. For instance, it is difficult to think that a credit assignment algorithm may be obtained in a standard way, by using an objective function and an optimization procedure.

Heuristics used to solve the credit assignment problem have to consider that some difficult situations may occur, such as the following:

(i) a complex environment state may occur only occasionally,

(ii) the number of environmental states is very large and a certain, useful sequence of states might be observed very rarely, or even only once.

15.4.1.1 Bargaining procedure

The bucket brigade algorithm treats the strength allocation problem as a *bargaining procedure.*

The rules (classifiers) are considered as economic *agents*. The rule strength may be considered as the agent's *capital.*

The rules are treated as economic agents producing (i.e., sending) and consuming (i.e., receiving) messages. An agent receives payments from his *consumers* (i.e., the consumers of his messages) that are winning agents (i.e., fired rules).

A winning agent is rewarded by a payoff from the environment.

When the condition part of a rule is matched by a message, the rule does not directly place a message on the message list. Having the condition part matched by a message qualifies the rule to compete for activation.

The competition of matched rules for firing may be described as an *auction* process. To participate in the auction, each agent (matched classifier) makes a *bid* proportional to its strength.

The probability that an agent wins the competition for firing is proportional to its bid.

Transactions have to be *cleared*. A *winning agent*, i.e., a rule selected for activation, must clear its payment through the *clearing house*. It must pay its bid to its suppliers (the agents that sent it matching messages).

The bid is divided among all the suppliers.

15.4.1.2 Bid and winning probability

The bid b_i of the classifier C_i is a function of its current strength (wealth, fitness) w_i. A constant ρ determines the amount the classifier is prepared to lose in one auction.

Definition

The *specificity* s_i of a rule (classifier) is the proportion of non-wild card symbols in the condition part of the rule.

Definition

The *bid* of the classifier C_i is expressed as

$$b_i = \rho\, s_i\, w_i,$$

where

* ρ is a parameter of the method, $0 < \rho \leq 1$;

* s_i is the classifier specificity, $0 \leq s_i \leq 1$;

* w_i is the classifier strength.

Remarks

(i)   The constant ρ may be interpreted as a kind of *learning rate* of the classifier.

(ii)   The specificity is constant for a given rule and measures the *specialization degree* of the rule.

(iii)   The expression of the bid indicates that highly specialized rules are preferred over non-specialized (general) rules.

The rule agents may be selected deterministically, according to their bid values. However, probabilistic selection seems to be more convenient.

The *winning probability* p_i of rule C_i may be defined as its *relative bid*; an *effective bid* is usually used to define p_i.

The *effective bid* may be defined by considering a random *noise term*.

If an additive, normal, random noise is used, we may define the *effective bid B_i* of rule C_i as follows:

$$B_i = b_i + N(0, \sigma),$$

where

- b_i is the classifier bid,

- σ is the noise standard deviation.

Remarks

(i)   A *multiplicative* noise may also be considered.

Using a lognormal perturbation, we may write the effective bid as

$$B_i = b_i \, e^{\tau N(0, \sigma)},$$

where τ is a constant.

(ii)   A *power* effective bid may be sometimes useful.

In this case, we have

$$B_i = (b_i)^m,$$

where m is an integer constant, $m \geq 2$.

Definition

The probability p_i that the agent (rule, classifier) C_i wins the competition may be defined as

$$p_i = \frac{B_i}{\sum\limits_{j=1}^{n} B_j},$$

where n is the number of competing agents.

15.4.2 Updating strength of a winning classifier

Let us consider a winning classifier C_w.

The *updated strength* $s_w(t+1)$ of this classifier is calculated according to the following correction rule:

$$s_w(t+1) = s_w(t) + R - b_w(t),$$

where

- R is a *reward*,

- $b_w(t)$ is the current classifier bid.

Remarks

(i) The reward may be a payoff from the environment.

(ii) The environmental payoff is distributed among the winners.

Let us denote by $W(t)$ the set of winning classifiers at the moment t and by P the *environmental payoff*.

The update of a winning classifier strength is now expressed as follows:

$$s_w(t+1) = s_w(t) + \frac{P}{\text{card}(W(t))} - b_w(t).$$

Remarks

(i) The payoff may also be negative.

(ii) A negative 'reward' penalizes an inappropriate action.

15.4.3 Updating strength of a producing classifier

Let us now consider a *producing* classifier C_p.

This classifier will pay a tax T_p.

The strength of a producing classifier is modified according to the rule:

$$s_p(t+1) = s_p(t) + b_p(t) - T_p(t),$$

where

- $T_p(t)$ is the current tax to pay,

- $b_p(t)$ is the current classifier bid.

15.4.3.1 Income tax

The *tax* may be considered proportional to the classifier bid or to the classifier strength.

In the former case, we may write

$$T_p(t) = I\, b_p(t),$$

where I is an *income tax rate* on all payments received from other classifiers.

We may thus write

$$s_p(t+1) = s_p(t) + (1 - I)b_p(t).$$

Remark

The income of a classifier is taxed in order to suppress *free-riders*.

15.4.3.2 Property tax

Let us consider a property tax.

In this case, we have

$$T_p(t) = p\, s_p(t),$$

where p is a *property tax rate* and $0 < p < 1$.

This taxing mechanism means that we tax the wealth (property) or the strength of a rule.

15.4.4 Updating strength for remaining situations

Let us now consider a classifier C_i that is neither winning nor producing.

In order to eliminate rules that are never utilized, we have to penalize the classifier C_i. The unique possibility is to penalize their strength.

The correction rule for the strength of the classifier C_i may be written as

$$s_i (t+1) = s_i (t) - T_i(t),$$

where T_i is the tax to pay.

As the wealth (strength) is penalized, we have

$$T_i(t) = p \, s_i(t),$$

where p is the *property tax*.

The updated strength now becomes

$$s_i(t+1) = (1 - p) \, s_i(t).$$

15.4.5 Taxing the winners. Updating strength revisited

Let us observe that the winners were not taxed. But generally each rule is taxed in order to prevent the population from being biased toward the most productive rules.

If a tax is considered, the strength of a winning classifier is adapted according to the correction rule:

$$s_w(t+1) = s_w(t) + \frac{P}{\text{card}(W(t))} - b_w(t) - T(t).$$

It is natural to tax a winning rule proportionally to its strength (wealth). Thus, we may write

$$T(t) = p \, s_w(t),$$

where $0 < p < 1$.

The updated strength of a winning classifier is now

$$s_w(t+1) = (1 - p) \, s_w(t) + \frac{P}{\text{card}(W(t))} - b_w(t).$$

15.4.5.1 Remarks on bucket brigade algorithm

- The bucket brigade algorithm is based on local information only. The involved rules are only the winning classifiers and the rules directly linked with the winners. As the strength of rules does not change drastically, the learning process is gradual.

- The bucket brigade algorithm also supplies the fitness of the rules.

- Classifier systems are not intended to obtain the fittest rules, but a population of rules that cooperatively solve a task. Therefore, proportional selection or elitist selection mechanisms are not useful.

- Some selection models replacing similar population members or other strategies inducing multimodal optimization could be helpful.

15.5 Pittsburgh classifier systems

Classifier systems from the Pittsburgh family (Smith, 1980) assume that each individual in a population represents the complete set of rules (a rule base). The individuals compete using the fitness values.

Therefore, the Pittsburgh approach may be considered as an evolutionary algorithm applied to a specific learning problem.

The key problems within the Pittsburgh approach are representation and fitness calculation. If an objective function may be used, the fitness calculation problem becomes trivial.

The rule base discovery problem is solved by generating a new set of rule bases at each generation. A relatively large amount of training is necessary. Therefore, the Pittsburgh approach is not suitable for on-line learning situations.

15.6 Fuzzy classifier systems

A fuzzy classifier is a learning system using fuzzy rules.

15.6.1 Fuzzy Michigan classifier systems

The components of a fuzzy Michigan classifier system are

- a fuzzy rule base,

- an apportionment of credit system,

- a fuzzy rule discovery system.

A fuzzy rule language is used to express knowledge in the production system, including the rule database of the system.

The fuzzy rule discovery system is an evolutionary algorithm (usually a genetic algorithm).

The actual rule discovery system of the evolutionary algorithm depends on the class of problems.

As the apportionment of credit algorithm, a fuzzy relative of the bucket brigade algorithm may be used.

15.6.2 Fuzzy Pittsburgh classifier systems

The main categories of learning in a fuzzy Pittsburgh classifier system are

- learning fuzzy set memberships only,

- learning fuzzy rules only,

- learning both fuzzy rules and fuzzy set memberships in different stages,

- learning both fuzzy rules and fuzzy set memberships simultaneously.

In what follows, some approaches of previous learning categories will be reviewed.

15.6.2.1 Learning fuzzy memberships

Karr (1991) considered the problem of tuning membership functions of a fixed set of fuzzy rules.

The membership degrees of condition variables and action variables are represented as triangular functions and are defined by their base-points (the triangles are considered to be isosceles).

A genetic algorithm with a small population has been used to create an adaptive fuzzy controller for the *cart-pole-balancing* problem.

15.6.2.2 Learning fuzzy rules with fixed fuzzy membership functions

Fuzzy rules using fixed membership functions may be used to evolve a fuzzy control strategy (Thrift, 1991).

Pham and Karaboga (1991) described a system that learns fuzzy rules and output membership functions simultaneously using fixed input membership functions.

15.6.2.3 Learning fuzzy rules and membership functions separately

Learning fuzzy rules and membership functions simultaneously may be difficult due to complex interactions.

Kinzel, Klawonn and Kruse (1994) proposed an alternative three-stage approach:

- An initial rule base and membership functions are selected heuristically.

- A genetic algorithm is applied to the rules (membership functions are fixed).

- The genetic algorithm is applied for fine tuning of membership functions within the obtained good rule bases.

15.6.2.4 Learning fuzzy rules and membership functions simultaneously

Lee and Takagi (1993) used a genetic algorithm to simultaneously optimize a variable-size fuzzy rule base and fuzzy set membership functions. A Takagi-Sugeno fuzzy controller model is used.

Carse, Fogarty and Munro (1996) describe a Pittsburgh-style fuzzy classifier that simultaneously learns fuzzy relations and membership functions.

Fuzzy rules are encoded in the genome. Variable-length genomes are considered. Fuzzy rules and fuzzy set memberships are encoded as real numbers rather than considering the usual binary string encoding.

Cordon and Herrera (1996) proposed a hybrid, *genetic algorithm-evolution strategy* method for establishing the knowledge base of a fuzzy controller that learns from examples.

References and bibliography

Carse, B., Fogarty, T.C., Munro, A., (1996), Evolving temporal fuzzy rule-bases for distributed routing control in telecomunication networks, *Genetic Algorithms and Soft Computing*, F. Herrera, J.L. Verdegay (Eds.), Physica-Verlag, Heidelberg, 467-488.

Cordón, O., Herrera, F., (1996), A hybrid genetic algorithm- evolution strategy process for learning fuzzy logic controller knowledge bases, *Genetic Algorithms and Soft Computing*, F. Herrera, J.L. Verdegay (Eds.), Physica-Verlag, Heidelberg, 251-278.

Goldberg, D.E., (1989), *Genetic Algorithms in Search, Optimization, and Machine Learning*, Addison-Wesley, Reading, MA.

Herrera, F., Verdegay, J.L., (1996), *Genetic Algorithms and Soft Computing*, Physica-Verlag, Heidelberg.

Holland, J.H., (1986), Escaping brittleness: The possibility of general-purpose learning algorithms applied to parallel rule-based systems, *Machine Learning*, 2, R.S. Michalski, J.G. Carbonell, T.M. Mitchell (Eds.), Morgan Kaufmann, Los Altos, CA, 593-624.

Holland, J.H., Reitman, J.S., (1978), Cognitive systems based on adaptive algorithms, *Pattern Directed Inference Systems*, D.A. Watermann, F. Hayes-Roth (Eds.), Academic Press, New York, 313-329.

Karr, C., (1991), Design of an adaptive fuzzy logic controller using a genetic algorithm, *Proc. 4th Int. Conf. on Genetic Algorithms*, R.K. Belew, L.B. Booker (Eds.), Morgan Kaufmann, San Mateo, CA, 450-457.

Kinzel, J., Klawonn, F., Kruse, R., (1994), Modifications of genetic algorithms for designing and optimizing fuzzy controllers, *Proc. 1st IEEE Int. Conf. on Evolutionary Computation*, IEEE, Piscataway, NJ, 28-33.

Lee, M.A., Takagi, H., (1993), Integrating design stages of fuzzy systems using genetic algorithms, *Proc. 2nd IEEE Int. Conf. on Fuzzy Systems*, IEEE, San Francisco, CA, 612-617.

Michalewicz, Z., (1992), *Genetic Algorithms + Data Structures = Evolution Programs*, Springer-Verlag, Berlin.

Pham, D.T., Karaboga, (1991), Optimum design of fuzzy logic controllers using genetic algorithms, *Journal of Systems Engineering*, 1, 114-118.

Smith, S.F., (1980), A Learning System Based on Genetic Adaptive Algorithms, Ph.D. Thesis, University of Pittsburgh, PA.

Thrift, P., (1991), Fuzzy logic synthesis with genetic algorithms, *Proc. 4th Int. Conf. on Genetic Algorithms*, R.K. Belew, L.B. Booker (Eds.), Morgan Kaufmann, San Mateo, CA, 509-513.

16

Applications of evolutionary computation

16.1 Introduction

This chapter presents an overview of some applications of evolutionary computation. Evolutionary algorithm applications are limited only by the ability to encode a problem adequately and to establish a proper solution evaluation procedure (a fitness function or a different quality measure).

EC applications include practically all the fields in which traditional optimization methods and AI-based techniques (especially machine learning methods) are used.

The large number of relevant applications makes any selection really incomplete.

Many early EC specific applications are described in detail, for instance, in Davis (1991).

A wide spectrum of applications can be found in Bäck, Fogel and Michalewicz (1997).

A selection of applications of genetic programming is contained in the book of Banzhaf, Nordin, Keller and Francone (1998).

16.2 General applications of evolutionary computation

Search and optimization methods based on evolutionary computation have a large spectrum of practical applications in different domains. A list of some important application domains is given below.

Distributed and parallel computation systems

Evolutionary computation applications deal with time estimation and optimization of inter-processor or inter-process communication in a distributed computation environment, processor configuration, and automated tests for numeric circuits.

A very interesting application is the automated parallelization of sequential programs.

Chemistry

Chemistry applications try mainly to optimize production processes and strategies. Evolutionary computation methods are also used for technology and installation design, and data analysis and interpretation. Further applications address chemical process control in laboratory or industrial conditions, and environmental control (e.g., pollution control).

Engineering

The domain of engineering applications is vast and it includes technology design, simulation, testing, real-time process control, telecommunications (network optimization, traffic control, device design), image processing (handwritten character recognition, fingerprint recognition and voice recognition), and recognition of complex scenes.

Business

Business applications focus on the modeling of complex economic systems, and system prediction. Possible financial uses are modeling based on time series, and market prediction.

Medicine

Medical applications deal mainly with medical imagery and data analysis, and automated diagnosis (detection of signals indicating epilepsy, for instance).

Management

Some important practical management applications have been proposed. Most of them appear in an industrial setting with emphasis on production. This seems to be very natural, since production actually involves complex optimization tasks.

Some hybrid systems integrating evolutionary computation with artificial neural networks and fuzzy set theory have also been developed.

Other domains

There are several more applications like those regarding resource allocation, scheduling, transportation optimization, optimal object location, etc.

16.3 Main application areas

Some specific applications of the evolutionary computation approach are indicated below. A taxonomy of these applications is based on the task to be fulfilled. However, domain ranges are not disjoint.

Optimization

- numerical optimization problems

- integer programming

- combinatorial optimization problem

  o multiple-knapsack problems

  o packing and grouping problems

  o cutting problems

- real-world optimization problems

  o database query optimization

  o job shop problems

  o iterated and strategic games

  o portfolio optimization

  o power flow optimization

  o fuel cycle optimization

Design (general and industrial)

- circuit design

- pipeline systems design

- communication lines design

- evolutionary design of computing machines

- design of hardware controllers

- aircraft design

- packing

- circuit simplification

- decision diagrams

- designing low-cost sets of packet-switching communication network links

- local and wide-area network design

- on-line reassignment of computer tasks across a suite of heterogeneous computers

Planning, routing and scheduling

- routing in communication design

- routing in manufacturing

- general production process scheduling

- decentralized production scheduling

- scheduling in flexible manufacturing

- maintenance scheduling

- job shop scheduling problem

- facility layout problem

- location planning

- general scheduling and planning

  o school timetable problem

o   exam scheduling problem

o   scheduling patients in a hospital

o   mission planning

Automated programming

- obtaining sorting algorithms

- sorting networks

- caching algorithms

- recursion

- automated generation of programs for a given problem

- parallelization of sequential programs

Machine learning, classifier systems

- neural network design

- neural network training

- cellular automata rules detection

- deduction of rules for solving different problems

- game playing

- decision trees

Pattern recognition

- feature extraction

- feature selection

- filtering

- noise filtering

- signal filtering
- clustering
- classification
- character recognition

Control (general, process, robots and agents)

- control strategy programs
- process engineering
- control for robot motion and obstacle avoidance
- movement in a maze
- navigation algorithms
- deduction of control rules
- fuzzy control
  - synthesis of fuzzy controllers
  - optimization of fuzzy controllers
- autonomous vehicle controller
- autonomous agents
- autonomous robotic agents
  - evolution
  - learning
- bargaining agents

Simulation and identification

- simulation of complex system behavior

- simulation of population genetics and ecology
- deduction of control rules
- complex system identification
- decision making
- chaos exploration

Analysis of complex data and time series prediction

- chaotic system prediction
- weather prediction
- financial prediction
- market evolution prediction
- software fault prediction
- protein core detection
- protein structure prediction
- data mining
- structure discovering
- data compression
- data encoding
- signal identification

Modeling

- model induction
- model identification of some complex processes in
  o economics

- o politics

- o neurology

- o ecology

- o biotechnology

- o biochemistry

- o population genetics

Management and business

- personnel scheduling

- inventory control

- optimal load management

- analyzing customer data

- location planning

- distribution

- models of consumer choice

- planning models

- scheduling transportation

- intelligent and cellular manufacturing systems

- optimizing decision variables

- line balancing in the metal industry

- multi-objective production planning

- sequencing orders in the electrical industry

- sequencing orders for the production of engines

- production scheduling
- optimized power flow in energy supply networks
- maximizing efficiency in power station cycles
- scheduling aircraft landing times to minimize cost
- elevator dispatching
- parameter optimization of a simulation model for production planning
- optimization tools for intelligent manufacturing systems
- job shop scheduling
- underground mine scheduling
- general production scheduling
- decentralized production scheduling
- buffer optimization in assembly system
- dynamic solutions to a strategic market game
- optimizing distribution networks
- analyzing efficient market hypothesis
- determining good pricing strategies for the market

Finance and trade

- financial analysis
- credit scoring
- filtering credit card applications
- filtering insurance applications

- assessing insurance risks
- risk management
- time-series prediction
- bargaining
- trade and financial strategies
- trade models
- optimal investment strategies
- evolving neural network predictor to handle pension money
- credit card transaction fraud detection
- optimal allocation of personnel in a large bank

Natural language

- language processing
- language decision trees
- text processing
- text classification

Signal and image processing

- signal filtering
- signal modeling
- image analysis
- feature extraction
- image compression
- image enhancement

- image and signal recognition

16.4 Optimization and search applications

The general philosophy concerning optimization/search applications of evolutionary algorithms is considered.

16.4.1 Optimization

Genetic algorithms were preeminently used in the first research to solve optimization problems. (Fitzpatrick and Grefenstette, 1988; Grefenstette, 1986). Evolution strategies and evolutionary programming may also be used for optimization problems.

Evolutionary computation has become a more and more important instrument for finding good (sometimes optimal) solutions to large optimization problems.

Evolutionary algorithms have proved to be superior to conventional optimization methods, especially in the case of multi-modal functions (involving the detection of several optimum points) and non-stationary optimization problems.

Combinatorial optimization deals with problems that involve different discrete objects. Therefore, the function variables involved in combinatorial optimization are discrete. In this particular case, optimization requires mechanisms of coding, recombination, and comparison of solutions.

Evolutionary algorithms were successfully applied to tackle classical problems of combinatorial optimization, like the *traveling salesman problem* (to find the shortest way to visit a specified group of localities) or the *packing problem* (to arrange a number of objects in a given space in an optimal way).

The packing problem has numerous practical applications and it is also related to the *cutting* problem. An interesting application of this problem regards the design of VLSI circuits (Fourman, 1985).

16.4.2 Search

Evolutionary techniques represent efficient methods to explore the problem state space. These methods are extremely attractive for standard and nonstandard artificial intelligence systems.

In standard symbolic AI systems, the movement in the problem space is described as a set of rules.

In *production systems*, the rules are represented by pairs of the type:

(condition, action).

For this kind of search, the chromosomes describe the states of the problem space. The criterion function, or a different mechanism, supplies an evaluation for each state.

In the next section, we will describe how evolutionary computation can be used in a specific search problem. The examined problem concerns the optimization of sequential decision-making strategies.

16.5 Choosing a decision strategy

Evolutionary algorithms can be successfully applied to optimize strategies for sequential decision-making problems.

A *strategy* can be represented as a set of rules of the type *(condition, action)*. Each proposed strategy can be evaluated by means of a decision-simulating model.

An evolutionary algorithm can be used to search for the best strategies. For systems with a large number of states, the emphasis is placed on rules, rather than on states.

Grefenstette (1991) has considered the application of genetic algorithms for solving the control problems that appear in *multi-agent* systems.

The interactions among the autonomous agents make these systems extremely complex and impossible to describe completely. Even when a complete mathematical description is feasible, traditional methods cannot provide a real-time solution.

The SAMUEL (*Strategy Acquisition Method Using Empirical Learning*) system uses a genetic algorithm to optimize the decision strategies.

A set of sensors supplies the information about the system's current state. The decision of an agent establishes the values of some control variables.

In the SAMUEL system, a *strategy* is a set of rules (condition, action) of the form:

$$\text{if } (c_1 \wedge c_2 \wedge ... \wedge c_n),$$

$$\text{then } (a_1 \wedge a_2 \wedge ... \wedge a_m),$$

where

- c_i is a condition concerning a sensor,

- each action a_j specifies the value of a control variable, and

- $\wedge$ represents the logic AND operator.

Grefensette (1991) indicated how the SAMUEL system can learn some manipulating techniques by which a simulated aircraft is able to avoid a rocket (that is also simulated).

The evolutionary algorithm can use variable-length chromosomes. A chromosome represents a strategy. Within the problem model, each strategy (chromosome) is evaluated with respect to a set of tasks.

The corresponding results are used to manipulate the aircraft in simulated interactions of the aircraft and the rocket. In this way, the fitness value of every chromosome is calculated. The used search operators generate new plausible strategies from parents with good performance.

16.6 Neural network training and design

Evolutionary computation and neural computing interact considerably. Evolutionary algorithms can be used for neural network training (i.e., to establish the weights of the synaptic connections) and for network design.

16.6.1 Neural network training using evolutionary computation

Let us consider a neural network having a given architecture (topology). We assume that the network is feed-forward and has hidden layers. In this case the network can be trained using the *backpropagation* algorithm.

Unfortunately, the backpropagation algorithm may stop the training process at a local minimum point of the criterion function. In this case, the error may be unacceptable.

If we combine the backpropagation algorithm with an evolutionary algorithm, we can prevent the learning process from stopping at a local minimum point. This is just the simplest and most natural neural-evolutionary computation hybridization method.

Evolutionary algorithms may be successfully applied for a large class of neural computation purposes.

16.6.1.1 General applications

Some of the most natural applications of evolutionary algorithms for neural learning purposes and network design are listed below:

- to establish the initial weights of the networks,

- to design neural networks (i.e., to establish the network architecture) for a given task,

- to establish the network parameters (learning rate, training set, maximum number of iterations, etc.),

- to establish the learning rule,

- to surpass the local minimum points,

- to establish the weights of a specified network,

- to achieve the progress of the search in the early stages of the training process,

- to resume the training process with modified parameters (if the obtained error at the end of the training process is too large),

- to combine an EC optimization algorithm with classical learning algorithms (e.g., an algorithm based on gradient information or another kind of local information) to obtain a hybrid algorithm that integrates the advantages of both methods.

16.6.1.2 Evolutionary algorithms as training procedures

Evolutionary computation can be used as an independent instrument to establish the neural network weights. We assume that the network architecture is known.

Compared to classical methods, the advantage is that the objective functions may be as complicated as necessary, no matter if they are derivable or convex.

In this case, we do not use any local information like gradient information or second-degree derivatives. In some situations (complex objective functions), this information is difficult to obtain.

Another interesting idea is to use evolutionary computation to compare different criterion functions used for network training.

In this way, the training strategy can be equipped with an adjusting mechanism that allows us to choose the most appropriate strategy.

Suppose the architecture of the network is known. A vector made up of connection weights represents a chromosome.

The easiest way is to consider a real representation for chromosomes.

We could also choose a bi-dimensional representation of chromosomes. A chromosome describes the network weight matrix. In this case, special search operators are needed.

16.6.2 Establishing neural network architecture

To establish an appropriate architecture for a network designed to solve a given problem is a difficult task and there is no universal method to solve it.

The use of evolutionary computation allows consideration of some different aspects of the neural network architecture simultaneously.

The number of hidden layers and the number of units in each layer can be varied.

The network architecture can be represented by a chromosome-vector formed by some sub-chromosomes. Each sub-chromosome may correspond, for example, to a layer of the network.

The search takes place in the space of the possible network architectures. Each solution (architecture) can be evaluated for the problem that the network must solve.

It seems that evolutionary programming and evolution strategies represent searching methods in the network architecture space more appropriately than simple genetic algorithms.

This is natural if we think of how complicated it is to associate an intuitive meaning with the recombination of two neural networks. (This is exactly the case of finite automata and the Turing machine.)

Mutation seems to be the operator capable of creating new realistic and acceptable network architectures.

The evaluation of different architectures uses an adequate *lose function*. This function may be a particular one or may be independent of the actual problem to be solved by the network.

16.7 Pattern recognition applications

Evolutionary algorithms represent an extremely appropriate instrument in data analysis and especially in *pattern recognition*. The syntagma 'pattern recognition' mainly designates a corpus of theories and methods used to solve clustering and classification problems.

A *pattern* is usually represented by a vector in the space of the characteristics.

16.7.1 A simple genetic algorithm for fuzzy clustering

Consider the data set $X = \{x^1, x^2, ..., x^P\}$. Each object from X represents a pattern in a space with a finite number of dimensions.

The most frequent case is $x^j \in \mathbf{R}^s$, where $s \geq 1$ is the dimension of the Euclidean space, x^i_k is the value of the kth characteristic in the object x^j.

A class (or cloud or cluster) of objects is described by a subset of the set X. The central problem in data analysis is to detect the natural grouping of objects in the data set. An obvious requirement is that similar objects are in the same class and dissimilar objects are in different classes.

In real-world problems, classes do not have uniform and precise bounds. That is why it is useful to describe classes as fuzzy sets.

A *fuzzy set A* over the universe X is a function

$$A : X \rightarrow [0,1].$$

$A(x)$ is called the *membership degree* of the object x to the fuzzy set A.

The *cluster structure* of X can be described as a fuzzy partition $P = \{A_1, A_2, ..., A_n\}$ of X.

For a particular choice of fuzzy set operations, P is a fuzzy partition of X if and only if

$$\sum_{i=1}^{n} A_i(x^j) = 1, \quad j = 1, 2, ..., p.$$

(For details, see Dumitrescu, Lazzerini and Jain, 2000.)

We assume that each fuzzy class A_i is represented by the prototype $L^i \in \mathbf{R}^s$. We write

$$L = \{ L^1, L^2, \ldots, L^n \}$$

to denote the representation of the fuzzy partition P.

The clustering problem can be now formulated as an optimization problem with the variables P and L.

The inadequacy of the representation of the partition P by L (denoted by $J(P,L)$) can be described as

$$J(P, L) = \sum_{i=1}^{n} \sum_{j=1}^{p} A_i^2(x^j) d^2(x^j, L^i), \qquad (16.1)$$

where d is a suitable distance on the data space X.

Solving the clustering problem is reduced to the minimization of the criterion function J.

If the representation L is fixed, then the optimization problem

$$J(\cdot, L) \rightarrow \min$$

has the solution (see Bezdek, 1981):

$$A_i(x^j) = \frac{1}{\sum_{k=1}^{n} \dfrac{d^2(x^j, L^i)}{d^2(x^j, L^k)}}. \qquad (16.2)$$

To determine the optimum prototypes a genetic algorithm has been proposed (Bezdek and Hathaway, 1994).

A chromosome c is a vector containing the coordinates of the n prototypes:

$$c : (L^1, L^2, ... L^n).$$

Since genetic algorithms are designed to maximize functions, we will consider the fitness function f defined as

$$f(c) = Max - J(P, L),$$

where Max is a constant used to ensure that

$$f(c) \geq 0, \forall c.$$

Bezdek and Hathaway (1994) have considered a binary linear representation of chromosomes and a constant population of 50 chromosomes in each generation.

The proposed selection mechanism automatically transfers the best 25 chromosomes of the current population into the new generation.

The search operators are crossover and mutation.

The considered mutation probability is

$$p_m = 0.002.$$

The number of classes is supposed to be known. The chromosomes evolve toward the class prototypes.

After a reasonable number of generations, chromosomes will overlap and only n distinct prototypes, one for each class, will remain.

Remark

We have to observe that the number n of optimal clusters is included in the fitness calculation. This explains how the number of distinct prototypes converges to n.

After the prototypes are established, the corresponding fuzzy classes are calculated using formula (16.2).

A heuristic rule to generate a classical partition of X may also be employed.

Another possibility is to use a multidimensional representation (Dumitrescu, Stan and Dumitrescu, 1997). In this case, crossover is obtained by changing blocks within the chromosome matrix.

16.7.2 Other approaches

Blekas and Stafylopatis (1996) and Dumitrescu, Dodu and Dodu (1997) have proposed a real representation for chromosomes. This representation seems to be more natural and suitable for solving clustering problems. Experimental results emphasize a better convergence rate.

It is also possible to consider a search mechanism in which a chromosome population (of L type) is used in order to determine the prototypes.

Another independent population (of P type) generates the classes (Dumitrescu and Stan, 1996).

The procedure convergence is slower in this case if the criterion function is (16.1).

The method is more general and can be applied for any criterion function.

Indeed, the objective function may be nondifferentiable with respect to the membership degrees or the derivation may be very complicated, requiring complex calculations.

The method may be considered a *coevolutionary* one: a population of partitions and a population of prototypes coevolve.

16.8 Cellular automata

Cellular automata represent a class of distributed computational systems. The interaction of cellular automata and evolutionary algorithms is investigated.

16.8.1 Basic notions

Cellular automata (CA) were conceived by Ulam and von Neumann in the 1940s to provide a means of investigating complex extended systems (von Neumann, 1966).

Cellular automata represent a class of spatially distributed dynamical systems where many simple elements interact to produce complex behavior patterns.

Cellular automata represent a strong and versatile computational method. Typically, CA are decentralized systems characterized by high parallelism, discrete time and spatial extension, and the ability to perform various computational tasks.

Such systems could be very efficient for different computational and learning purposes.

The simplest class of highly parallel systems having spatial extension is the one-dimensional cellular automaton.

A binary one-dimensional cellular automaton can be represented as follows (the broken rectangle delimits a cell's neighborhood).

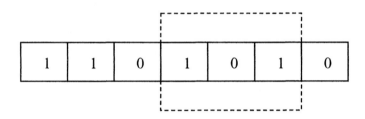

Generally, a cellular automaton is a spatial system composed of cells whose behavior changes in time in discrete steps (see Toffoli and Margolus, 1987; Wolfram, 1994). The cells are connected in regular structures (cellular arrays, lattices, or grids).

The cellular array is *n*-dimensional (usually, *n* = 1, 2, 3). The cells directly connected to a certain cell are the neighbors of that cell. At any instant, a cell is characterized by its state.

The states of all cells composing the automaton are updated synchronously in discrete time steps according to a local *interaction rule* (or *transition rule*, or *transition function*). The next state of a cell is determined by its current state and by the current state of its neighbors. Each cell computes its new state and communicates it to the neighbors.

The new states are computed using a *transition rule* that characterizes each cell of the system. The transition rule is basically a finite state machine, with an entry for each possible neighborhood configuration of states.

When the states are only 0 and 1, we have a *binary-state* cellular automaton. In this case, the transition rule is expressed as a Boolean function.

16.8.2 Specification of a cellular automaton

A cellular automaton is a system specified by the following elements:

Structure of the interconnection lattice

The most frequent lattices are one-, two- and three-dimensional. They have rectangular and cubic shapes. Other useful grids are triangular, hypercubic, or tree lattices.

Neighborhood of each cell

Consider a grid. The neighborhood of a cell is usually defined as a sphere with the center in that cell and a fixed radius.

Boundary conditions

Usually, cellular automata are represented as finite lattices. In this case, it is necessary to specify how to build the neighborhood of the cells placed on the grid border. There are two usual approaches:

(i) the *null limit conditions*,

which suppose that the grid is surrounded by cells with the 0 state;

(ii) the *cyclic limit conditions*,

which consider that the cells placed on the opposite sides of the border are adjacent.

The latter approach assumes that the opposite sides touch each other or the lattice becomes circular by means of closing to infinite.

Evolution (transition) rules

The state of each cell at time t is a function of the states of the cell neighborhood at time $(t - 1)$.

A cellular automaton is called *uniform* if all its cells have the same evolution rule. More often, the cells follow different transition rules.

Initial conditions

Frequently, we suppose that the evolution of a cellular automaton starts from a certain predefined configuration.

The automaton considered in the previous section has the following characteristics:

- number of states per cell: 2;

- radius dimension: 1 (i.e., each cell has two neighbors, one to the left and the other to the right);

- table of transitions (for instance),

$$000 \rightarrow 0$$
$$001 \rightarrow 0$$
$$010 \rightarrow 1$$
$$011 \rightarrow 1$$
$$100 \rightarrow 0$$
$$101 \rightarrow 1$$
$$110 \rightarrow 1$$
$$111 \rightarrow 1.$$

Now we are able to give the following formal definition of a cellular automaton.

Definition

A *cellular automaton* is a system

$$A = (S, G, D, F),$$

where

S is the finite set of states,

G is the cellular neighborhood,

D is the dimension of the cellular automaton (grid dimension),

F is the transition function.

Remark

In uniform CA, the transition function F is identical for all cells. For non-uniform CA, the function F may differ for different cells.

16.8.3 CA applications

Cellular automata are pre-eminently used to provide a useful model of well-characterized collective phenomena with a high degree of complexity as they appear in physics, biology, and computer science. Such highly nonlinear phenomena may be connected with chaotic and fractal behavior of complex systems.

Some applications of cellular automata are listed below:

- fluid dynamics,

- turbulence,

- ordering of complex systems,

- chaos,

- symmetry-breaking in elementary particle physics,

- fractal behavior,

- crystal growing,
- study of magnetic spin systems,
- models for galaxy formations,
- models for chemical oscillations,
- explanation of the genesis of some biological forms (e.g., the shell of the shellfish),
- cell dynamics,
- parallel language recognition,
- parallel image processing,
- logical circuit testing,
- neural network design and training.

16.8.4 Determining transition functions

Evolutionary algorithms can be used to evolve cellular architectures and to establish the transition rules for a given cellular automaton.

16.8.4.1 CA rule detection

Rule detection is a difficult task because the search space has a high dimension.

For example, let us consider a binary cellular automaton. Suppose that the neighborhood radius is one. Every cell has two neighbors. Therefore the next state of each cell is established as a Boolean function of three variables: the present state and the state of the two neighboring cells.

As the function has three binary variables, there are 2^3 possible combinations of the three values.

Hence the transition function is a Boolean function

$$f : D \to \{0,1\},$$

where D is the set of all possible combinations of three binary values. It is easy to prove (by induction) that there are

$$m = 2^{|\text{card } D|}$$

$$= (2)^{2^3}$$

$$= 256$$

different Boolean functions.

Therefore the transition function of each cell must be selected through 256 different functions.

If we have a neighborhood with radius two, then the transition Boolean functions have five variables and the search space dimension is

$$m = (2)^{2^5}$$

$$= 2^{32}.$$

In the case of a neighborhood with radius three, there are

$$m = (2)^{2^7}$$

$$= 2^{128}$$

transition functions.

This means that the transition function of every cell must be chosen from a search space with 2^{128} elements.

In order to deduce the rules for a cellular automaton, the application of evolutionary algorithms can be done in different ways depending on the considered problem.

There are two possibilities regarding the choice of the chromosomes:

(i)   Each chromosome corresponds to a cellular automaton.

In this case, the value of the gene i identifies the rule for the cell i of the automaton.

(ii)   A chromosome corresponds to a cell's rule.

In both cases, the fitness value is calculated by executing the resulting cellular automaton for T time steps. The number of cases in which the behavior is satisfied will contribute to computing the fitness.

Let us consider the case in which chromosomes describe transition rules.

An evolutionary algorithm to determine the CA rules is the following:

AN EVOLUTIONARY ALGORITHM TO ESTABLISH THE RULES FOR A CELLULAR AUTOMATON

S1. Initial configuration:

set $t = 0$,

initialize the population $P(0)$ with transition rules that are randomly generated.

S2. **while** (termination condition not satisfied) **do**

    begin

        S2.1.   Calculate the fitness value for each rule.

        S2.2.   Select the best E rules ('the elite') and copy them unchanged into the new generation $P(t+1)$.

        S2.3.   Apply the crossover and mutation operators to the elite rules that are selected with an adequate mechanism (e.g., proportional selection).

                 The new rules enter the population $P(t+1)$.

        S2.4.   Set $t = t+1$.

    end

Remark

The number E is a parameter of the algorithm.

When each chromosome corresponds to a CA, each gene has a number of possible values equal to the number of possible rules. Two parents are selected for crossover using an appropriate method.

By crossover, only one descendant is obtained. The value of each gene comes from either one parent or from the other.

The parent is chosen randomly. Mutation is achieved by a random selection of a gene and randomly changing its value.

The value of the objective function associated with each chromosome is calculated by executing the appropriate CA for T consecutive time instants (T functioning steps).

Each run will provide a result. The fitness value can be defined, for example, as the ratio of the number of favorable (acceptable) results and the number of unfavorable results (unacceptable for the current problem).

16.9 Evolutionary algorithms vs. other heuristics

It seems very difficult today to predict if evolutionary algorithms will produce results superior to those of similar modern heuristics. Currently, evolutionary algorithms are more and more integrated as optimization modules in large software products.

The combination of evolutionary computation with neural networks and fuzzy logic generates a new extremely promising direction: *intelligent computation*. This tends to be a powerful paradigm of Artificial Intelligence and can generate many other interesting applications.

References and bibliography

Bäck, T., Fogel, D.B., Michalewicz, Z., (1997), *Handbook of Evolutionary Computation*, Institute of Physics Publishing, Bristol, Oxford University Press, Oxford.

Banzhaf, W., Nordin, P., Keller, R.E., Francone, F.D., (1998), *Genetic Programming*, Morgan Kaufmann, San Francisco, CA, and dpunct.verlag, Heidelberg.

Bezdek, J.C., (1981), *Pattern Recognition with Fuzzy Objective Algorithms*, Plenum Press, New York.

Bezdek, J.C., Hathaway, R.J., (1994), Optimization of fuzzy clustering criteria using genetic algorithms, *Proc. 1st IEEE Conference on Evolutionary Computing*, Orlando, FL, 589-594.

Blekas K., Stafylopatis, A., (1996), Real-coded genetic optimization of fuzzy clustering, *Proc. EUFIT'96*, Aachen, 461-465.

Davis, L. (Ed.), (1991), *Handbook of Genetic Algorithms*, Van Nostrand Reinhold, New York.

Dumitrescu, D., (2000), *Mathematical Principles of Classification Theory*, Academy Publishing House, Bucharest.

Dumitrescu, D., Bodrogi, L., (1997), *A New Evolutionary Method and its Application in Clustering*, 'Babes-Bolyai' University, Seminar on Computer Science, 2, 127-126.

Dumitrescu, D., Costin, H., (1996), *Neural Network*, Teora, Bucharest.

Dumitrescu, D., Dodu, C., Dodu, V., (1997), *Comparative Study of Genetic Algorithms*, 'Babes-Bolyai' University, Seminar on Computer Science, 2, 115-126.

Dumitrescu, D., Lazzerini, B., Jain, L.C., (2000), *Fuzzy Sets and Their Application to Clustering and Training*, CRC Press, Boca Raton, FL.

Dumitrescu, D., Lazzerini, B., Marcelloni, F., (1999), Olfactory signal classification based on evolutionary computation, *Proc. IJCNN'99, Int. Joint Conf. of Neural Networks*, Washington DC, 313-316.

Dumitrescu, D., Stan, I., (1996), Genetic Algorithms in Neural Networks and Clustering, *Artificial Intelligence Methodology, Systems, Applications*, A.M. Ramsay (Ed.), IOS Press, Amsterdam, 134-140.

Dumitrescu, D., Stan, I., Dumitrescu, A., (1997), Genetic Algorithms for Fuzzy Clustering. Multidimensional Encoding, *Proc. EUFIT'97*, Aachen, Vol. 1, 705-708.

Fitzpatrick, M.J., Grefensette, J.J., (1988), Genetic algorithms in noisy environments, *Machine Learning*, 3, 101-120.

Fourman, M.P., (1985), Compaction of symbolic layout using genetic algorithms, *Proc. 1st Int. Conf. on Genetic Algorithms*, J.J. Grefenstette (Ed.), Lawrence Erlbaum, Hilsdale, NJ, 141-153.

Grefenstette, J.J., (1986), Optimization of control parameters for genetic algorithms, *IEEE Trans. on Systems, Man and Cybernetics*, 16, 122-128.

Grefenstette, J.J., (1991), Strategy acquisition with genetic algorithms, *Handbook of Genetic Algorithms*, L. Davis (Ed.), Van Nostrand Reinhold, New York, 186-201.

Hall, L.O., Ozyurt, I.B., Bezdek, J.C., (1999), Clustering with a genetically optimized approach, *IEEE Trans. on Evolutionary Computation*, 3, 103-112.

Koza, J.R., (1992), *Genetic Programming*, MIT Press, Cambridge, MA.

Mange, D., Tomassini, M., (1998), *Bio-Inspired Computing Machines*, Press Polytechnique et Universitaires Romandes, Lausanne.

Mitchell, M., (1996), *An Introduction to Genetic Algorithms*, MIT Press, Cambridge, MA.

Nissen, V., (1997), Management applications and other classical optimization problems, T. Bäck, D.B. Fogel, Z. Michalewicz (Eds.), *Handbook of Evolutionary Computation*, Institute of Physics Publishing, Bristol, and Oxford University Press, Oxford, F1.2:1-F1.2:50.

Toffoli, T, Margolus, N., (1987), *Cellular Automata Machines: A New Environment for Modeling*, MIT Press, Cambridge, MA.

von Neumann, J., (1966), *Theory of Self-Reproducing Automata*, University of Illinois Press, Illinois.

Wolfram, S., (1994), *Cellular Automata and Complexity*, Addison-Wesley, Reading, MA.

Index

allele, 2
  dominant, 255
ARGOT system, 220, 246

Baldwin effect, 291
bias, 117
Boltzmann selection, 93–96
breakpoint, 105
brood recombination, 310
brood recombination
  algorithm, 310
brood size, 310
bucket brigade algorithm, 11,
  328–337
building block, 36, 313
building block hypothesis, 36,
  178

caching the best mechanism,
  18
canonical genetic algorithm,
  28–30

Cauchy distribution, 208
Cauchy perturbation, 274, 279
cellular automata, 365–374
cellular model, 289
chromosome
  diploid, 252
  exon, 3
  haploid, 252
  intron, 3, 220, 312–313
  junk DNA, 3
  messenger RNA, 3
  non-coding DNA, 3
  transfer RNA, 3
classifier, 324
classifier system (*see also*
  learning classifier system),
  323–340
closure property, 303
coding function, 12
coevolution, 25, 290–291
  competitive model, 290
  cooperative model, 290–291

coevolutionary selection, 44, 97
conservative operator, 15
correlated mutation, 273
credit, 291
credit assignment system, 11
crossover, 104–125
    adaptive, 110
    bias, 117
        distributional, 118
        positional, 118
    diagonal, 116
    diagonal multi-parent, 196
    heuristic, 198
    local, 194
    multi-parent uniform, 116
    non-uniform convex, 193
    N-point, 108–110, 121–123
    one-bit-self-adaptation, 115
    one-point, 104–107
    point, 105
    punctuated, 110–112
    punctuation, 111
    random respectful
        recombination, 116
    reduced surrogate, 116
    scanning, 116
    segmented, 112–113
    setting parameter, 120
    shuffle, 113–114
    simplex, 198
        random, 199
    two-point, 107–108, 110
    uniform, 114–115
    uniform convex, 193
crossover point, 105

crossover punctuation, 111
crowding, 287

delta coding, 220, 247–251
    real-valued, 247–248
deme, 287
    overlapping, 294
diffusion model, 289, 294
diploidy, 5, 252, 257
dominance, 253–254
    evolving map, 256
    function, 256
    map vector, 256
dominance relation, 254, 256

elitist selection, 86–87
energy surface, 25
evaluation window, 222
evolution strategies, 8
evolution strategy, 261–275
    (μ,λ), 268, 269
    $(\mu+\lambda)$, 268, 269
    $(\mu+1)$, 268
    $(1+1)$, 263–268
    1/5 success rule, 264–268
    Cauchy perturbation, 274, 279
    correlated mutation, 273
    multimembered, 268–275
evolutionary algorithm, 1
    parallel implementation, 292
evolutionary computation
    applications, 343–374

decision strategy, 355–357

neural network design and training, 357–360

optimization, 354

pattern recognition, 360–365

search, 355

cellular automata, 365–374

evolutionary programming, 7, 275–279

Cauchy mutation, 274–275

exon, 3

exploitation, 22, 42

exploration, 22

fitness

implicit evaluation, 43–44

scaling, 42

fitness calculation, 307–309

fitness case, 307

fitness function, 12, 13, 24, 42–43

adaptive, 224

implicit, 25

noisy, 63

remapping, 64–65

fitness landscape, 25

fitness sharing, 284–287

niche count, 286

shared fitness, 286–287

sharing function, 286

forma, 180

forma analysis, 180

full method, 306

function set, 302

fuzzy classifier system, 337–340

fuzzy clustering, 361–364

fuzzy logic controller, 225

fuzzy system, 217

gamete, 257

gene, 2

dominance, 5

dominant, 253

epistasis, 4

orthogonal, 4

pleiotropy, 4

polygeny, 4

recessive, 253

generation gap, 27

generational selection, 85, 91

genetic algorithm, 7

adaptive, 223

canonical, 28–30

metalevel, 220

simple, 148–149

genetic drift, 37, 98

genetic programming, 9, 299–320

basic algorithm, 317–320

generational, 318

steady-state, 319–320

brood recombination, 310

brood recombination algorithm, 310

brood size, 310

building block, 313

closure property, 303

fitness calculation, 307–309
fitness case, 307
full method, 306
function set, 302
graph structure, 304–305
grow method, 306
intron, 312–313
    artificially inserted, 312
island model, 317
linear structure, 305
macromutation, 314
micromutation, 314
mutation, 313–315
parallel fitness evaluation
    model, 317
parallel implementation,
    317
population model, 316
ramped half-and-half
    method, 306
selection, 315–316
terminal set, 301
tree structure, 304, 305–307
genome, 3
genotype, 3
graph structure, 304–305
greedy over-selection, 96–97
grow method, 306

haploid organism, 5
Holland system, 326
homologous chromosomes, 5
host-parasite relationship, 290
hybridization, 215–216

implicit parallelism, 36
innovative operator, 15
intelligent computing, 374
intrinsic adaptation, 25
intron, 3, 220, 312–313
    artificially inserted, 312
island, 287
island model, 287, 293, 317

junk DNA, 3

learning classifier system, 10,
    323–340
    Michigan approach, 10,
        324–337
        bucket brigade algorithm,
            328–337
        Holland system, 326
    Pittsburgh (Pitt) approach,
        11, 325–326
linear structure, 305
linkage problem, 234–236

macromutation, 314
mating, 120–121
    cloning, 121
    inbreeding, 120
    line breeding, 120
    negative assorting, 121
    outbreeding, 121
    positive assorting, 121
    random, 120
    self-fertilization, 121
mating pool, 41

messenger RNA, 3
messy encoding, 236–237
messy genetic algorithm, 233–
    245
    competitive template, 239
    cut-and-splice operator, 239
    cut operation, 239
    generalization, 244–245
    initialization phase, 243
    juxtapositional phase, 244
    mutation, 242–243
    over-specification, 237
    primordial phase, 243
    probabilistically complete
        initialization, 244
    recombination, 239–242
    splice operation, 240
    under-specification, 237
Metropolis algorithm, 202
micromutation, 314
Monte Carlo selection method,
    48–49
mutation, 133–149, 313–315
    neutral, 132
    non-uniform, 139–141,
        202–206
        adaptive, 142
    rate (probability), 134, 144–
        145
        fitness-dependent, 141
        self-adaption, 142–145
        time-dependent, 139–141
    silent, 132
    strong, 135, 136–137
    weak, 136, 138

mutation rate (probability),
    134, 144–145
mutation step, 264

neural network, 217
niching method, 284
non-coding DNA, 3
non-uniform convex
    crossover, 193

operator
    clone, 30
    inversion, 146
    mutation, 14
    recombination, 13
    reproduction, 30
    SBX, 195–196
    selection, 22
    selection for recombination,
        14
    selection for replacement,
        14
operator tree, 220
overlapping degree, 27

parallel evolutionary
    algorithm, 292
parallel fitness evaluation
    model, 317
parallel implementation, 317
parameter control
    adaptive, 219
    blind, 219
    self-adaptive, 219

parameter encoding
  dynamic, 246
parameter setting
  adaptive, 223
partially enumerative
  initialization, 31
phenotype, 4
point mutation, 314
polyploidy, 3
population model, 316
premature convergence, 22,
  37, 50
prey-predator relationship, 290
production rule, 323
production system, 323, 355
proportional selection, 46–53
punctuation list, 110

ramped half-and-half method,
  306
real-valued encoding, 188–211
recombination (*see also*
  crossover)
  average, 191
  complete continuous, 192
  continuous, 191
  convex (intermediate), 192–
    194
  discrete, 190
  fitness-based, 197–199
  intermediate, 192–194
  multiple-parent, 196
representation
  adaptive, 224, 247
  diploidic, 254

quadrallelic, 256
  specific, 214–215
  triallelic, 254–256
  variable-length, 233–234
representation space, 11
roulette method, 48–49

SAMUEL system, 356–357
scale transformation, 50, 58–
  59
  dynamic, 58–59
  linear, 59
  logarithmic, 60
  power law, 60
  sigma scaling, 61–62
  sigma truncation, 61–62
  static, 58
  window scaling, 62–63
    dynamic, 62–63
scaling window, 63
schema, 33, 155–183
  above-average, 161–163
  average fitness, 156
  below-average, 161–163
  building block, 176–177
  defining length, 35, 155
  disruption probability, 163–
    166
  dynamics, 157–176
  fitness, 35, 157
  instance, 34, 156
  linkage, 178–179
  order, 35, 155
  representative, 156
  survival probability, 166

theorem, 175
well-defined symbol, 34
schema theorem, 36
    generalization, 180–181
selection, 315–316
    Boltzmann, 60, 93–96
    coevolutionary, 97
    conservative, 85
    disassortative, 78
    dynamic, 86
    effectiveness, 54
    elitist, 84
    elitist strategy, 86–87
    extinctive, 85
    for replacement, 41
    for reproduction, 41
    generational, 85, 91
    greedy, 45, 96
    linear ranking, 66–72
        selection pressure, 70
        selection probability, 66
        takeover time, 70
    Michalewicz, 92–93
    nongenerational, 85
    nonlinear ranking, 72–74
        biased exponential, 74
        exponential, 73
        general, 74
        geometric distribution, 73
    non-overlapping model, 87
    overlapping degree, 88
    overlapping model, 88
    parallel recombinative
        simulated annealing, 95
    pure, 84
    rank-based, 65–74

ranking
    score-based, 78
    response to, 54
    simulated annealing, 95
    static, 86
    tournament
        binary, 75–77
        Boltzmann, 77
        deterministic, 75–76
        probabilistic, 76–77
        q-tournament, 78–79
        score-based, 78
    truncation, 54
selection operator
    adaptive, 224
selection pressure, 44–45
selection probability, 46–48
simulated annealing, 202, 217
slow convergence, 51
steady-state algorithm, 89–91
    basic, 89
    generalized, 90
steady-state selection, 31
stepping stone population
    model, 289
stochastic sampling with
    partial replacement, 52
stochastic universal sampling,
    53
strategy, 356

tabu search, 217
takeover time, 45
target sampling rate, 53, 67
terminal set, 301

test case, 43
total fitness, 47
tournament
    binary, 75–77
    Boltzmann, 77
    deterministic, 75–76
    probabilistic, 76–77
    q-tournament, 78–79
    selection, 75–80
    size, 78
    trial, 75
transfer RNA, 3
tree structure, 304, 305–307

full method, 306
grow method, 306
mutation, 314
    macromutation, 314
    micromutation, 314
ramped half-and-half
    method, 306
trial, 75

uniform convex crossover,
    193